Praise for previous editions of

Kansas
Off the Beaten Path®

"[This book] uses detailed maps, lists the top ten attractions in each region, gives an extensive list of more conventional places to stay and eat (along with the more colorful, highlighted ones in the text), and points out spots worth a visit. The fresh look, level of detail, and helpful organization make the guide a must for any Kansas traveler."

—*The Wichita Eagle*

"This little handbook offers a varied menu of historic sites . . . and natural attractions for the visitor to Kansas. . . . The book is an intriguing guide to 'many of the state's unique points of interest. . . . For those who choose to stop and smell some roses, this little gem should serve them well."

—*Western Library*

"Whether your trip into Kansas is for a weekend or a week, it is sure to be more enjoyable with this guidebook along. Covering a range of sights, the volume always includes a touch of the flavor and history of each region."

—*St. Joseph* (Mo.) *News-Press*

Help Us Keep This Guide Up to Date

Every effort has been made by the author and editors to make this guide as accurate and useful as possible. However, many things can change after a guide is published—establishments close, phone numbers change, and facilities come under new management.

We would love to hear from you concerning your experiences with this guide and how you feel it could be improved and be kept up to date. While we may not be able to respond to all comments and suggestions, we'll take them to heart and we'll also make certain to share them with the author. Please send your comments and suggestions to the following address:

The Globe Pequot Press
Reader Response/Editorial Department
P.O. Box 480
Guilford, CT 06437

Or you may e-mail us at:

editorial@globe-pequot.com

Thanks for your input, and happy travels!

OFF THE BEATEN PATH® SERIES

Kansas

SIXTH EDITION

Patti DeLano

The Globe Pequot Press

GUILFORD, CONNECTICUT

Text design by Laura Augustine
Illustrations by Cathy Johnson
Maps created by Equator Graphics © The Globe Pequot Press

ISSN 1542-443X
ISBN 0-7627-2684-9

Manufactured in the United States of America
Sixth Edition/First Printing

Dedicated to Tom Stapleton,
who asked for my hand
to lead me through the Heartland.

—Patti DeLano

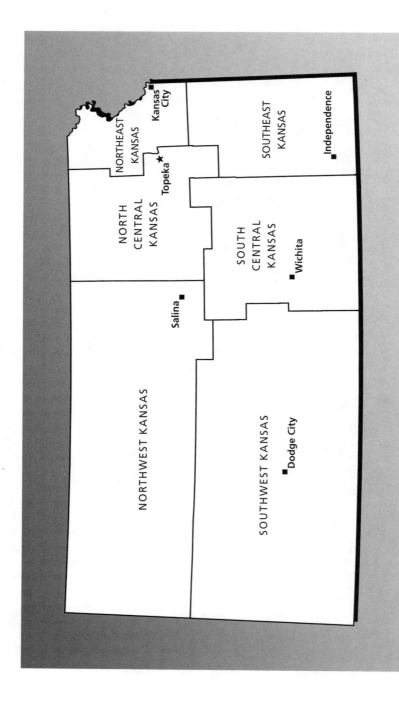

Contents

Acknowledgments

Thanks to the Kansas Department of Commerce Division of Travel and Tourism in Topeka, and all of my friends in Kansas for their help and advice. Many thanks to every Kansas restaurant owner, innkeeper, retailer, park ranger, historian, and museum curator who took time from their busy schedules to visit with me. The book would not have been possible without your help.

—Patti DeLano

Introduction

You'll find that the Kansas landscape can be surprising if you were weaned on *The Wizard of Oz*. The real Heartland in Kansas, the state Dorothy and Toto couldn't wait to come home to, has tall limestone monoliths, red buttes that mimic the Southwest, and flint outcroppings forming long, bony escarpments. There are rich, mixed forests, rolling hills, fast-flowing rivers, and bottomless springs.

Once, prairie grasses blew like the ocean in billowing waves, with few natural landmarks; courses were set by the sun and stars. One woman, forced to move to Colorado, complained bitterly that her view of the sky was blocked by the Rocky Mountains. William Inge, Kansas playwright, echoed her sentiments when he said that in other places the "heavens are trimmed down like a painting to fit a smaller frame." Here, "as far as the eye can see" is a long way; you sense the meaning of infinity.

The endless skies can be an innocent blue, and then, like an unruly child, they can send havoc to a peaceful scene. Blizzards, tornadoes, hail, and relentlessly burning sun ride in on the Kansas winds, destroying crops as quickly as an Old Testament curse.

But when it's right, it's right. Solid gold sunsets reflected in the summer wheat fields melt into the horizon. Acres of sunflowers and the sweet smell of prairie grass after a spring rain delight each of the senses. The ever-changing prairie is covered with the colors of its wildflowers: the sunflower, of course, and the buttercup, primrose, wild daisy, gayfeather, and wild onion—each a different color and each lasting only a few days.

Wheat fields stretch mile after golden mile across the state. There are no crowds here. It takes the combined population of all seven Plains states to equal the population of New York City.

The waves of prairie grasses reflect the prehistoric inland sea that once covered the state; the bedrock is salted with fossils of sharks and oysters with 3-foot shells. Kansas is a great place to hunt fossils, arrowheads, and—because of the openness of the terrain—meteorites. The largest Pleistocene meteorite ever found is here.

This is a state known for its sunshine; western Kansas has been known to have as many as 300 clear days in a year. The mountains in nearby Colorado block the rain, making this part of the state sunny and dry. Temperatures may be warm (or even hot), but a low relative humidity in the western part of the state makes summer days more comfortable than you would expect and the nights cool and pleasant.

INTRODUCTION

Gentle sun, pleasant warm days, and cool nights make the spring and fall weather almost perfect. The many bed-and-breakfast inns get you out of the motel rut and onto working farms (some of them in Amish communities) or into elegant Victorian homes across the state, where a country breakfast means fresh eggs from the barn and bread made with wheat ground from the field next door. Kansas is the breadbasket of the world. Sheltered by the mountains, the Heartland beats a slow, steady rhythm year after year.

Interstate 70 is more than a fast way to Colorado. It is a path rich with history. From 1830 to 1854 the region was Indian Territory. It was inhabited by Native Americans displaced from other parts of North America; by indigenous tribes, among them the village builders—the Pawnee, Osage, Kansa, and Wichita; and by nomadic hunters—the Cheyenne, Comanche, and Arapaho.

The 1870s brought settlers. Both the Oregon Trail and the Santa Fe Trail cut through this state. The Santa Fe Trail was called "The Big Lonely," and Kansas was the jumping-off place. It was where the railroads broke ground heading west and cattle drives from Texas ended. The Wild West was wildest in Cimarron and Dodge City, where you can relive the legend on Front Street, filled with the ghosts of buffalo hunters, railroad workers, cowboys, and drifters, the "baddest" of the bad guys laid to uneasy rest at Boot Hill Cemetery. Wild Bill Hickok, Bat Masterson, and Buffalo Bill Cody called Kansas home.

But the frontier spirit didn't die with the Old West. The Kansas–Nebraska Act gave the people of the territory the right to choose whether slavery would be permitted in the future state of Kansas. Many people came to try to influence the decision, among them abolitionist John Brown and the infamous Southern sympathizer William Quantrill and his band of marauders.

Temperance leader Carry Nation swung her bar-busting hatchet here, too. But then, the women of Kansas have always been ahead of their time. The first woman mayor in the country—in the world, they say— was elected here. The first woman to be elected to the Senate, the first black woman to be admitted to the American Bar Association, the first woman dentist in the world, and Amelia Earhart, that brave lady of the skies, were from the state of Kansas.

When Joan Finney served as governor (1991–95), Kansas became the first state in U.S. history to have a female governor, a female senator (Nancy Landon Kassebaum), and congressperson (Jan Meyers) all at once. Dorothy would be proud to come home to today's Kansas.

There are canoe trails and hiking trails, bike trips and trail rides, and even a covered-wagon jaunt for real history buffs tough enough to measure themselves against our forebears as they journeyed west to claim the land.

What can we say about Kansas? Plenty. Spend some time here, and you will understand why Dorothy and Toto wanted to leave the Land of Oz and return to the state that is called the Heartland.

Welcome to Kansas!

The prices and rates listed in this guidebook were confirmed at press time. We recommend, however, that you call establishments before traveling to obtain current information.
Maps provided are for reference only and should be used in conjunction with a road map. Distances suggested are approximate.

Northeast Kansas

Sure, Kansas has the reputation of being flat, but Northeast Kansas's Smoky Hills, where the Kansas and Missouri Rivers meet, is anything but. From the bustle of Kansas City to the quiet of farmlands, these rolling hills offer a variety of lifestyles.

Some of the suburban communities of Kansas City are stylish and sophisticated, others are small-town friendly. The city of Overland Park, for example, is a shopper's paradise, with unusual shops offering designer clothes and upscale merchandise.

But as you leave Kansas City and head west into Kansas, you will experience the dramatic change from big-city life to the quiltwork of fields and fences of the Kansas countryside. This is the most agriculturally productive section of the state, the soils thick and fertile.

Greater rainfall in the eastern part of the state makes it favorable for a wider variety of crops than can be grown in the west. Northeast Kansas is an ideal location for growing fruit. In a good year, orchard-graced Doniphan County can produce more than four million pounds of apples.

Trivia
The Kansas River is known as the Kaw River around here. The tribe the state was named for, the Kansa, is known as the Kaw Native American Tribe.

Northeast Kansas is also home to several Native American tribes: The Sac, Fox, Kickapoo, Horton, and Potawatomi have reservations in this area. From 1830 to 1854 the region was unsettled by whites and designated as Indian Territory. The Native Americans who inhabited the area were displaced from other parts of the country as relentless waves of settlers moved west. Kansas began to attract settlers in the 1870s. Many of them were Mennonites from Russia, who brought the seeds of Turkey Red wheat. The seeds took well to the prairie soil, turning a wild and unsettled land into America's breadbasket.

The river heritage here is strong. The Kansas (called the Kaw) and the Missouri Rivers join here to rush together to the Mississippi. Meriwether Lewis and William Clark camped on the Kansas side of the Missouri

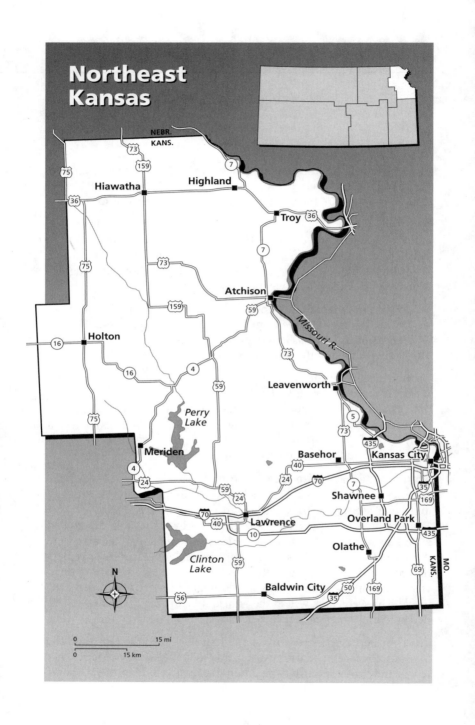

Northeast Kansas

NEBR.
KANS.

Hiawatha
Highland
Troy
Atchison
Holton
Leavenworth
Perry Lake
Meriden
Basehor
Kansas City
Shawnee
Lawrence
Overland Park
Olathe
Clinton Lake
Baldwin City

Missouri R.

MO.
KANS.

N

0   15 mi
0   15 km

River several times in June and July 1804 while exploring the Louisiana Purchase.

This region was crossed by settlers on the California, Oregon, and Santa Fe Trails. Businessmen and railroad tycoons made fortunes here in those early days and left grand homes to mark their journey through life in Kansas.

Kansas City Metro Area

Kansas City suffers from a split identity. Most of the metropolitan area is actually in Missouri, although a lot of people across the country think otherwise. Kansas City, Kansas, is a good-sized city in its own right, with its own downtown and the brand-new **Kansas Motor Speedway,** west of Kansas City near the junction of Interstates 70 and 435. Fans can watch NASCAR racing (Winston Cup and Busch series) at the 1½-mile tri-oval track as well as Indy cars. For information, call the Kansas Speedway Corp. (913–328–7223), or check the Web site at www.kansasspeedway.com.

Speedway fans love to stop by **Wyandotte Café** at 7731 State Avenue in KCK (as it is affectionately called by residents) for a home-cooked meal and a cold beer. It's open twenty-four hours a day, so no matter how late the races run, the cafe is waiting for you. Call (913) 788–7851. Or, if the scent of cinnamon rolls, fudge brownies, carrot cake, apple and cherry strudel, and cookies of all kinds calls you, look for **Mema's Specialty Bakery** at 7634 Leavenworth Road. Mema's has—of course—povotica bread, too. If you have never tasted this Croatian delicacy, be sure to try it. Call (913) 299–9121.

If you've got kids in tow, stop at the **Children's Museum of Kansas City,** at its new location at 9601 State Avenue (Indian Springs Marketplace, I–635 and State Avenue). More than one hundred hands-on activities are perfect for children ages two to eight. They can put on a play complete with costumes, makeup, and lights; don hard hats or drive trucks as part of a construction crew; push child-size carts through a grocery store; or check out an emergency room. Hours are 9:30 A.M. to 5:00 P.M. Tuesday through Saturday, 1:00 to 5:00 P.M. Sunday. Admission is $3.50 per person ages two and up; children must be accompanied by an adult. Call

---

AUTHOR'S TOP TEN IN NORTHEAST KANSAS

Downtown Lawrence

Jalisco Restaurant, Kansas City

Perry State Park

Deanna Rose Children's Farmstead, Overland Park

Apple Valley Farm, Perry

Stan Herd's Earthwork, Atchison

Davis Memorial, Hiawatha

Frontier Army Museum, Fort Leavenworth

Gates BBQ, Kansas City

Valomilk

Trivia

Kansas City, Kansas, is the hometown of Olympic track and field champion Maurice Green.

(913) 287–8888, or visit the Web site www.kid muzm.org for information.

The city is actually a consolidation of eight towns, and so the streets are not in a grid pattern. There are many main streets and residential neighborhoods as well as several ethnic communities worth a visit, such as the Strawberry Hill neighborhood, a Slavic settlement. You can learn the history of these people at the **Strawberry Hill Museum** (913–371–3264) at 720 North Fourth Street. A completely restored, high-Victorian–style home built in 1872, the museum houses ever-changing exhibits of Croatian artifacts from the peoples of Eastern Europe. The gift shop offers a variety of unique ethnic items. It is open on Saturday and Sunday from noon to 5:00 P.M. Admission is $5.00.

Another part of the city's melting pot is the Argentine District, a Mexican-American neighborhood. You can't miss the *Anthology of Argentina* mural, painted on a wall more than 200 yards long, at Thirty-first and Metropolitan Streets. Nearby, you'll find the **Jalisco Restaurant,** which serves soft, handmade tortillas, homemade tamales, real Mexican chili with pieces of tender pork (no hamburger in this stuff), chicken mole, Mexican beer, and sopapillas for dessert. Juan Hernandez owns this restaurant and the other branch of Jalisco. His brother Javier manages the 1411 South Twenty-sixth Street restaurant. It's tricky to find, but worth the effort. The 5000 State Avenue site (913–287–9268) is more on the beaten path (and more crowded). The tortillas are made at the State Avenue restaurant. You can watch them being made one day a week. Call (913) 831–9001 for more information. Jalisco restaurants are open seven days a week. Hours are from 11:00 A.M. to 10:00 P.M. Sunday through Thursday, and until midnight on Friday and Saturday at the State Avenue site, and from 11:00 A.M. to 9:00 P.M. Sunday through Thursday, and until 10:00 P.M. Friday and Saturday at the Twenty-sixth Street location.

What's in a Name?

The term Huron *is not really the name of a Native American tribe but a somewhat derisive nickname bestowed by the French. The Wyandot people wore a traditional headdress that reminded the French of the bristly hairs on the back of a wild boar.*

Because this region was Indian Territory for years, there are several places to do research on Native American genealogies. The **Huron Burial Ground** was established by the Wyandot Indians in 1843, after they were moved west from Sandusky, Ohio. The burial ground is in downtown Kansas City on Armstrong and Seventh Streets.

The historic **White Church** (913–299–4056) at 2200 North Eighty-fifth

NORTHEAST KANSAS

Street includes an exhibit of Native American relics. A Delaware Indian cemetery is on the grounds. It is open from 6:00 A.M. to 6:00 P.M. weekdays. Church services are still held here on Sundays.

Settlers came and began to push the Native Americans west. The *Grinter Place State Historic Site* (913–299–0373), at 1420 South Seventy-eighth Street, was built around 1862 by Moses R. Grinter and his wife, Anna. Their family included ten children. Grinter is credited with being the first permanent white settler in what is now Wyandotte County and one of the earliest settlers in Kansas.

The house is modeled after a Kentucky farmhouse built in 1800 by Grinter's uncle. Structural timbers are made of native walnut. The woodwork inside is walnut and white pine hauled from Leavenworth with an ox team. Open Wednesday through Saturday from 10:00 A.M. to 5:00 P.M., Sunday from 1:00 to 5:00 P.M. Admission is free, although donations are welcome. For more information, check the Web site at www.kshs.org.

Kansas City is famous for its barbecue, and the Kansas side has its share of great places in both the city and suburbs. *Gates BBQ* at 1026 State Avenue (913–621–1134) is one of the top choices in Kansas City; Ollie Gates has served some of the finest meat in the area for more than fifty years. Featuring 100-percent hickory-smoked meats to eat there or carry out, the menu also includes all the usual trimmings. Hours are from 11:00 A.M. to midnight weekdays, until 2:00 A.M. on Friday and Saturday for after-hours cravings, and until 11:30 P.M. on Sunday. Visit www.gatesbbq.com on the Internet.

You and the children will enjoy *Fritz's Union Station* restaurant at 250 North Eighteenth Street, where food is delivered to each table by model train. Railroad paraphernalia is everywhere—on shelves, for sale behind the counter, and hanging on the walls. Each employee wears a ticking-striped engineer's uniform,

---

TOP ANNUAL EVENTS IN NORTHEAST KANSAS

May
Riverbend Art Fair and Antique Airplane Fly-In,
Atchison; (800) 234-1854

June
Great Lenexa Barbeque Battle,
Lenexa; (913) 888-1414

July
Amelia Earhart Festival,
Atchison; (800) 234-1854

August
Civil War on the Western Frontier,
Lawrence; (888) 529-5267
McLouth Threshing Bee and Steam Engine Show,
McLough;
www.mclouththreshingbee.homestead.com

September
Grinter Applefest,
Kansas City; (913) 299-0373

September–October
Lawrence Indian Arts Show,
(785) 864-4245;

October
Wild, Wild West,
Mahaffie Farmstead and Stagecoach Stop, Olathe;
(913) 782-6972

November–December
Festival of Poinsettias,
Lawrence; (785) 865-4411;
Thanksgiving through December

---

complete with cap. Children wear paper engineer hats. Call (913) 281–2777 for more information. Hours are from 6:00 A.M. to 9:00 P.M. Monday through Saturday, with train service beginning at 11:00 A.M.

Leaving metro Kansas City, the drive south along State Line Road will take you to *Fairway.* The *Shawnee Indian Methodist Mission* (913–262–0867), at 3403 West Fifty-third Street, Fairway, was established in 1830 by the Reverend Thomas Johnson and became a school for Native American children. The first territorial legislature met in these stately redbrick buildings in 1855. The Oregon and Santa Fe Trails passed through the mission complex, and it served as a camp for Union soldiers during the Civil War. It is open year-round Tuesday through Saturday from 10:00 A.M. to 5:00 P.M., Sunday from 1:00 to 5:00 P.M. Admission is free, but donations are accepted. Visit the state historical society's Web page for more information (www.kshs.org) or e-mail shawneemission@kshs.org.

State Line Road also crosses the suburb of *Mission Hills,* filled with showplace mansions on acres of grounds. At about Forty-fifth Street and State Line is a cluster of very fine antiques shops on both the Kansas and Missouri sides of the street. You can spend an entire day browsing this area. *Show-Me Antiques and Consignments* (913–236–8444) is at 4500 State Line Road and is open Wednesday through Saturday from 11:30 A.M. to 4:30 P.M., as are most of the shops in the area. Other stores include *Old World Antiques,* 4436 State Line Road (913–677–4744) and *Welling Antiques,* 1905 West Forty-fifth Street (913–432–4333). Most of the shops are located in buildings dating from the 1920s and 1930s and carry eighteenth- and nineteenth-century European and American furniture and accessories.

If you leave Kansas City on Highway 69 toward the south, you'll go through the city of *Mission,* a very upscale suburban community. There is no shortage of places to shop or eat.

The Coyote Grill (913–362–3333) at 4843 Johnson Drive in the Mission

The First Newspaper in the State Was Native American

*T*he state's first newspaper was the Shawnee Sun, *a monthly paper published in 1835 at the Shawnee Indian Methodist Mission. It was printed in the* Shawnee language by the missionary Jotham Meeker. *The first weekly newspaper was the* Kansas Weekly Herald, *published in Leavenworth in 1854.*

NORTHEAST KANSAS

WORTH A VISIT

*Linn County Park
at La Cygne Lake—
near La Cygne*

*Great Mall of the
Great Plains—Kansas City*

*Prairie Center State
Park—Olathe*

*Constitution Hall
State Historic Site—
Lecompton*

*Ottawa Antique Mall
& Restaurant*

Mall reflects the Santa Fe Trail's terminus in both menu and decor. Once you eat here, it will become a regular stopping spot if you are soft on Southwestern specialties. This is not just a taco-and-enchilada place; owners Paul Khoury and Bill Crooks offer dishes such as grilled shrimp in cilantro-lime sauce, Squawking Nachos (chicken-topped cheese favorites), Navajo beef, and tequila pasta. It is open Monday through Thursday from 11:00 A.M. to 10:00 P.M., Friday and Saturday from 11:00 A.M. to 11:00 P.M., and Sunday from 10:00 A.M. to 9:00 P.M. Brunch buffet on Sunday is from 10:30 A.M. to 2:30 P.M.

A nightspot you might want to visit is *The Roxy* at 7230 West Seventy-fifth Street. There's live music every night, a mix of classic rock and roll and blues. The Roxy is open seven days a week from 11:00 A.M. to 2:00 A.M. You can grab a quick burger here and enjoy the music. Call (913) 236–6211.

Shopping is the sport of choice in *Overland Park,* especially on 119th Street and 135th Street between Metcalf and Roe. The neighborhood is filled with designer shops, gourmet foods, huge health-food stores, and choices upon choices of places to spend money on anything you can imagine.

When you are ready to slip away from the shops for lunch, and if you have never had slow-cooked goat or are having a craving for a hot and spicy chicken dish served with a homemade flat bread, try the lunch buffet from 11:00 A.M. to 2:30 P.M. seven days a week at *Ruchi Indian Restaurant.* This restaurant at 11168 Antioch Road (College and Antioch) in Overland Park is run by Nirjen Reddy, from India, of course, so the food is authentic, unusual, and delicious. Dinner is served from 5:00 to 10:00 P.M. every day. Call Nirjen at (913) 661–9088.

In Overland Park, the *Deanna Rose Children's Farmstead* (913–897–2360) at 13800 Switzer is a tribute to a local policewoman. Rose, who loved animals, was killed making a routine traffic stop. This minifarm has every kind of farm animal you can think of. When members of the Epsilon Iota chapter of Beta Sigma Phi opened the park in 1977, they didn't know how popular it would become. It soon grew beyond petting animals and looking at flowers.

The city of Overland Park now operates the replica of an 1850 Kansas farmstead. The farmstead also has a nature trail through a wooded area with many native Kansas birds, including the great horned owl, red-tailed hawk, and grouse. A working windmill recirculates water through a tank, and vegetables and perennial flowers grow in a community garden. A chicken coop and horse-drawn farm equipment are on display. There's even a fishing pond and pony rides. The children's farmstead is open from 9:00 A.M. to 5:00 P.M. March to Memorial Day and from 8:00 A.M. to 8:00 P.M. Memorial Day to Labor Day. Admission to the facility is free.

Eight times a week, fifty-two weeks a year, the *New Theatre Restaurant,* 9229 Foster, Overland Park, treats an audience of about 600 to Broadway comedies and musicals and five-star cuisine. Nationally known stars including Don Knotts, Loretta Swit, Bonnie Franklin, Jamie Farr, and Tom Poston have performed here. Five different shows are produced each year. Make reservations by calling (913) 649–SHOW. For other information, call (913) 649–0103, or check the Web site at www.newtheatre.com.

Visit the *Overland Park Arboretum and Botanical Gardens,* 300 acres on the edge of Overland Park's residential neighborhood. The seven ecosystems in the park can be enjoyed from asphalt walks and chip-and-bark trails. Walk past lonely water gardens and through dense forests along Wolf Creek, which runs past 30-foot bluffs. A family of pileated woodpeckers draws a lot of visitors. A meadow features waterfalls, pools, a butterfly garden, and a wildflower collection. Less than one-third of the total acreage has been touched. The arboretum is on 179th Street just west of Antioch Road, about ½ mile west of Highway 69, which is a continuation of Metcalf Avenue. The park is open daily from 7:00 A.M. to 8:00 P.M. April 1 through October 31, 7:00 A.M. to 5:00 P.M. November 1 through March 31. For more information, call (913) 685–3604, or check the Web site at www.opkansas.org.

Brown v. Topeka Board of Education

*T*he city of Merriam has an interesting bit of history attached to it: Brown Park is named for Esther Brown, a local Jewish woman who led a court fight in 1946 at the Walker Grade School, now the Philadelphia Missionary Baptist Church (9430 West Fiftieth Terrace) to demand integration. This was one of nineteen known cases that preceded the Brown v. Topeka Board of Education *case decided in 1954 by the U.S. Supreme Court, which made segregated schools illegal across the country. Although Esther Brown was not one of the Browns named in that landmark case, she is honored for her extensive work and fundraising for the NAACP.*

If you're leaving Kansas City toward the southwest on Interstate 35, you'll pass through Merriam, Lenexa, and Olathe. At the turn of the twentieth century, **Merriam** was known as the playground of Kansas because of its amusement park. President Ulysses S. Grant dedicated Merriam Park in 1880, and for two decades, rail travelers came by the thousands to enjoy boating, baseball, tennis, a merry-go-round, and a zoo. The Hocker Grove area still has some of the beautiful summer homes of the wealthy families who visited from Chicago and Denver. Kansas City built its own amusement parks in the early 1900s, drawing away the tourists, but trolley service extended to the Hocker Grove neighborhood soon attracted many permanent residents.

If you have a sweet tooth, Merriam today is dear to your heart because of the gooey sweet produced by **Sifers Candy Company,** founded in 1903. Owner Russell Sifers and his son have become the fifth generation to use the original copper pots and recipe. One day in 1931, an employee (who, they say, sampled too much of the bourbon vanilla) botched up a batch of marshmallow filling. The marvelous result was the Valomilk, known to Midwesterners as the favorite thing to find in your "dinner bucket" at school. These shells of blended light and Brazilian dark chocolate filled with super-sweet marshmallow goo are sold only (and everywhere) in the Midwest and through a few specialty catalogs. There are no factory tours because there are only six employees (and even the boss gets in the way sometimes), and there is no outlet store. But once you're hooked, you can order them by the box (in cool weather) by writing Russell at 5112 Merriam Drive, Shawnee Mission, 66203 or by calling (913) 722–0991. There's also a Web site (www.valomilk.com).

Old Shawnee Town, at 11501 West Fifty-seventh Street in **Shawnee,** has seventeen original and replica buildings from the nineteenth and twentieth centuries, as well as period gardens. See the first jailhouse in Kansas, dating from 1843, the 1878 Hart House, Amos Undertakers, All Faiths Chapel, Franke Barber Shop, and the Shawnee Fire Barn. Old Shawnee Town is open Tuesday through Saturday from noon to 5:00 P.M. Call (913) 248–2360 for information.

The Legler Barn Museum, at 14907 West Eighty-seventh Street Parkway, Shawnee, was originally located on the old Santa Fe Trail. Using stone from the original barn, it was rebuilt and restored in the fifty-three-acre Sar-Ko-Par Trails Park. On the grounds of the barn is more history, including the old Frisco Railroad depot. The museum also contains a gift shop. Hours are Tuesday through Friday 10:00 A.M. to 4:00 P.M. and Saturday and Sunday 1:00 to 4:00 P.M. Call (913) 492–0038 for information. There's no admission fee, but donations are welcome.

If you're traveling with kids, be sure to stop at the *Wonderscope Children's Museum,* at 5705 Flint in Shawnee. Kids can make a tornado, experience an emergency operating room, lift their body weight on giant pulleys in the Science Lab, freeze their shadows, paint their faces, broadcast the news in the TV studio, or maneuver a wheelchair in the What if . . . Maze. There also is a Small Wonders Play Space for kids age three and younger. Hours are Tuesday through Saturday from 10:00 A.M. to 5:00 P.M., Sunday from noon to 5:00 P.M.; March through August the museum is open seven days a week 10:00 A.M. to 5:00 P.M. Admission is $5.00 for adults and children age three and older, $2.50 for children under age three. Call (913) 268–4176 for more information.

The Machine Shed restaurant is a tribute to the hard-working farmers of Kansas and the pioneer spirit of the people who settled here. The homemade food is served in a comfortable setting and wins numerous awards. Antique farm implements and a country gift shop give the kids someplace to wander while the food is prepared. Most popular is the Sunday brunch served from 8:00 A.M. to 2:00 P.M. But Tuesday night is a personal favorite—fried chicken night, and their recipe is the crisp, juicy kind you wish your mama made. Wednesday is barbecue night, Friday is fish night, and all of this is just $7.99—and they just keep serving until you ask them to stop. The Machine Shed is at 12080 South Strang Line Road (I–35, exit 220). Call (913) 780–2697.

Shawnee is also home to the *Prairie Center,* where the rich natural history of Kansas has been preserved with 300 acres of native tallgrass prairie. Six miles of hiking trails wander through woodlands and across creeks and are open for cross-country skiing. A five-acre lake provides fishing, and the park is open daily from dawn to dusk at 26325 Prairie Center Road (135th and Cedar Niles Road). For more information contact the Kansas Department of Wildlife and Parks at (913) 894–9113, extension 13.

For more organized beauty, stop by *Whittaker Flower Farm* at 15855 West 183rd Street and behold six acres of field-grown flowers and herbs, everything from old-fashioned zinnias to exotic leonotis, to be cut all year. There are more than 125 different plants to touch and smell. In the fall the pumpkin patch lets you find the perfect jack-o-lantern. The kids can visit Larkwhistle Cottage and the Children's Garden. The garden is open from 10:00 A.M. to 5:00 P.M. April through October, closed Mondays. Gaye and Gary Whittaker can be reached at (913) 592–3229.

Neon beer signs glimmer in the windows of *Side Pockets*, at 13320 West Eighty-seventh Street, in *Lenexa,* but this is not your neighborhood bar and pool hall. It is a billiard parlor, and even though the players are perhaps drinking a beer, they are there for a serious game. Many players carry their own cues in cases as they come through the door. They pay $7.00 per hour for professional-size tables (only 75 cents for regular bar-size tables). You can hold the table for the evening, or if you are competitive, you can play at the challenge tables, where a better player can come after you.

There are twenty-four tables in the 10,000-square-foot hall, and it is filled with groups of women, men, and couples. You can have a sandwich or a steak dinner and watch the action while listening to the classic rock and roll from the jukebox. Hours are from 10:00 A.M. to 2:00 A.M. every day. Call Keith Robinson and Rich Hawkins at (913) 888–7665.

Looking for some povotica? Find the Croatian bread at *Strawberry Hill Povotica* (913–631–1002), at 8609 Quivira Road, Lenexa. Hours are 9:00 A.M. to 5:00 P.M. Tuesday through Friday, 9:00 A.M. to 2:00 P.M. Saturday.

Everywhere in the state are reminders of the history of the area, and *Olathe* is no different, despite its nearness to metropolitan Kansas City. Just off Highway 7, about 3 miles north of town, is the lonely grave of a baby boy who died nearly a century and a half ago on the Santa Fe Trail. Several years ago a Boy Scout troop cleaned the grave site and surrounded it with a small pipe fence. Sometimes fresh flowers can be seen on the grave of nine-month-old Asa Smith, born November 15, 1856, died August 30, 1857.

Olathe has a fine collection of charming old homes within just a few blocks of each other on West Park Street (the city's first street) and South Pine Street. West Park was part of the Santa Fe Trail and boasts some of the oldest homes in the county. For more information on the town, stop at the Tourist Information Center at Strang Line Road and 119th Street, just off the 119th Street exit of I–35.

Mahaffie Farmstead and Stagecoach Stop (913–782–6972), 1100 Kansas City Road, Olathe, was the first "home station" (stop providing meals for travelers) on the Santa Fe Trail. It's also the only remaining stop preserved and open to the public. Still standing on the fifteen-acre farmplace, which dates from 1865 and is on the National Register of Historic Places, are the original farmhouse, a wood-peg barn, and a stone icehouse. A stagecoach and prairie schooner are there, too. Hours are 10:00 A.M. to 4:00 P.M. Monday through Saturday, noon to 4:00 P.M. Sunday, April through December. Closed in January, open weekdays only in February and March. Admission is $3.00 for adults, $1.75 for children ages five to eleven.

Along the Oregon Trail

Between the 1840s and the 1870s, about 300,000 hardy souls walked the Oregon Trail to the northwest in the greatest peacetime migration in the history of the world. The 1,172-mile journey still makes an exciting tour. In Kansas the trail passes through the towns of Olathe, Lenexa, Lawrence, Topeka, St. Mary's, Manhattan, Wamego, Westmoreland, Blue Rapids, and Marysville. They have historic sites that date from that great migration, and wagon ruts are still visible in several places.

Michael and Lenore Brumet have a beautiful bed-and-breakfast at 507 West Park Street, Olathe. The *Pickering House* is on the National Register of Historic Places; it was built in the 1870s for Major Isaac Pickering, who liked to give glamorous affairs. The cupola above the front porch was built to house a string quartet, in which Major Pickering played cello. Three sets of French doors in the large living room open onto the veranda for summer parties. A watchtower atop the house allowed Pickering to oversee the town when he was mayor. These days, guests can bask in a hot tub in the atrium or relax in a gazebo in the courtyard. Breakfast is an event in itself. Lenore prepares a four-course gourmet breakfast, which may include such wonders as Danish abelskivers (ball-shaped pancakes), blintzes, scones, crepes, and French eggs in a phyllo shell. Rooms are $110. For more information, call (913) 829–7800, or check the Web site at www.pickeringhouse.com or e-mail pickeringhousebb@cs.com.

Also on your route through Olathe on Interstate 35, you will pass the *Old Olathe Naval Air Museum* in New Century Air Center, Kansas, near Olathe. It is housed in the former Commanding Officer Quarters, one of the few original structures of the Olathe Naval Air Station. The museum displays memorabilia from World War II, and from the Korean and Vietnam Wars. It is funded entirely by the donations of former servicemen and servicewomen. Museum hours are April through October noon to 4:00 P.M. Weekends only and by appointment anytime. Call (913) 768–1153 for more information.

The *Rose Garden Cafe* at 11695 Blackbob Road, Olathe, is a ranch-style home, and five of the rooms are devoted to antiques. Barbara and Harrison Sharifian are the owners of this unusual shop. Two rooms serve as a cafe offering quiche, salads, soups, sandwiches, and desserts. Hours are 11:00 A.M. to 2:00 P.M. Monday through Saturday. Call (913) 393–3232.

The Dolphin Song in *Gardner* makes its home in a building at 102 South Elm, at the corner of Main and Elm Streets. It is an "environmentally conscious" shop, with hand-carved toys, pottery, jewelry, and crafts. Owner Linda Meisinger purchases many items through international programs dedicated to promoting cultural understanding with

Eastern Europe and Asia. Wander in and spend hours browsing from 10:00 A.M. to 5:00 P.M. Tuesday through Saturday. Call (913) 856–7513.

Sunrise Soap Company, at 204A East Main Street in Gardner, is where Terry and Judy Michaelis make and sell all kinds of homemade soap and lotions. You can watch the soap being made right there in the shop—using the best ingredients, such as vegetable oils and goat's milk—as well as candles, lotions, and bath products scented to match the soaps. Some of their specialties include Bath Bursts (like scented Alka Seltzer in your tub) and Sunrise Sprinkles (a powdered bath oil that fizzes). Judy even has "gourmet dish soap" in a pretty glass bottle. Everyone who visits the shop leaves with a free sample. Hours are 10:00 A.M. to 6:00 P.M. Monday through Friday and to 5:00 P.M. on Saturday. Call (913) 856–7923.

Things I Love, at 212 East Main Street, is a store that Nancy Schaefer jam-packs with collectibles. Along with home-decor items and candles, Nancy has Willow Tree Angels and Boyd's Bears. At Christmas time the entire store is changed and filled with holiday things. Hours are 10:00 A.M. to 6:00 P.M Monday through Saturday, with extended hours during the holiday season. Call (913) 856–9988.

Schartner's Corner, 202 East Main Street, is unique, and big, so you have to see it yourself. Owner Lynn Hails carries Thomas Kinkade art, the famous Kansas City Cows, Heritage Lace, Roman Angels, and such odds and ends as teapots, sewing notions, and fishing gear . . . well, you just have to see it for yourself. Christmas Shop in the back open year-round. Hours are 10:00 A.M. to 6:00 P.M. Monday through Friday and to 5:00 P.M. on Saturday. Call (913) 856–7882.

Experience old-time country education at *Lanesfield School Historic Site* (913–893–6645), 18745 South Dillie Road in *Edgerton* on Highway 56, a one-room stone schoolhouse built in 1869. It is the only structure left on the town site of Lanesfield, a mail stop on the Santa Fe Trail, and it has been restored to serve as a living-history classroom for Johnson County children. Hours are Tuesday through Sunday from 1:00 to 5:00 P.M. Admission is free.

Tonganoxie wins the prize for the best town name in Kansas; it has a catchy sound to it that stays in your brain for days. Tonganoxie,

> **Trivia**
>
> *Several colleges were chartered in the 1800s when Kansas was a territory. Only three of these are still in existence. They are Baker University in Baldwin City, Highland Junior College in Highland, and St. Benedict's College in Atchison.*

Tonganoxie, your brain whispers to you over and over. So, of course, you have to stop in the heart of Tonganoxie for lunch at **Badd Jack's Southwest** or you won't be able to sleep tonight. Anyway, the Southwest food and atmosphere are good, prices are reasonable, and there's even an outdoor cantina in the works. Badd Jack's is at 416 East Fourth Street, (913) 845–8779. Hours are Tuesday through Thursday from 11:00 A.M. to 9:00 P.M., Friday to 10:00 P.M., Saturday from 3:00 to 10:00 P.M., and Sunday from 1:00 to 7:00 P.M. Go to www.baddjacksouthwest.com for a look at Jack Cronemeyer's place.

Saturday nights in Tonganoxie get lively thanks to **Glen's Opry**, at the corner of Fourth and Main Streets downtown. You have a "good time guaranteed or your money back" here in this newly remodeled auditorium that boasts theater seating and the latest in sound systems, and that's a safe offer if you like country music. According to Glen, it all began when he listened to Grand Ole Opry every Saturday night back when he was growing up. Then he had Friday night jam sessions at his house until it grew to where the house wasn't big enough. Doors open at 6:30 P.M. and the show begins at 7:30. Admission is $7.50 for adults, $7.00 for seniors, and $4.00 for children under age twelve, so bring the whole family for some good, clean entertainment—guaranteed. Call (913) 631–2591 for reservations.

Kaw River Road

Around **Baldwin City** are places that are worth the short drive. Douglas County State Lake has excellent fishing, sailing, canoeing, and boating 2 miles northeast of Baldwin City; the Ivan Boyd Prairie Preserve, 3 miles east of Baldwin City, is a good place to see virgin tallgrass prairie as well as the ruts carved by the thousands of wagons that traveled the Santa Fe Trail. The ruts are easier to see in early spring when the grass is short. Park at the roadside lot and walk.

Another interesting stop in Baldwin City is Baker University. The **Clarice L. Osborne Memorial Chapel** on the campus was constructed in 1864 in Sproxton (pronounced "Prose-ton"), England, and had fallen into disrepair. The university discovered the chapel was for sale and with the help of a $1 million donation from R. R. Osborne the chapel was disassembled, moved, and reconstructed. Named in memory of Osborne's wife, it now stands as the spiritual heart of the campus.

Interesting facts about the move: A time capsule was found in the cornerstone. The original pump organ and stained glass have been restored.

New to the chapel is the English garden, which brightens the surrounding landscape. It is, as you would guess, very popular for weddings.

The former British prime minister Margaret Thatcher visited the campus in 1996 to dedicate the chapel. Thatcher's father had served as a lay minister at the English chapel in the 1930s. Call (785) 594–4553 for more information.

Also at Baker University is the *Old Castle Complex,* a three-story native limestone edifice built as a college in 1858. It could be seen for miles over the treeless prairie by the pioneers traveling the historic Santa Fe Trail. Noting Kansas's prevailing southern winds, the nineteenth-century builders designed a concave south wall to withstand them. The Old Castle houses an outstanding museum.

Other buildings of note on the campus include Case Hall, built of native blue limestone, and Parmenter Hall, a sandstone structure that is famous locally for the grasshoppers that stacked themselves as high as the building's foundation—18 inches—during an 1870s plague of the insects. The Old Castle, Case Hall, and Parmenter Hall are all on the National Register of Historic Places.

Both you and the children will enjoy the famous "train to nowhere," which leaves Baldwin City, rain or shine, on Saturdays, Sundays, and Thursdays from Memorial Day weekend through October. This excursion train runs on a line constructed in 1867 and travels to Norwood, crossing a 200-foot trestle 24 feet above a stream. The *Midland Railway Depot,* on the National Register of Historic Places, is next to the grain elevator at 1515 West High Street (8 blocks west of downtown Baldwin City).

All aboard; the train leaves the depot at 10:30 A.M. Thursday mornings, and at 11:30 A.M., and at 1:30 P.M., and 3:30 P.M. on Saturdays, Sundays, and holidays. During April, May, September, and October the train also departs at 11:00 A.M. and 1:00 P.M. on Fridays. During the Maple Leaf Festival, the third weekend in October, the train runs hourly from 11:00 A.M. to 5:00 P.M.. Then there's the nighttime Halloween Train at 6:30, 8:00, and 9:30 P.M. Call (800) 651–0388 for fare information.

If you're a history buff, ask at the chamber of commerce for a guided tour of Baldwin City. You will be put in touch with local experts on the Santa Fe Trail, abolitionist John Brown, and the Civil War. You can even find the site of the Battle of Black Jack, where Captain Pate and his Westport Sharpshooters tried but failed to capture John Brown.

There are two very nice Victorian bed-and-breakfasts in Baldwin City. Just down the street from an antiques store is the *Grove House* at 807

Grove Street. The B&B, which dates from 1907, has two private suites. The upstairs suite has a fireplace and claw-foot bathtub, while the downstairs suite offers a whirlpool tub. Step back in time by watching a vintage movie from the house collection or listening to an old Victrola. Your hosts can even arrange for you to tour the town in the backseat of an antique car. Private candlelight dinners are available by special arrangement. Room rates are $90 to $95, including breakfast. Visit the Web site at www.baldwin-city.com/grove, call (785) 594–2947 or (785) 594–6495 in the evenings, or e-mail rhaskey@sprintmail.com.

The **Three Sisters Inn** at 1035 Ames was built in 1905. It has been restored with elegance, charm, and antiques. There are four rooms with private baths; rates range from $79 to $129, including full breakfast. Innkeepers Diane and Jim Niefoff offer packages including gourmet picnic baskets to be enjoyed in the privacy of the gazebo, Victorian high tea, and massage. Check the Web site at www.threesistersinn.com for details, or call (785) 594–3244.

The city of **Lawrence** on Interstate 70 is more than just the home of the fierce University of Kansas Jayhawks. It is also a very livable city, nestled between the valleys of the Kansas and Wakarusa Rivers.

Drop by the **Lawrence Visitor Information Center,** located in a renovated Union Pacific depot dating from 1888. The center is at North Second and Locust Streets, just north of downtown along the Kansas River or about a mile south of exit 204 on Interstate 70/Kansas Turnpike. Summer hours are Monday to Saturday from 8:30 A.M. to 5:30 P.M. and Sunday from 1:00 to 5:00 P.M.; hours are shorter in winter but still daily. Call (785) 865–4499 or 888–LAWKANS for information. The official Web site for the city is www.visitlawrence.com, where you will find a current calendar of events as well as information on accommodations, dining attractions, and the city's history.

An entire neighborhood, bounded by Tennessee and Indiana Streets on the east and west and Sixth and Ninth Streets on the north and south, all within walking distance of downtown, is designated as a historic district. Old West Lawrence contains some of the finest nineteenth- and early-twentieth-century houses around. The architectural styles range from Italianate and Queen Anne to Gothic Revival and Neoclassical. The gentle slopes of the hills have an atmosphere of nineteenth-century

New England, with broad lawns and brick and stone mansions. A map is available from the visitors center.

The settling of Kansas was different from that of any other state because of the Kansas–Nebraska Act, which allowed settlers to vote and choose between being a free or slave state. Many came to Kansas Territory to make it free, and the result was violent border wars with neighboring (proslavery) Missouri. The number of proslavery proponents who crossed the border to Kansas resulted in a proslavery territorial government. The antislavery people refused to obey the new legislature. A new constitution was written, and Kansas entered the Union as a free state in 1861. When the Civil War erupted, Kansas had the largest proportion of fighting men in the Union Army.

The sacking of Lawrence by the pro-South William Quantrill's Raiders in August 1863 was one of many skirmishes along the Kansas–Missouri border. His band of marauders, including "Bloody" Bill Anderson, Dick Yeager, and the James Boys, laid Lawrence to ashes. More than 200 men and boys died, and the town was devastated. The bloodshed is remembered each August with living-history events during Lawrence's Civil War on the Western Frontier.

Set aside time to stroll historic downtown Lawrence, where shops, galleries, and eateries line Massachusetts Street (referred to as "Mass" here) from Sixth to Eleventh Streets. Yes, Lawrence is a college town, home of the much loved/hated Jayhawks of the University of Kansas. But downtown Lawrence is much more than that; it is a honeycomb of activity ranging from the familiar to the bizarre. You can have it all—from a

Quantrill Was a Schoolteacher

At the age of only twenty-six, William Quantrill was the leader of the violent proslavery guerrillas called Quantrill's Raiders. Before conducting his infamous assault, Quantrill was a schoolteacher in the Lawrence system. He spent the school year of 1859–1860 living in the city to learn the local geography necessary to plan a successful assault on Lawrence. In August 1863, he as-sembled 450 men in Missouri and launched a perfect attack. The order was to burn every house and kill every man. Women and children were robbed but not harmed. Four hours of looting, burning, and murdering made Quantrill's raid what many historians call the greatest atrocity of the Civil War. It left 85 women as widows and 250 fatherless children. Damage was estimated at $2.5 million.

massage at Lunaria to a tattoo at Skin Illustrations. You can enjoy a double dip of ice cream at Sylas & Mady's or a double martini at Teller's. Or if you want more action than that, you can do a swan dive into a mosh pit at Bottleneck and follow it up with tango lessons at the Flamingo Dance Academy. It's all here: farmers and professors, wine-sipping artists and beer-drinking sports fans. What's more, almost everything is locally owned with a blue-million small shops carrying unique items. At **Waxman Candles,** 609 Massachusetts (785–843–8593), Bob Werts has been pouring candles for thirty years (his wares can be seen at www.waxmancandles.com). Sarah Fayman at **Sarah's Fabrics,** 925–927 Massachusetts (785–842–6198), has offered quilting classes nearly as long. **The Topiary Tree,** 716 Massachusetts (785–842–1181), specializes in European antiques, while at the **Lawrence Antique Mall,** 830 Massachusetts (785–842–1328), you might find something reminiscent of Grandma's attic. Check their Web site at www.lawrenceantiquemall.com. Hours are Monday through Saturday 10:00 A.M. to 6:00 P.M. and Sunday 1:00 to 5:00 P.M. **The Bay Leaf,** at 725 Massachusetts Street, (785–842–4544), is a favorite for kitchenware and table settings. Hours are Monday through Saturday 9:30 A.M. to 5:30 P.M., but owner Geri Reikhof keeps the place open on Thursday nights until 8:30 P.M. and is open on Sunday from noon to 5:00 P.M. Colorful murals are painted in the breezeways between the buildings in the 700 and 800 blocks, where you can shop for fine jewelry and crafts at **Silver Works and More,** at 715 Massachusetts (785–842–1460), or American Indian jewelry and fine arts at **Southwest and More,** 727 Massachusetts (785–843–0141), and then on to the unique **Vormehr & Youngquist Gallery,** at 914 Massachusetts, featuring KU-inspired jewelry and Harley Davidson–style art. Then walk to number 919 to visit the **Phoenix Gallery** (785–843–0080), where local artists have been showing ceramics, wood, jewelry, textiles, glass, prints, and much more. This colorful gallery specializes in custom stained glass. Call Downtown Lawrence, Inc. (785–842–3883) for information on store hours for these and other businesses in the area.

Around Twelfth Street and Massachusetts is South Park, where you can catch an outdoor band concert on a summer evening. The last concert of the summer always includes the *1812 Overture* with real cannon fire and the ringing of church bells. On the other side of South Park is **Footprints,** 1339 Massachusetts Street (800–488–8316), known for its Birkenstocks and its murals by local artist Missy McCoy in a style inspired by regionalist painter and Kansas native John Steuart Curry.

The Eldridge Hotel at Seventh and Massachusetts Streets, built in 1855, was first called the Free-State Hotel and housed abolitionists who were building homes in Lawrence. It was a symbol of defiance of the laws passed by the proslavery territorial legislature. Proslavery forces burned it in 1856 and again in 1863 as raiders tore "Bloody Kansas" asunder.

This die-hard hotel has been restored to its 1925 grandeur, including a molded plaster ceiling and a splashing fountain and goldfish pond in the lobby piano bar. The all-suite hotel contains forty-eight units with such luxuries as wet bars and coffeemakers. Shalor's restaurant serves a seasonally varied menu of regional favorites. If you order the chicken breast baked in Flint Hills clay, the waiter cracks the shell open at your table. Very impressive. Suites are $78 to $235. Call (785) 749–5011 or (800) 527–0909.

The Castle Tea Room (785–843–1151) is a seventeen-room limestone mansion at Thirteenth and Massachusetts Streets. Built in 1894, it is listed on the National Register of Historic Places. The walnut, birch, pine, oak, and sycamore woodwork and exquisite carving were done by the Englishman Sidney Endacott. The tearoom opened in 1947 and serves American, Italian, and Bohemian cuisines. Libuse (Libby) Kriz Fiorito (who says she is "knocking eighty" and has been here since it opened) is the proprietor. Dining is by reservation only, and reservations must be made a couple of days in advance. Lunch is served for eight or more people only, and dinner is served from 6:00 to 7:30 P.M. if you are lucky enough to have a reservation.

Or try the *Paradise Cafe* (785–842–5199) at 728 Massachusetts Street, where the diners are as interesting as the decor. You can get some terrific vegetarian food here in addition to the everyday fare—if by everyday you mean a muffuletta sandwich, a seafood kabob, or a Philly steak. (Give them a call; you'll chuckle when they answer with "This is Paradise!") Paradise is open Monday through Saturday from 6:30 A.M. to 2:30 P.M. On Wednesday through Saturday dinner is served from 5:00 to 10:00 P.M. Sunday hours are 8:00 A.M. to 2:30 P.M. The owner is Steve McCoy.

Now that you have worked up a thirst, you'll need something cold. The *Free State Brewing Company* (785–843–4555), at 636 Massachusetts Street (in a converted trolley barn just north of the Liberty Hall Opera House), is the oldest brewery in the state because in 1880 Kansas was the first state to pass a constitutional prohibition against alcohol. (Kansas had 113 breweries in the days before Prohibition, due to the large population of German and Slavic immigrants.)

The beer is brewed on the premises in huge, stainless-steel tanks behind a glass wall, and great foods are served. All ages are welcome in the bright glass, cedar, and brick building. Brewmaster Steve Bradt and owner Chuck Magerl offer five types of house beer on tap or in carry-out kegs. Wheat State Golden, Ad Astra Ale, and Hefe-Weizen are standard beers available most times, with special brews introduced from time to time to keep it interesting. In the fall there is an Oktoberfest beer and in the winter a holiday stout.

The brewery is open Monday through Saturday from 11:00 A.M. to midnight and on Sunday from noon to 11:00 P.M. Visit the Web site at www.freestatebrewing.com.

For lunch or dinner, head to *The Tellers' Restaurant* in a beautiful 1877 bank building at 746 Massachusetts Street. The rest rooms are in the vault, so you will feel very safe while washing your hands.

Chef Robert Dewalt describes his eclectic menu as "spirited Italian and French cuisine." The wood-fired brick ovens are enclosed in glass so patrons can watch the chef at work. This is an eating experience to remember. Lunch is served from 11:00 A.M. to 4:00 P.M., dinner from 4:00 to 10:00 P.M. Sunday through Thursday and to 11:00 P.M. Friday and Saturday. Call (785) 843–4111.

Although the city was twice sacked and burned in the first ten years of its life, Lawrence has risen like the fabled phoenix to become the educational center of the state. "Rock Chalk Jayhawk!" is the cry heard in Lawrence, where the red-roofed limestone buildings of the *University of Kansas* can be seen on the summit of Mt. Oread, as the hill is known locally.

What to do at KU? Start at the *Dyche Hall and Museum of Natural History* on Jayhawk Avenue. Here's why:

Almost everyone knows about Lieutenant Colonel George Armstrong Custer's last stand on June 25, 1876, at the Little Bighorn River in what is now Montana. Well, there was one lone survivor of that bloody clash of the Seventh Cavalry and the Sioux and other Native Americans—a cavalry horse named Comanche. Several days after the battle, the men of the Seventh Cavalry found the horse, severely wounded, standing over the body of his master. They took the horse back to the fort and nursed him back to health.

When Comanche died at Fort Riley in 1891, the men of the Seventh Cavalry employed a taxidermist to prepare the horse for permanent display. Today Comanche stands proudly in the museum, along with one of the largest collections of fossils and mounted animals in natural habitats. The museum is open year-round Monday through Saturday from 10:00 A.M. to 5:00 P.M. and Sunday from noon to 5:00 P.M. Call (785) 864–4540, or visit the museum's Web site at www.nhm.ukans.edu/. The e-mail address is hunhm@ukans.edu. Admission is free.

The *Helen F. Spencer Museum of Art,* at 1301 Mississippi Street, also on the KU campus in Lawrence, is one of the finest university museums in the country. Its collection ranges from medieval to modern art. Hours are 10:00 A.M. to 5:00 P.M. Tuesday, Wednesday, Friday, and Saturday. On Thursday it is open until 9:00 P.M. Sunday hours are noon to 5:00 P.M. Admission is free.

Not far from KU is *Haskell Indian Nations University,* at Haskell Avenue and Twenty-third Street. It opened in 1884 as an elementary school and has evolved into an intertribal university that attracts Native American students from 150 tribes and 35 states. The 320-acre campus includes twelve National Historic Landmarks as well as the American Indian Athletic Hall of Fame and a 24-foot-tall medicine wheel totem pole. For more information, call (785) 749–8404, or check the Web site at www.haskell.edu.

At the *Halcyon House*, 1000 Ohio Street, Lawrence (785–841–0314 or 888–441–0314), Ester Wolfe and her daughter Constance offer an elegantly renovated, century-old bed-and-breakfast close to the Kansas University campus and downtown. This light-blue, three-story, European-style hotel is only 3 blocks west of the "Mass" Street shopping area.

Nine guest rooms featuring walnut woodwork, some with a private bath, some with a king-size bed, are on three floors. Coming down to the big kitchen, with its brick floor and window-lined wall, for the house specialties (Morning Glory Pie and homemade biscuits) will get you off to a good start. Prices are from $50 for the rooms with semiprivate bath to $149 for the rooms with private bath and king-size bed.

Just outside town, 4 miles south and 0.7 mile east of Twenty-third and Iowa Streets, is *Wells Overlook County Park*, which features a 27-foot-tall wooden tower with a spectacular view of the countryside. Hike the trails or enjoy this perfect spot for a quiet picnic.

If you would like to surround yourself with open space on a grand scale, try the *Circle S Ranch and Country Inn,* which covers endless acres of rolling hills, waiting to be explored. There's biking, bird-watching, and fishing on the property of this elegant country inn, where romantic fires burn in cool weather. Mary Beth Cronemeyer will welcome you to the 1,200-acre ranch, home to the 400 head of cattle that wander over the tallgrass prairie. More than twenty ponds dot the ranch, and heavy timber surrounds it. Exploring the ranch reveals signs of early settlement, including several old stone walls. You can even bring your own horse for a trail ride through the countryside.

The inn is built to resemble a Kansas barn and has twelve guest rooms, each with a private bath and beautiful view. Some have claw-foot tubs or fireplaces. Complimentary breakfast is served; dinner is available at additional cost by reservation. The ranch is at 3325 Circle S Lane, in Lawrence. Call (800) 625–2839 or (785) 843–4124, visit the Web site at www. CircleSRanch.com, or e-mail circlesinn@aol.com. The ranch is located east of Wellman Road (County Road 1045) 2 miles along a county road. Barbed-wire fencing with wooden fence posts will guide you to the old-fashioned archway entrance. Rooms are from $155 to $215.

Clinton Lake has high bluffs and a wooded shoreline. The roads follow the contour of the land, and everything is planned to have as little impact on the natural landscape as possible.

This lake is unique in the number of recreational opportunities available. There are more than 400 campsites, and the Rockhaven area is the trailhead to 30-plus miles of bridle paths and hiking trails. The Woodridge area has 450 acres for backpackers who enjoy roughing it. There is a total of 9,000 acres of public hunting lands with mourning doves, quail, and small game, as well as waterfowl, and plenty of fishing coves. There is also a full-service marina. It is just 4 miles west of Lawrence on High-

Sailing a Hobie Cat

*V*isitors are often surprised to learn that sailing is a popular summer pastime in Kansas. While natural lakes are few, the state boasts numerous reservoirs and plenty of wind.

At Perry State Park, Hobie Cats are a common sight. The twin-hulled catamaran sailboats have a trampoline between the hulls, nothing more. On windy days, the boat reaches very high speeds, and heels, or tilts, to the point where the sail touches the water

and the hull you sit on can be 5 to 8 feet above the water. That's called "flying a hull" and can result in the boat tipping over. Fortunately, the boat is easily turned right side up again.

Fleet 149, a group of local Hobie Cat sailors with a passion for sailing and racing, holds annual regattas open to other Hobie Cat enthusiasts. The sport is a great way to cool off in Kansas's summer heat.

way 40 and 2 miles south on K–10. For information, call Clinton State Park at (785) 842–8562.

Take Highway 59/159 north from Lawrence to **Old Jefferson Town,** on Highway 59 at **Oskaloosa.** A collection of vintage buildings moved from other locations throughout the county, the town is a replica of early Jefferson County settlements. Old Jefferson Town includes a two-story Victorian home, an 1887 schoolhouse, a 1909 jail, a blacksmith shop, a general store, and the Edmonds Church, built in 1891 and still used for Easter sunrise services and weddings. The 125-year-old iron **Bow String Bridge** is also here. It is open May through September on Saturday mornings and Wednesday evenings, and by appointment. For more information, visit the Web site at www.usa.net/kansasnet.com/jefferson, or call (785) 863–2070.

In the hills of northeast Kansas, a century-plus-old barn that once put up Buffalo Bill and his horse waits for you. **The Barn Bed and Breakfast** at 14910 Bluemound Road in **Valley Falls** is owned by Tom and Marcella Ryan, who along with their daughter Patricia offer you a chance to get away for some peace and quiet while still near the big cities and Lake Perry.

The Barn has twenty guest rooms and will sleep fifty-three people, so groups are welcome. Breakfast is served in the all-glass east dining room, where you can watch the sun come up and enjoy a good, old-fashioned country breakfast with homemade bread. But that's not all. Guests also get supper in the evening—country cooking done by the whole family. The bedrooms in the hayloft have king-size beds and private baths. You'll also find fitness equipment, an indoor 20-by-40-foot heated pool, and a conference room. It is open year-round. To find the Barn, turn north at Milepost 354 on Highway 4. Call (800) 869–7717 or (785) 945–3225. The cost is $111 per room, double occupancy, Monday through Thursday, $117 Friday through Sunday. Additional charges apply for extra people in the room. For more information, check the Web site at www.thebarnbb.com.

Off Highway 24 and Ferguson Road, near **Perry,** you'll find **Apple Valley Farm** at 9252 Apple Valley Lane (785–876–2114). The old barn is now a melodrama and antiques shop and saloon. The Homestead is a farmhouse restaurant. An airy space filled with windows, it has a country-kitchen motif, complete with red-checked tablecloths. Knickknacks and crafts items abound. The deck is fine for a twilight dinner. Friday and Saturday evenings a buffet is offered at $11.25. The tickets for the melodrama are $12 and $14, depending on seating.

Melodramas begin at 8:30 P.M. The Grainery Saloon, also on the grounds, has a pool table and dance floor and serves appetizers—the cream cheese–stuffed jalapeños are great. In the dining room, you can order a steak that comes with a bushel basket full of steak fries. The menu also includes burgers. Hours are Friday and Saturday from 5:00 P.M. to 2:00 A.M. Call (888) 634–4219 for reservations or information.

Nearby *Perry Lake State Park* and *Slough Creek Park,* a recreational area administered by the Army Corps of Engineers, offer all kinds of outdoor fun. Perry Lake is great for sailboats (always plenty of wind on the prairie). There are miles of trails designated for specific uses, including a 25-mile-long equestrian trail, hiking trails, and all-terrain-vehicle trails. On the east side of the lake, hikers can connect with a National Hiking Trail. A state park pass is required for admittance to the park. Call the state park office at (785) 246–3449 or the Army Corps of Engineers at (785) 597–5144.

Sharon's "Billtown" Cafe (785–597–5541) is on Highway 24 just before the turnoff to Lake Perry. This place has great food, and the prices are right. Breakfast here is popular with the lake crowd.

In *Lakewood Hills,* north of Perry, is a fascinating shop called *Jesterday's* (8717 Hilltop Road), where Christine Shively makes jesters, angels, and character dolls from fabric. She sells her creations at art fairs across the country and has won numerous awards. Call (785) 876–2804 for studio hours and directions.

Reservation Country

North and west of Atchison are the reservations of several Native American tribes. The Prairie Band of the Potawatomi nation is located in Jackson County. A casino (785–966–7777) is a popular attraction here. Three more reservations, the Kickapoo, Sac and Fox, and Iowa, are in Brown County. Inquire locally for a schedule of powwows and other events open to the public.

Holton, north of Topeka on Highways 75 and 16, is a Victorian town with original brick sidewalks, historic lighting, and a lovely courtyard square. There are several antiques and gift shops, an old-fashioned five-and-dime store, and a number of accommodations to choose from. *The Hotel Josephine* has been in operation at Fifth and Ohio Streets since 1890 and retains its early charm but with modern comforts (it's air-conditioned but filled with antiques). It is 1 block off the square. Rooms are $50; call (785) 364–3151. The hotel is a good starting point for a stroll around the square to visit the antiques shops and eating places there.

The Parsonage is at 425 West Fourth Street (785–364–2240). This 1870 home served as a parsonage until 1996. It features five guest rooms with private baths and televisions. Hosts Joni and Dennis White will help you decide where to explore in the downtown area and nearby lakes and can point you toward the casinos. Rooms are $79 to $129, including a continental breakfast on weekdays and a full breakfast on weekends. E-mail at jwhite@holtonks.net. There is a new shop in the B&B, too, called The Pastor's Study (what it was when the home was actually a parsonage). Joni carries inspirational gifts as well as antiques.

Tucked into 560 acres of farmland, *Country Reflections B&B* is 3.5 miles from Holton at 20975 R Road (785–364–3747). Three rooms in a guest house near the farmhouse offer private baths and entrances. There's even a two-and-a-half-acre fishing pond. A private balcony gives you a splendid view. Wake up to a country breakfast served by host Novena Newman. Rates are $70 to $80.

Called the "City of Beautiful Maples," *Hiawatha*'s tree-lined streets display hard maples planted and cultivated by the residents through the years. Visitors from throughout the Midwest travel here to enjoy the fall splendor. But the lovely maples are not the real reason for coming to Hiawatha. The Mount Hope Cemetery in Hiawatha, 3 blocks north of the Highway 36/73 junction, contains the *Davis Memorial*, eleven life-size statues made from Italian marble showing Mr. and Mrs. John M. Davis at various stages of their lives.

The first pair of statues shows the couple newly married; the next four show them at later stages in their lives. The last pair, done before Mrs. Davis's death, reveals the aged couple sitting in overstuffed parlor armchairs. The final statue is of granite instead of marble and shows Mr. Davis, with a long white beard, sitting alone in his great armchair, beside which stands an empty chair.

The ten marble statues were carved from photographs sent to an Italian artist in Rome; the final granite statue was done by a Vermont sculptor. The memorial was built in the early 1900s by this wealthy farmer, who is said to have spent over $100,000 on this tomb. Mr. and Mrs. Davis had no children. To some, the memorials are an enduring record of the couple's love, although some locals have a different story. Mrs. Davis's will, they say, stipulated that her husband build a fitting memorial and return the remaining funds to the estate to be distributed to other relatives; Mr. Davis was careful to spend it all. It is open year-round in daylight hours.

At the **Brown County Agricultural Museum,** at 301 East Iowa Street, is an unusual tribute to area farmers. More than forty full-size windmills, each erected by family or friends of local farmers in their memory, turn briskly in the wind. Each windmill is a little different; the tallest reaches 65 feet. Admission is $3.00 for adults, $5.00 for couples, and $1.00 for children. Call the museum for more information at (785) 742–3702.

On Highway 136 just off Highway 36, 2 miles east of **Highland,** is the **Highland Presbyterian Mission,** built for the Iowa, Sac, and Fox Indians in 1837. It was the first white settlement in Doniphan County, 2 miles west of Wolf River. The mission followed the removal of Native Americans from lands as distant as north of the Great Lakes, as well as from northwestern Missouri. It is open year-round Tuesday through Saturday from 10:00 A.M. to 5:00 P.M. and Sunday from 1:00 to 5:00 P.M.

If you're interested in staying in Highland overnight, try **Meadowlark Bed and Breakfast & Tea Room** at 207 South Ives. Gene and Sally Rush invite you to take it easy in this quiet residential neighborhood. The homemade cinnamon rolls make a tasty breakfast, and a country dinner is available by reservation. The tearoom provides light lunches for parties or clubs. Three rooms are available for $65, all with private bath. Call (785) 442–3727.

Missouri River Valley

The town of **Troy,** on Highway 36 southeast of Highland, is in the fertile hills of the Missouri River valley. Thousands of acres here are planted in apple orchards. On the lawn of the Doniphan County Courthouse is the wooden sculpture of an Indian with an interesting story to tell. Hungarian-born sculptor and writer Peter Wolf Toth's statue *Tall Oak* is part of the **Trail of the Whispering Giants.** Toth has produced one for each of the fifty states; this was his twenty-ninth. (He also is in *Ripley's Believe It or Not;* Kansas is a pretty incredible place.) The burr oak sculpture stands 35 feet high and weighs about ten tons. Toth now has erected a total of sixty-seven such carvings throughout the United States and Canada.

Go south on Highway 7 to the city of *Atchison,* where the Lewis and Clark Expedition camped in 1804. The town lies on the west bank of the Missouri River in an area scooped out during the glacial epoch and surrounded by low hills. In 1958 two flash floods in two weeks wiped out downtown Atchison but earned it the reputation of "the town that refused to die." A 10-foot wall of water swept through the city's downtown after torrential rainfall saturated the hills surrounding it.

But plans for rebuilding the town were begun even before the mud had dried. Now Atchison has twenty-five watershed dams on the city perimeter, with recreational facilities and one of the first downtown pedestrian shopping malls, turning the destruction into 2½ blocks of tree-lined walks and a mall shaded by concrete canopies with benches, fountains, and old-fashioned street lights.

The 120-year-old limestone *Atchison, Topeka & Santa Fe Depot* at 200 South Tenth Street has been renovated and now houses the visitors center, Historical Museum (its exhibits include firearms dating from the Revolutionary and Civil Wars), and gift shop. There is a walking and driving tour to see the city's magnificent mansions, historic buildings, and churches. The depot also is the starting point of the *Atchison Trolley.* The fully enclosed trolley is wheelchair accessible and operates May through October. Trolley fare is $4.00 for adults, $2.00 for children ages four to twelve; kids age three and younger are free. The center is open Monday through Friday from 9:00 A.M. to 5:00 P.M., Saturday from 10:00 A.M. to 5:00 P.M., and Sunday from noon to 5:00 P.M. Call the visitors center (913–367–2427 or 800–234–1854) for information about the trolley and other attractions, or visit the city's Web site at www.atchisonkansas.net.

Amelia Earhart was born in Atchison in 1897, and people have not forgotten "Lady Lindy," America's First Lady of Flying, the lost lady of the sky. The *Amelia Earhart Birthplace Museum* at 223 North Terrace Street overlooks the Missouri River; the house was constructed in 1861. It's been renovated and is open to the public year-round. The house is owned by the 99s, an international organization of women pilots. Earhart was its first president in 1929. The house is restored to the era in which she lived. Tour hours are 9:00 A.M. to 4:00 P.M. Monday through Friday; Saturday and Sunday hours are 1:00 to 4:00 P.M. Admission is $2.00.

The *International Forest of Friendship* was founded and maintained by the 99s and the city of Atchison. The quiet forest overlooks Warnock

Lake and is made up of trees from fifty states and forty-one foreign countries. It is dedicated to a special dream of Earhart—peace on earth and the fellowship of humanity—embodied in the poem "Let There Be Peace on Earth, and Let It Begin with Me." A tree grown from a seed that traveled to the moon on *Apollo 14* is in the center of a memorial to the ten American astronauts who lost their lives in space exploration.

The *Evah C. Cray Historical Home Museum*, at 805 North Fifth Street, a three-story Victorian mansion and carriage house built in 1882, contains nineteenth-century period rooms, special children's displays, and a country store. This castle-like home designed by Alfred Meier contains a bracketed cornice above the second floor, mansarded third level, and lantern tower of late-Victorian origin. The round tower on the northeast side has a battlement-topped crown and was added after the owner became fascinated with Scottish castles. All this and a magnificent porte cochere on the north side make it an astonishing sight. Tours are conducted daily May through August, and Friday through Monday March, April, September, and October. Admission is $2.00 for adults, 50 cents for children under age twelve. Hours are 10:00 A.M. to 4:00 P.M. Monday through Saturday, 1:00 to 4:00 P.M. Sunday. For current information on winter hours, call (913) 367–3046.

> ### Trivia
>
> *The first library in the state was established in 1859.*

The Muchnic Gallery (pronounced mush-nik), at 704 North Fourth Street, a striking fourteen-room Victorian brick structure, was built in 1885 and features parquet floors of walnut, mahogany, and oak, intricately carved woodwork, and huge, ornate newel posts. The doors have bronze hardware with windows of leaded glass, and there are many unusual fireplaces. The gallery is filled with works of art and is a project of the Atchison Art Association. It's open Wednesdays from 10:00 A.M. to 5:00 P.M. and Saturday and Sunday from 1:00 to 5:00 P.M. Call (913) 367–4278.

> ### Trivia
>
> *Mother Xaviar Ross was founder of St. Mary College, St. John's Hospital, and the Sisters of Charity of Leavenworth. She was born Ann Ross, the daughter of a Methodist minister. When she converted to the Catholic faith as a teenager, her brothers used to lock her in the closet to prevent her from attending Mass.*

Consider staying at a former governor's mansion while you're visiting Atchison. *The Tudor Inn at Glick Mansion,* at 503 North Second Street, was built in 1873 by Governor George Glick. The mansion underwent renovations that transformed it from a Victorian-style home to a Tudor Revival manor. Innkeepers Joyce and Ray Barmby have

A Pop Counter-Culture Quiz

*W*hat do Kansas City boss Tom Pendergast, George "Machine Gun" Kelly, "Bugs" Moran, Manuel Noriega, and Leonard Peltier have in common? Okay, here's a hint: Throw in Robert Stroud, the "Bird Man of Alcatraz." You guessed it. The prisons in Leavenworth and Lansing (south of Leavenworth on Highway 45) have been home to many infamous criminals. Stroud worked with his birds for twenty-eight years here before being transferred to Alcatraz. "Rocky" Graziano got his start in boxing while incarcerated here. The Kansas State Penitentiary was also home to Richard Hickock and Perry Smith, whose tale was chillingly recounted in Truman Capote's In Cold Blood.

created a warm atmosphere of a past era with the modern conveniences of today. The four rooms each have a private bath and the comfortable mansion gleams with 110 windows. The rooms range from $99 to $129 a night, including breakfast, which might consist of Joyce's Mediterranean omelet with tomato/basil aioli, or her Fiesta omelet with mango salsa and fresh fruit. Evenings offer tea or wine with hors d'oeuvres (maybe little crab puffs). This lady can really turn out fine food, and it is no surprise since she has recently opened the **Windsor Tea Room** at 517 Commercial Street, on the mall, featuring a Euro-classic menu and all the elegance of high tea by the Thames. White linens, crystal, and china show off scones, quiche, soups, salads, and some fine sandwiches. "Cream tea" and "High Tea" are served daily with scones, biscuits, finger sandwiches, fresh fruit, and sweet delicacies of all kinds. Joyce Barmby will spoil you with the attention this new little place offers. Call Joyce for hours of the restaurant or inn reservations at (913) 367–9110.

Stan Herd is a well-known artist who creates magnificent works in the fields of Kansas. His "paintings" are made with plow and plantings and usually last just one season. **Stan Herd's earthwork** near Warnock Lake, about 3 miles southwest of Atchison, is the first permanent one he created. You don't have to fly over this one to see it, as you do his other incredible displays in wheatfields, because a viewing stand has been built so that you can look down and see the one-acre portrait of Amelia Earhart.

If you're hungry, the **Marigold** (913–367–3858) at 715 Commercial Street is a fine bakery and cafe. For something more substantial, try the **River House,** at 101 Commercial, offering fine dining and a view of the Missouri River. Chef Michael's signature sandwich, Chef

Michael's River House Veggie Sandwich, is a favorite at lunch time. You can enjoy a glass of wine or a cocktail with dinner. Hours are from 11:00 A.M. to 9:00 P.M. Monday through Saturday. Call (913) 367–1010.

About 8 miles east of Holton, *Larkenburg* is on Highway 116, but you have to look quickly to see it—it is just two streets, at right angles to the highway (162 Highway 116). But here is the kind of place many folks, for some reason, love to spend hours in: a hardware store. *Wheeler's Hardware* is a "farmer's hardware store," the owners say. They carry farm implements, feed, lumber, 3-inch roofing nails, and specialty tools designed for everything. You can walk up and down the aisles and see most any size bolts and all kinds of twine and wire. When Jerry Wheeler's dad, Winston, ran the store, he used to restock by buying out old hardware stores, which accounts for some of the unusual items in the inventory. Hours are 8:00 A.M. to 5:00 P.M. Monday through Friday. Call (785) 872–3515.

Take Highway 7/73, the tree-lined scenic route from Atchison to Leavenworth, once the center for steamboat and river traffic on the west bank of the Big Muddy. Three Mile Creek flows through the town, which in 1883 spread out over the high bluffs and rolling hills.

This land was inhabited by the Kansa, Osage, and Delaware Indians, and many streets are named after these and other Native Americans. The fort on the bluffs of the Missouri played an important role in keeping the peace between the various tribes and the increasing number of settlers headed west.

Trivia

Fort Leavenworth was established in 1827 on the bluffs of the Missouri River as a frontier post to protect trade on the Santa Fe Trail. Today it is the oldest U.S. Army fort west of the Mississippi and the home of the U.S. Army Command and General Staff College, considered the finest senior tactical school in the world for advanced military education.

In 1854 *Leavenworth* became the first city in Kansas. One of the more famous residents was Buffalo Bill Cody, who spent part of his youth here as a Pony Express rider and army scout. Pick up a brochure for a self-guided walking or driving tour at the city's Welcome Center off Highway 73.

Fort Leavenworth and the federal penitentiary are the two best-known places in Leavenworth. The prison, known as "The Big House," was built in 1906 and is still in use. There are no tours of this towering city of gray stone and redbrick buildings, of course, but you can take photos from across the street (just keep off prison property). A small buffalo herd west of the main building can be seen from a pull-off on Metropolitan Avenue and Santa Fe Trail Road.

Leavenworth has been called "the mother-in-law of the army" because of the number of locals who have married officers stationed at the fort. Fort Leavenworth was built to protect covered wagons and prairie schooners headed west; it was established in 1827. The Main Parade has been beautifully preserved, and the *Frontier Army Museum* (913–684–5604) houses an exhibit on the fort's history from the 1800s to the present and a collection of horse-drawn vehicles covering everything from Conestoga wagons to Abraham Lincoln's black buggy.

There are self-guided tours of the post, the oldest in continuous operation west of the Mississippi. The museum is open Monday through Saturday from 10:00 A.M. to 4:00 P.M., Sunday and holidays from noon to 4:00 P.M.

Leavenworth is full of things to see. The *Buffalo Soldier Monument* on Grand Avenue has brought national attention to the Ninth and Tenth Cavalries, made up of black soldiers when the army was segregated.

The grand old Harvey Residence, circa 1883, is being restored and is home to the *National Fred Harvey Museum* at 624 Olive Street. It was put on the National Register in 1972. The home is filled with the finest arts and comforts of the era when the family observed the custom of English afternoon tea and evening high tea. Who in the world was Fred Harvey? He was a man who emigrated from England in 1850 and began as a dishwasher in a New York City restaurant. He had vision, though, and in 1876 he opened a small restaurant of his own. Later he contracted to supply food along the Santa Fe rail lines. Eventually the restaurants opened in depots and then airports across the country, staffed by the well-recognized "Harvey Girls." His policy of "maintenance of standard regardless of costs" grew into the first restaurant chain in the country. Call (913) 682–1866 to arrange for a tour of this work in progress, or go to the Web site at www.firstcitymuseums.org.

The Historic Skyview Restaurant at 504 Grand Avenue is an 1892 home-turned-restaurant furnished with Victorian antiques. This restaurant is known for its decor and cuisine. Owners Mike and Sara Niemann seat customers Wednesday through Saturday from 5:30 to 8:30 P.M. Diners are welcome to stroll the restaurant's extensive perennial and herb gardens while they wait. Reservations are requested; call (913) 682–2653.

Rather have something Mediterranean? Try the *Oasis Cafe,* at 604 Cherokee. Owner Muhammad Hamid will introduce you to appetizers including falafel and *baba ghanouj.* Choose among beef, chicken, seafood, pasta, and lamb entrees. Call (913) 772–0888 for reservations. Hours are Tuesday through Friday 11:00 A.M. to 2:00 P.M. and 5:00 to 9:00 P.M.

The Tea Room (913–682–0777) is a good place to stop for lunch Monday through Saturday from 10:30 A.M. until 4:00 P.M. This tea-room is located in the **Leavenworth Antique Mall** (seventy dealers on three floors), at 505 Delaware (913–758–0193). Hours are 10:00 A.M. to 6:00 P.M. Monday through Saturday.

Not far from Leavenworth is the town of **Basehor,** near Highway 24/40, where you can stop in for wine tasting, or bring a picnic lunch and purchase a bottle to enjoy with it at the **Holy-Field Vineyard and Winery** (158th Street and State Avenue). Holy-Field makes twelve wines and has won fifty international awards. The winery uses grapes from the twelve-acre vineyard of Les Meyer and his daughter Michelle Meyer Havey. Free walking tours of the vineyards are available on summer weekends by appointment. The winery is open from 11:00 A.M. to 6:00 P.M. Monday through Friday, 9:30 A.M. to 6:00 P.M. Saturday, and noon to 6:00 P.M. Sunday. It's open later in the summertime and has a deck to enjoy the good weather. Call (913) 724–9463.

Trivia

When Bishop John Baptist Miege was appointed bishop to the West, he sent the appointment back and asked the pope to reconsider, writing that he would be a thousand times more willing to go back to Europe than take on this task. The pope insisted, and the new bishop eventually built a cathedral in Leavenworth that was the largest house of worship in the United States up to that time.

Bonner Springs, just west of Kansas City on Interstate 70, is the home of the annual **Renaissance Festival,** held each fall for seven weekends beginning Labor Day weekend. It is a huge festival covering acres of wooded land, with roving troubadours and lots of food. You become part of the action as you watch craftspeople at work and meet wandering characters such as the Rat Lady, Mad Tom from Bedlam, and various storytellers and ladies-in-waiting. Royalty abounds—handsome knights in full armor, princesses, and a king who will greet ladies with a kiss on the hand (guaranteed to make you blush). Misbehave and find yourself pilloried and wearing a sign around your neck accusing you of a crime too unmentionable to speak of— lying, stealing, adultery—while strolling jesters taunt you and more blameless citizens eat turkey drumsticks as they discuss your obviously guilty face. If you and your family have never experienced a Renaissance Festival, this is a must. Admission is $13.95 for adults, $6.95 for children ages five through twelve. Call (800) 373–0357 for more information.

Visit a museum dedicated entirely to American farmers, the *National Agricultural Center and Hall of Fame,* 630 Hall of Fame Drive (North 126th Street), Bonner Springs. Along with antique farm implements and a gallery of rural art, is a re-created early-twentieth-century farm town, including a farmstead, general store, one-room school, blacksmith shop, poultry hatchery, and railroad depot. An Agricultural Hall of Fame honors Luther Burbank, George Washington Carver, John Deere, Cyrus McCormick, Eli Whitney, and thirty other individuals for their contributions to agriculture. Open Monday through Saturday from 9:00 A.M. to 5:00 P.M., Sunday 1:00 to 5:00 P.M. mid-March through November. Admission is $6.50 for adults, $5.00 for senior citizens, and $3.00 for children ages five through sixteen. Call (913) 721–1075, or visit the Web site at www.aghalloffame.com.

There are two bed-and-breakfasts in Bonner Springs. *Back in Thyme* at 1100 South 130th Street is a Queen Anne with a wraparound veranda on ten acres of parklike grounds. As you can guess by the name, the B&B has herb gardens and an herb shop; also a fishing pond and a hiking trail, where you might spot deer, wild turkey, or fox. Inside, a parlor with fireplace and a sun room with a tin ceiling are just a couple of the interesting features of this home. Hosts Clinton and Judy Vickers serve appetizers, dessert, and a full breakfast to their guests. There are three rooms with private baths. They range from $100 to $155. Call (913) 422–5207 or visit their Web site at www.backinthyme.com.

Carol's Candlelight Cottage at 626 North Nettleton is a charming 1934 house. There are fireplaces to lounge by and a full gourmet breakfast in the morning. Innkeeper Carol Hiatt loves to show off her house full of Victorian lace and French Provincial furnishings. The house is yours to roam, to enjoy the handcrafted hardwood floors and luxurious carpets. Curl up by a fireplace and read a novel. There are three rooms available with private bath, and a television in every room. Rooms are from $75 to $95. Call (913) 441–6646 days, (913) 411–6646 nights.

Lost your marbles in northern Kansas? Here comes the spot to replace them and find many more. *Moon Marble,* 600 East Front Street (on Highway 32 west of Highway 7) in Bonner Springs, has a gift shop full of any marble-related merchandise you can suggest, and of course, marbles galore. You can actually watch marbles being made if you come on the right day.

Bruce Breslow is a marble maker by trade and does demonstrations in this retail shop, especially around holiday time. Co-owner Lynda

Sproules has all sorts of marble-related games and toys, unusual gifts, and collectibles. (What is more collectible than marbles? you might ask. Well, there are Pez dispensers, nostalgic and retro toys, and tin toys, the list goes on.) Collectors come from all over the Midwest to see antique marble toys and thousands upon thousands of machine-made marbles and a fine collection of artists' hand-made marbles, although people who live in Bonner Springs might not even know this little shop exists.

Call (913) 441–1432 to see when there are marble-making demos or look at the Web site at www.moonmarble.com. The shop is open Tuesday through Friday from 10:00 A.M. to 5:00 P.M. and on Saturday from 10:00 A.M. to 3:00 P.M. You can also e-mail them at moonmarble@msn.com. There are extended holiday hours for gift shoppers and for children to watch the marble-making demos.

PLACES TO STAY IN NORTHEAST KANSAS

ATCHISON
Comfort Inn,
502 South Ninth Street,
(913) 367–7666
or (800) 228–5150

BONNER SPRINGS
Holiday Inn Express,
13031 Ridge,
(913) 721–5300 or
(888) 206–2066

HIAWATHA
Country Squire Motel,
2000 West Oregon Street,
(785) 742–2877

Gateway Inn Express,
207 Lodge Road,
(785) 742–7450

Hiawatha Heartland Inn,
1100 South First Street,
(785) 742–7401

KANSAS CITY
Best Western
Country Inn—North,
2633 Northeast Forty-third
Street, (816) 459–7222

Best Western
Flamingo Motel,
4725 State Avenue,
(913) 287–5511 or
(800) 528–1234

Days—Inn South,
11801 Blue Ridge Boulevard,
(816) 765–1888

Motel 6—Southeast
(allows pets),
6400 East Eighty-seventh
Street, (816) 333–4468

LAWRENCE
Baymont Inn & Suites,
740 Iowa Street,
(785) 838–4242

Ramada Inn,
2222 West Sixth,
(785) 842–7030 or
(800) 272–6232

Travelodge,
801 Iowa Street,
(785) 842–5100

LEAVENWORTH
Hallmark Inn,
3211 South Fourth,
(913) 651–6000
or (800) 540–4020

Ramada Inn,
Third & Delaware,
(785) 842–7030

Super 8 Motel,
303 Montana Court,
(913) 682–0744 or
(800) 800–8000

LENEXA
Days Inn,
9630 Rosehill Road,
(913) 492–7200 or
(800) 329–7466

La Quinta Inn,
9461 Lenexa Drive,
(913) 492–5500

Wellesley Inn & Suites,
8115 Lenexa Drive,
(913) 894–5550

OLATHE
Best Western Hallmark Inn,
211 North Rawhide Drive,
(913) 782–4343

Econo Lodge,
209 East Fleming Road,
(913) 829–1312 or
(800) 424–4777

Fairfield Inn by Marriott,
12245 Strang Line Road,
(913) 768–7000

OVERLAND PARK
Club House Inn,
10610 Marty,
(913) 648–5555
or (800) CLUB–INN

Doubletree Hotel,
10100 College Boulevard,
(913) 451–6100

**PLACES TO EAT IN
NORTHEAST KANSAS**

ATCHISON
Lopez de Mexico,
112 South Sixth Street,
(913) 367–2422

Mueller's Locker Room,
120 South Second Street,
(913) 367–2727

Paolucci Restaurant,
113 South Third Street,
(913) 367–6105

BASEHOR
Doc & Brutie's Pizza,
15510 State Avenue,
Suite K,
(785) 728–2000

HIAWATHA
Heartland Restaurant,
1100 South First Street,
(913) 742–7401

HOLTON
Trails Cafe,
606 Arizona Avenue,
(785) 364–2786

KANSAS CITY
Alvarado's Casa de Tacos,
7516 State Avenue,
(913) 334–TACO,
(live Latin jazz music)

Jennie's Restaurant,
402 North Fifth Street,
(913) 621–4222

Selected Chambers of Commerce and Visitors Bureaus

**Call (800) 2–KANSAS, ext. 243
for a free travel guide to the entire state.**

Lawrence Convention & Visitors Bureau,
*734 Vermont, Suite 101, P.O. Box 586,
Lawrence 66044–0586; (785) 865–4411 or
(800) 529–5267, fax (785) 865–4400;
e-mail info1@visitors.lawrence.ks.us*

Kansas City Convention & Visitors Bureau,
*727 Minnesota Avenue; (913) 321–5800 or
(800) 264–1563*

Atchison Chamber of Commerce,
*200 South Tenth, P.O. Box 126, Atchison 66002;
(913) 367–2427 or (800) 234–1854,
fax (913) 367–2485*

Lenexa Convention & Visitors Bureau,
*11180 Lackman Road; (913) 888–1414 or
(800) 950–7867*

Overland Park Convention & Visitors Bureau,
*9001 West 110th Street; (913) 491–0123 or
(800) 262–7275;
opcvb@opks.org*

Hiawatha Chamber of Commerce,
602 Oregon; (785) 742–7136

Wyandot Barbeque #1,
8441 State Avenue,
(913) 788–7554

LAWRENCE
Munchers Bakery,
925 Iowa Street,
(785) 749–4324

Paisano's Italian
Ristorante of Lawrence,
2112 West Twenty-fifth
Street, (785) 838–3500

LEAVENWORTH
High Noon Saloon,
206 Choctaw Street,
(913) 682–4876

LENEXA
Callahan's,
12843 West Eighty-seventh
Street, (913) 894–1717

OLATHE
Crown House,
920 South Harrison,
(913) 768–0625

Mom's Kitchen,
530 East Santa Fe,
(913) 782–3542

OVERLAND PARK
Boardroom Bar-B-Q,
9600 Antioch Road,
(913) 642–6273

Mulvaney's Beef N Brew,
7955 East Frontage Road,
(913) 648–6005

Santa Fe Cafe,
9946 West Eighty-seventh
Street, (913) 648–5402

Southeast Kansas

When the tallgrass prairie was as high as a bison's eye and dry as tinder by autumn, wildfires raged across this region, traveling as fast as a horse could run. Black smoke darkened the sky; crackling tongues of fire devoured everything, leaving only charred desolation. Wild animals and birds fled before the wall of flame. Often crazed coyotes and rabbits would turn suddenly and run into the flames to die. But after the fire the prairie bloomed with new life.

Settlers fought fire with fire by burning out sections of land around their homes. (If you ever have wondered why Americans have an almost instinctive need for mowed lawns, the answer might be hidden here.) But most of the prairie is gone now, and most of the area is rocky and hilly and covered with trees.

Kansas depends on man-made lakes. Aside from the oxbows of the rivers and the occasional prairie sink, there are few natural lakes. In the southeast, many lakes are the result of strip mining for coal that supported the area for many years. They have been reclaimed into beautiful state parks, wildlife refuges, and hunting areas. There are some really fine fishing lakes all around here, and fishermen come from miles around to enjoy them. Nearby tree-covered wildlife areas are a mecca for hunters.

You can leave the Kansas City area on Highway 69, an old military road that runs along the Missouri border through the Ozarks of Kansas. It is a great road now with very little traffic.

Military Road

ouisburg originally was called Little St. Louis; the post office asked that the name be changed to avoid confusion. The *Louisburg Cider Mill* (913–837–5202) is on Highway 68 about 3.5 miles west of town. You can watch the entire cider-milling operation in the shed. Cider and some tasty cider donuts are served daily from 9:00 A.M. to 6:00 P.M.

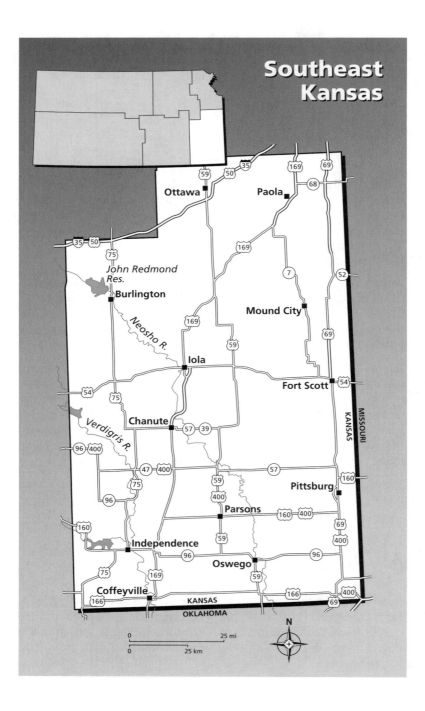

Southeast Kansas

Ottawa

Paola

John Redmond Res.

Burlington

Mound City

Neosho R.

Iola

Fort Scott

Chanute

Verdigris R.

Parsons

Pittsburg

Independence

Oswego

Coffeyville

KANSAS
OKLAHOMA

MISSOURI
KANSAS

0   25 mi

0   25 km

N

There is a retail shop at the mill, too, selling products made there. Come apple season, the annual Ciderfest is held the last weekend of September and the first weekend of October. This bash draws some 15,000 to 20,000 people for barbecue, crafts booths, skydiving, and other festivities.

Down the way a bit is the **Cattleman's BBQ House** (913–837–5361) at 2 West Amity, Louisburg (Amity is old Highway 68, and no one knows why it's called Amity). Just look for the junction of old Highway 69/68 and you will be there. The restaurant is said to have the best barbecue south of Kansas City. Owners Tom and Judy Jones have been smoking ribs here for twenty-four years. Well, not exactly here—the original place a couple of blocks away burned down a few years ago. But they still smoke without barbecue sauce, allowing the true flavor of the hickory to shine through. It's worth the drive if you are a true fan of smoked meats. Hours are Tuesday through Thursday from 11:00 A.M. to 8:45 P.M., Friday from 11:00 A.M. to 9:45 P.M., and Saturday and Sunday from 8:00 A.M. to 9:45 P.M. Closed Monday.

Powell Observatory is in Louis-Young Park. Take the Louisburg exit from Highway 69 to Highway 68. After about a mile, follow the maroon signs to Louis-Young Park. The 30-inch, f/4.5 Newtonian telescope was placed here by the Astronomical Society of Kansas City, a 225-member club, because it was the first town in Kansas where the Kansas City lights did not obscure the night sky. The telescope drive is computer-controlled to make it easy to find any object in the sky, and an ultra-low-light video camera is also used to show images of the night sky on a monitor. The scope has a 20-foot dome that rotates and opens every Saturday evening May through October, plus special observations twelve times a year. There is seating for thirty people, with three or four programs in an evening. Gates open at 8:30 P.M. Call (913) 837–5305 for a recording of programs for the month, or, if you are in Kansas City, you can call StarTouch Hotline (816) 889–STAR (7827) and give the category code 5400.

The Marais des Cygnes Wildlife Area (pronounced "mare deseen" here) near **Pleasanton** attracts birders from four states. French explorers came here about the same time as the establishment of the Province of Louisiana. The Marais des Cygnes was a route for trappers going west. The name probably comes from the Osage word *Maxackautsi,* which means "the spot abounding in wild swans" and translated as *marais des cygnes* or "swans' marsh." During fall and spring migrations, you may see thousands of ducks and geese, plus herons, pelicans, shorebirds, and warblers. Bring your binoculars and a thermos of coffee. The waterfowl are most active at sunrise and sunset. Also, be aware that some hunting is allowed here in season.

About 4 miles east of Pleasanton on 25939 East 1000 Road is the bed-and-breakfast **Cedar Crest Lodge.** Owners Matt and Laura Cunningham have redone the B&B in a rustic lodge style. It's surrounded by 113 acres of secluded countryside with trees and ponds and offers beautiful views. The twelve rooms, some with Jacuzzi and private bath, go for $89 to $129 a night. For more information, call (913) 352–6533 or (866) CEDAR00 (233–2700).

Traveling 5 miles north of Pleasanton on Highway 69, then 3 miles east on Highway 52, leads you to the **Marais des Cygnes Museum.** The river for which the museum is named plays an important role in the state; you'll find the museum at the site of a famous confrontation between proslavery and abolitionist forces that took place on May 19, 1858. The five victims of this massacre were immortalized as martyrs in the cause of freedom. The museum is open Wednesday through Saturday from 10:00 A.M. to 5:00 P.M. and Sunday from 1:00 to 5:00 P.M. Call (913) 352–6174, or check the Web site www.kshs.org for more information.

Nearby, on Highway 69, is the little town of **Trading Post,** an early Kansas settlement built on the Military Road, which connected a long line of frontier outposts. Because of its proximity to the border, it was the site of several skirmishes between pro- and antislavery groups, and near a battle between Union and Confederate soldiers. The **Trading Post Mu-**

Life in Kansas for Early Settlers

*L*ife was bountiful for the Native Americans indigenous to Kansas. They enjoyed a varied diet (including corn, pumpkin, and tomatoes) not known in other cultures, but for the settlers the going was rough. Crossing the fords with wagons and oxen was hazardous because everything could suddenly sink into the muck. Cholera and malaria were constant threats, and plagues of grasshoppers swarmed the land, mowing down all vegetation in their path. During droughts, the ferocity and speed of prairie fires could wipe out hundreds of miles of vegetation and wildlife.

SOUTHEAST KANSAS

seum Complex features a restored 1857 cabin, an 1887 schoolhouse, and artifacts from the "Bleeding Kansas" days. Next to the museum is a monument honoring victims of the Marais des Cygnes Massacre and a cemetery where four of the slain are buried. For hours and other information, call the Linn County Department of Economic Development in Mound City, (913) 795–2074.

Take a side trip off Highway 69 to little **Mound City,** birthplace of jazz saxophonist Harris "Sleepy" Johnson. It's nestled among the hills that give it its name, as though caught in a time warp. There are a beautiful old bandstand, old-style storefronts, the Linn County courthouse, the 1868 City Hall, and a cemetery where nearly one hundred Civil War veterans are buried. Mine Creek Battlefield, now a state historic site, is just outside town. In a city park on Highway 52, local volunteers are reconstructing the cabin of Col. James Montgomery, a conductor on the Underground Railroad. It's believed that several hundred former slaves hid under his cabin floor on their way to freedom. The cabin is an unusual vertical log style. Prizewinning author/filmmaker Gordon Parks, who grew up in nearby Fort Scott, filmed part of his autobiographical movie in Mound City. Call (913) 795–2074 for more information on the Mound City area.

Top Annual Events in Southeast Kansas

April
William Inge Festival,
Independence;
(316) 331–1400

June
Good Ol' Days,
Fort Scott;
(800) 245–FORT

August
Cowtown Days,
Baxter Springs;
(316) 856–3131;
first weekend

The Lane Fair, Lane;
(785) 869–2865;
first weekend

September
Little Balkans Days,
Pittsburg; (800) 879–1112;
Labor Day weekend

Buster Keaton Celebration,
Iola;
(316) 365–4765

October
Dalton Defender Days,
Coffeyville;
(800) 626–3357

The Battle of Mine Creek

*O*n October 23, 1864, Union and Confederate forces clashed at Westport, 100 miles from the present-day Pleasanton–Mound City area. About 6,500 Confederates retreated, with 2,500 Union soldiers in pursuit. Weighted down by wagonloads of loot plundered during their raids, the Confederates were unable to outrun the Union troops and employed only rear-guard action to keep their pursuers at bay. On October 25 the wagons became lodged in Mine Creek and the Union forces prevailed. The battlefield is a state historic site, with a new visitors center located on Highway 52, a mile west of the junction of Highways 69 and 52, or about 3 miles east of Mound City.

Trivia

*T*he **Shrine of St. Rose Philipine Duchesne** *is located 7 miles north and 5 miles west of Mound City on Keokuk Road. In 1838 about 900 Potawatomi people were forced from their homes in Indiana and marched 681 miles in 61 days to resettle at the Sugar Creek Mission. Thirty-nine people, mostly children, died on this "trail of death." In 1841 a nun of the Sacred Heart order, seventy-two-year-old Sister Rose Philipine Duchesne, was one of several nuns who came to teach the children. She was canonized by Pope John Paul II in 1988.*

The Victorian showplace of the Midwest is on the banks of the Marmaton River. *Fort Scott*'s brick streets and outstanding architecture can be seen from "Dolly the Trolley," a fifty-five-minute tour of the town and National Cemetery. It runs seven days a week from 10:00 A.M. to 4:00 P.M. Tickets are $5.00, but the free coupon book will pay that back in no time. The tour begins at the Tourist Information Station, 231 East Wall, and meanders down the main street and by the many restored homes and the fort; call (800) 245–FORT. The shaded streets are filled with architectural styles popular from 1865 to 1919. One of the most impressive is the Queen Anne at Sixth and Judson Streets. Nearby on Crawford Street are Eastlake-style homes, one with a window in the brick chimney. Many homes, both mansions and smaller houses, feature ornate woodwork, gingerbread, stained-glass windows, turrets, and eyebrow windows, as well as hitching posts and stepping-stones for carriages. Wealthy old Marblecrest Street has a panoramic view of the Marmaton River valley that is vivid with color in the fall.

Fort Scott has many celebrations drawing visitors from all over the four-state area: The Good Ol' Days, the first full weekend in June, is a street fair featuring arts and specialty foods with street dancing. It is a celebration of life from the 1840s through today. The Bourbon County Fair takes place the fourth week in July, and the Pioneer Harvest Fiesta the first full weekend in October. Homes for the Holidays offers visits to Victorian homes and the Old Congregational Church, all decorated for Christmas, and a candlelight tour of the Fort Scott National Historic Site.

The *Fort Scott National Historic Site* on Old Fort Boulevard is an 1840s military post built for peacekeeping efforts on the frontier. The restored military fort includes a hospital, officers' quarters, guardhouse, powder magazine, and museum. Living-history programs are offered Memorial Day, Independence Day, and Labor Day weekends. Call for dates and times of guided tours and interpretive talks. The fort also hosts four special events each year: Civil War Encampment, Good Ol' Days, American Indian Heritage Weekend, and Candlelight Tour. Contact the National Park Service, Fort Scott National Historic Site, Fort Scott, 66701; (620) 223–0310; Web site, www.nps.gov/fosc; e-mail, fosc_super intendent@nps.gov. Admission is $3.00 for adults, children free.

The site also contains a five-acre preserve of tallgrass prairie. An available brochure offers descriptions to help identify the most prominent grasses and wildflowers in a mixed-prairie area.

The *Fort Scott National Cemetery,* at the end of East National Street, is one of the original fourteen national cemeteries chartered by President Lincoln. It contains the graves of eighteen Native American scouts of the Indian Home Guard. Thirteen Confederate soldiers lie alone in a row to themselves. Mass graves honor bomber and tank crews who could not be identified individually. Row after row of white headstones pay moving tribute to those who gave their lives for their country.

The *Lyons' Victorian Mansion* at 742 South National in the city of Fort Scott is one of the Twin Mansions on the Prairie (a pair of side-by-side houses built for two sisters a century ago). It carries on a prairie tradition as a light in every window greets guests.

The brick Italianate mansion sits next to its twin on one of the highest spots on the prairie. Larry and Pat Lyons are famous in the area for the fine meals served in the large dining room (seats thirty-six easily).

Fort Scott

Dinner is available for guests by reservation. The mansion is popular for weddings and business meetings as well. Pat is a southern lady, and her breakfasts are legendary in Fort Scott. There is enough to feed a dozen, even if only two guests are spending the night, although her eight guest rooms are usually full. Ask about booking a "Mystery in the Parlor" party—they're great fun.

Pat loves peacock feathers, and they appear everywhere. In fact, she has a stuffed peacock, about 8 feet long from head to tail, in the house. It took four years to build this house, and when you look around, you will see why: native black walnut woodwork in the north and south parlors, oak in the dining room, and six fireplaces. And now there is even more waiting for you. The **Paradise Day Spa** is part of the Lyons' Mansion, and here a massage therapist will make you feel like a new man, or woman, or even couple—they offer a couple's massage for those on first or second honeymoons. Check the Web site at www.lyonsman sion.com for more details and a peek at the mansion. The local number for Day Spa reservations is (620) 223–3644, and you can make bed-and-breakfast reservations, too. Call for reservations early (800–78–GUEST, or e-mail at lyonshse@terraworld.net). Rooms are $89 to $150.

Fort Scott has two more lovely, historic lodgings. **The Courtland Hotel Bed and Breakfast** at 121 East First Street is a beautifully restored 1906 railroad hotel with seven guest rooms and four suites. Look at the Web site at www.courtlandhotel.com. Rooms are modest in size and in price ($50 to $70), as befits a hotel with a history of serving the men riding the rails. Each room has a private bath and cable TV. King-size, queen-size, double, and twin beds are available. In the morning, owners Marlene and

The U.S. Army at Fort Scott

*T*he U.S. Army established **Fort Scott** in 1842 to protect what was supposed to be the Permanent Indian Frontier. Army troops stationed here fought in the Mexican War (1846–1848) and patrolled the Santa Fe and Oregon Trails. The fort was abandoned by the army in 1853, and two years later the buildings were sold at auction and the fort became the town of Fort Scott. Violence plagued the area during the "Bleeding Kansas" years, prompting the periodic return of troops to restore order. The Civil War brought the military back in full force; the town served as an important supply base and training ground for Union troops. The final period of military occupation came between 1869 and 1873, when soldiers camped south of town during the construction of a railroad to protect it from attacks by squatters.

WORTH A VISIT

Toronto Lake—*Fall River*
Big Hill Lake—*Cherryvale*
Pomona Lake—*Vasser*

Dean Gettler serve a fine continental breakfast with fresh fruit and yummy home-baked rolls and sweets. Call (620) 223–0098 for reservations, or e-mail dmgettler@terraworld.net.

The Chenault Mansion at 820 South National is another great choice. For a $5.00 fee, this gracious home, which has proudly stood here since 1887, when the Chenault family built it, is also open for tours. The Victorian parlor, period rooms, stained glass, and crystal chandeliers speak of an elegant time when graciousness was a daily routine. Bob and Elizabeth Schafer (only the third family to own it) take you back to that time when you enter through the double cherry doors. Fresh-baked cookies and tea or coffee are served each afternoon. All rooms include private baths and queen-size beds. Five guest rooms, each decorated for the era of its namesake, create a unique and peaceful haven. The tower room has a sunny sitting room furnished in white wicker; a corner room has a fireplace; a stately suite done in walnut also has a fireplace. Room rates range from $89 to $99, including a full breakfast. Call (620) 223–6800 for reservations, or e-mail chenault@terraworld.net. You can see the mansion at the Chenault's Web site: www.bbonline.com.

North Main Street is a covered walkway chock-full of nice little shops. *Country Cupboard* (620–223–5980) at 12 North Main is the biggest country store in the area, with an old-fashioned flavor and a large selection of crafts, fabrics, cards, candy, dolls, and gifts—many made by local hands. It is open Monday through Saturday from 9:00 A.M. to 6:00 P.M., Sunday from 11:00 A.M. to 5:00 P.M.

Hollister Wildlife Area, 8 miles southwest of Fort Scott on Highway 69, is open for hiking, bird-watching, and backpacking. Hunters, trappers, and fishermen are welcome, too. Call (620) 449–2539 for information.

Greenbush, on Highway 57 between Girard and St. Paul, was just a quiet prairie town until recently. Now it is home to the *Pittsburg State University–Greenbush Astrophysical Observatory* (620–235–4391), which has a 24-inch Cassegrain telescope more than 150 feet high. Skyviewing programs are held one Friday night each month. And there is more.

Dozens of school buses wend their way to the *Southeast Kansas Education Service Center.* In its instructional buildings is the nerve center for interactive classes, a kind of educational co-op, where students can communicate with NASA astronauts in Houston or students in Japan. The center has its own Web site—www.greenbush.org. Unique in the nation, the resources of many school districts have been pooled together so the center can offer what the individual small-town schools cannot afford alone. Schools pay an annual membership, and in return receive unlimited student access to the William L. Abernathy Science Education Center. There they can watch lizards and butterflies skittering through a humid rain forest with ninety species of plants from the Amazon, or visit the adjacent greenhouse. They can root around in the archaeological dig, which is "planted" with bones and pottery chucks from whatever civilization they are studying. The science center is open to the public weekdays from 8:00 A.M. to 4:00 P.M. Admission is free, but donations are welcome. Call (620) 724–6281 for information.

The Frontenac Bakery, 211 North Crawford in *Frontenac,* just off Highway 69 south of Fort Scott, is unusual because the company still produces Italian bread in the same manner as when it opened in 1900. George Vacca, a native of Valparga, Italy, started the bakery when he gave up coal mining in the area. Until recently the brick ovens were heated by wood but now have been converted to natural gas. The Duchess oven reaches 500 degrees Fahrenheit, then the fire is turned off, and the bread is baked with the heat retained in the bricks at about 400 degrees. The ovens are loaded with a custom-made "peel," the long paddle that is used to slide the loaves in and out. The floor of the oven is brick, and the bread is baked directly on it to give it a crisp crust. French bread is made from the same recipe but baked on pans to give it a softer crust. Most of the work is done by hand; visitors are welcome. The bakery is open every day from 6:00 A.M. to 9:30 or 10:00 A.M. except Tuesdays and Saturdays. Call (620) 231–7980.

For a place to stay in the region, try the *Madison House B&B* at 211 North Summit in *Girard,* west of Arma on Highway 57. Call Dan and Janice Herbert at (620) 724–4679. The three-story Victorian, built in 1907, has four guest rooms with private baths and is filled with antiques. The price of $75 includes a room with a private bath, along with a full breakfast.

The Gathering Place (620–231–2155), at 324 East Highway 126, just west of *Pittsburg,* is where owners Gail and Warren Deatherage and Jerry and Cathy Stockard have gathered together primitive antiques and dried floral arrangements in an authentically reconstructed old barn with an herb garden. The barn was taken apart and moved from another location, and with the help of 200 townspeople, it was raised again where it stands today.

The two couples have filled this unique shop with treasures they have found on their twice-a-year trips together. The herb garden provides herbs and flowers for one-of-a-kind home decorations offered in their store. Call for hours.

Trivia

There are many small towns in Crawford County because of all the small campsites surrounding the mines. Most camps had one school and one church. Some also had a theater and a bank.

The couples' most recent addition is the *Old Miner's Guesthouse,* built adjacent to the shop. The renovated miners' house is now a bed-and-breakfast. Gail and Cathy found the authentic two-room building, a house built in the late 1800s with a 1920s addition, and had it moved to the site in 1997. They added wiring and plumbing, which the original house did not have, and furnished it with primitive antiques. It includes a modern kitchen and bathroom. The rooms, one with a queen-size bed and the other with twin beds, are airy and immaculately clean and have every modern convenience without losing a bit of their old-fashioned character. Rooms are $60 for two people and $5.00 for each extra person. Guests are welcome to bicycle around the wooded acreage, fish for bass and crappie (dock access is available), paddleboat, or swim in the crystal-clear strip pit. Or they can just "set" on the spacious and shady deck that wraps around the back of the house. Great place for a family reunion. Call (620) 231–7733; e-mail gplace@apexcorp.com.

Two of the best chicken places in the state (and there are quite a few really, really good ones) are in Pittsburg—*Chicken Annie's,* 1143 East 600th Avenue, (620) 231–9460, and *Chicken Mary's,* 1133 East 600th Avenue, (620) 231–9510. They are about a block from each other and a zillion signs will direct you to them (north on Highway 69 then about 3.5 miles east on a rural road). Both have super onion rings and the choice of mashed potatoes or German potato salad. Both are open daily for dinner, and Sundays at noon. The competition is fierce and the opinions just as strong, so you will just have to eat at both places and decide for yourself.

On Main Street in *Scammon, Josie's Ristorante* (620–479–8202) is a family-owned and operated restaurant named for Mike Saporito's grandmother. Mike and his wife, Sally, have been cooking dishes such as ravioli and linguini for years. Some of the recipes are Josie's, some Sally's. The bread is baked fresh daily. The restaurant is open Wednesday through Saturday from 5:00 to 9:00 P.M. Scammon is 7 miles north of Columbus on Highway 7.

Columbus has a clock tower on the courthouse square with 4-by-8-foot windows so that passersby can see the works inside. An electric motor lifts the seventy-five-pound weights every twelve hours. The matching weights, which control the striker chimes, weigh 200 pounds each. Originally built in 1919, the clock was later dismantled and the parts stored. In 1983 Starr Smith found the rusted parts and rebuilt the old clock. A buff-brick tower with brown trim and mansard roof was erected by the town, and now the 1,200-pound bell again rings out each half hour. Come to town on Columbus Day and see the hot-air balloon regatta that has become an annual tradition. The motto here is "Help America discover Columbus."

Mary Holt and her daughter Marva hated to see the circa 1938 barn collapsing. It was sagging and had become home to raccoons and other critters. So they decided to save it for the next generation. Now the barn is filled with bed-and-breakfast guests who enjoy biscuits, sausage, and the works each morning. The *Country Loft,* 2193 Northeast Center Star Road, Columbus, has four bedrooms; the main floor is open, with a fireplace covering one end. There are four bedrooms at the top of the spiral staircase on the second floor. All are furnished with country antiques, handmade quilts, and knickknacks, and ferns and ivy thrive under skylights. Some guests come to shoot skeet at Shawnee Creek Preserve on the adjoining acreage owned by Marva's brother, Jon Holt. Room rates are from $30 to $55, or you can have the whole barn for $180. Call (620) 674–3348 for more information.

Maple Common, at 120 East Maple, is designed with business travelers in mind. A former downtown department store, it also housed a bar at one time. The dance floor is now the lobby. Suites with big living areas and luxurious bathrooms are $54 to $124; breakfast is not included. Call host Dina Dove at (620) 429–3130 or (620) 429–3131.

For lunch or dinner head for *The Lunch Box Café,* at 124 South Kansas in Columbus, where you can get really good down-home cooking. It occupies one of the oldest buildings in town, circa 1876. The original floors and tin ceilings are still there. It opens at 6:00 A.M. for the early

The Union Wins One

The Pittsburg Public Library, built in 1910, is listed on the National Register of Historic Landmarks as an example of the Prairie School of architecture. But there is another reason for its landmark status. It is the only library built by Andrew Carnegie that does not bear his name on the exterior. Here's why: Carnegie was anti-Union, *and Pittsburg was a Union stronghold. The Union supporters protested Carnegie's donation for the library. "You might as well put a skull and cross bones in the stained-glass windows," one Pittsburg woman was quoted as saying. Carnegie acceded to the city's wishes and built the library without his name.*

birds and stays open to 8:00 P.M. for the night owls, Monday through Saturday. Owner Jim Hodgson invites you to stop in and have a bite to eat. Phone (620) 429–3434.

Meriwether House, 322 West Pine, Columbus, is a cottage with two bedrooms and a two-room suite, all with private bath. Call (800) 238–1957 or (620) 674–3274, fax (620) 429–1790, or e-mail merico@columbus-ks. com. Rooms are $40 per night, including continental breakfast.

For some pheasant hunting or sporting clays, try *Claythorne Lodge* at 1329 Northwest 100th Street in *Hallowell.* (Drive 10 miles west of Columbus on Highway 160 and 1.5 miles north on 100th Street.) Sam and Frieda Lancaster offer sporting-clay courses as well as skeet, trap, and Fitasc. Hunt for quail, pheasant, and chukar (a bird somewhere between a pheasant and quail in size) in field and driven hunts. A full hunt is $295 to $395 to bag forty quail. Breakfast and lunch are included, as are hunting dogs, bird cleaning, and a round of sporting clays. Lodging is available, and there is a pro shop, too. Rooms are $75 inside the lodge and $60 in the bunkhouse. Seasonal hunting from September 1 to March 31. Call (620) 597–2568 for more details.

Thirteen miles from Columbus (that's 7 miles north of Columbus on Highway 7, 6 miles west on Highway 102) is *West Mineral,* the home of *Big Brutus*, who looms over the countryside in his vivid orange-and-black colors. At a height taller than a fifteen-story office building, Big Brutus was the world's second-largest electric mining shovel when he was built—he is a one-of-a-kind fellow. He weighs eleven million pounds and could scoop up 150 tons of rock and soil in a single bite of his giant bucket, enough to fill three railroad cars. He didn't dig coal, but removed the "overburden" (dirt and rock covering the coal seams); men using huge coal strippers and 120-ton trucks then moved in on the exposed seams.

Brutus cost $6.5 million and worked twenty-four hours a day. But he was a workhorse, not a racehorse, moving at 0.22 miles per hour. When the coal supply was exhausted, he was too big to move to another mining site and too expensive to dismantle, so, his motors silenced, Brutus looked for another line of work. None was found. His usable parts were removed, and rust ate at his shell. Birds nested in his cavernous interior. The pits he had dug filled with water.

But as Brutus watched, the stripped land became picnic areas and the pits became lakes. Boats appeared, children swam, and soon the Kansas Senate passed a resolution proclaiming Brutus a historical museum dedicated to the mining history of the state. Brutus was reborn and has been attracting visitors to West Mineral ever since. What a guy! You can

Big Brutus

climb steps 160 feet to the top of the Brute if you are age thirteen or older and weather permits, and get a good look at the land for miles around. In 1987 the American Society of Mechanical Engineers designated Big Brutus a Regional Historic Mechanical Engineering Landmark. He wears the honor with pride. Open daily from 9:00 A.M. to 8:00 P.M. from Memorial Day to Labor Day. Hours vary the rest of the year. Call (620) 827–6177, or check the Web site at www.bigbrutus.org.

Highway 166 runs to **Baxter Springs,** the first cow town in the West, according to locals. Whether they mean the first one you come to—it's just north of the Oklahoma border—or the first one established is up for discussion. If you would like to discuss this premise with locals, **Murphy's** on Military Avenue (620–856–3263), the main street, is the place to do it. It is renowned for the pies made from scratch—people travel miles out of their way for them.

Another popular eating place on Military Avenue is **Cafe on the Route,** the "route" being 66, of course. It's in a former bank building that was robbed by the notorious Jesse James in the 1870s. The menu includes pasta, seafood, steak, and ribs. It's open for breakfast, lunch, and dinner, and closed between meals. Call (620) 856–5646.

In 1863 Quantrill's Raiders attacked an army garrison in Baxter Springs. Eighty-seven men were killed; some of them are buried at Baxter Springs National Cemetery, where a granite monument stands.

Jim Bilke spends many of his days riding and roping in rodeos. When he's not doing that, he's at his hat shop, **Bilke's Hatter** at 1041 Military Avenue, one of only twenty-five or so hatmaking businesses in the country. Jim has been quoted as saying that a man's best friends are closer than his dog—they are his hat and boots. A life-size sculpted horse in front of the shop will catch your eye first, then you will notice the mural of a cattle drive painted on the street side wall. Inside is the fascinating business of hatmaking, where a new hat begins its life with a dorky-looking round top. When Jim finishes blocking, pressing, sanding, and "ragging" it (some say "pouncing" it) to make the felt stand up, then adding a brim flange and blocking it again, he's not finished yet. After a seven-day rest, the brim is cut off to the customer's preference—5-inch, 4-inch, or 3½-inch width. Then it is taken to the sewing room, where the sweatband is added. Powder color is dusted and brushed on, and there you have it, a custom hat. Jim will restore your favorite old Stetson for only $40 ("Men get attached to their hats"), but a custom hat will set you back as much as $325 (for a pure beaver hat).

The Legend of the Bloody Benders

*B*ack *when this region was sparsely settled, an old man, his wife, and their grown son and daughter lived just outside the little village of Galesburg. There they kept an inn. One of them would stop a traveler and tell him that he could not reach his destination by nightfall and invite him to stay at their house. In the course of the evening, Miss Kate Bender would deal the traveler a blow to the back of the head with a large hammer, then another blow to the temple with a small hammer. Then the men would drag the victim to a trap door, where Kate would cut his throat. After taking his valuables, they would allow the unfortunate's corpse to drop through to the cellar. This went on for many years.*

They were found out when a man left his wife in eastern Kansas to go to make arrangements for settling farther west. When he did not return, his wife set out to overtake him. She, too, stopped with the Benders. While there, she picked up a locket that was lying on a table. When she opened it, she was

surprised to see her own picture in it and that of her little girl opposite. The locket belonged to her husband and was worn as a charm on his watch chain. That night she looked out the window and saw the light of a lantern in the orchard. She stole softly out of the house and drew near the light, where she found a newly dug grave. She hid on the prairie all night and in the morning went to a neighbor's home and told her story. The alarm spread, and soon a crowd gathered at the Benders' but the family had vanished. The mob set off in search of them, but when they returned, none would say if he or she had found the Benders.

There was a large reward offered for each member of the family who might be brought back dead or alive. Why the neighbors remained silent is a mystery to this day.

If this story seems too incredible to be true, track down the historical marker to this episode in Kansas history. It's west of Parsons; call the city at (620) 421–6500 for directions.

Trivia

Nine miles east of Baxter Springs just off the access road that connects Highway 166 with Interstate 44, a marker indicates the spot where Oklahoma, Missouri, and Kansas meet. You can be in three states at one time if you are very agile.

Upstairs the *Bilke Western Museum* is open during business hours. Call (620) 856–5707. Shop hours are from 9:00 A.M. to 6:00 P.M. Monday through Saturday.

Baxter Springs is an avid baseball town. The *Little League Baseball Museum* is located on the grounds of Little League Park at Fourteenth Street and Grant Avenue. This is reputed to be one of the best Little League parks in the country and has been the site of many state and regional Little League play-offs. The museum is filled with baseball memorabilia dating from when wealthy paving contractor Harold Youngman and a friend named Harry Wells first knew Mickey Mantle, who worked for Youngman in the summertime. The museum is opened two hours before Little League games so visitors and players can visit, or by making an appointment with Wayne Metcalf (620–856–3903). The museum was built by a local industrialist who was a close friend and mentor of Mickey Mantle when Mantle was just beginning his baseball career. As a teenager, Mantle played ball for the Baxter Springs Whiz Kids (he was born and reared in nearby Commerce, Oklahoma).

Eight blocks east of Military on Twelfth Street is Kiwanis Park, where a granite home plate has been installed as a tribute to Mickey Mantle. It sits on the spot where Mantle reputedly hit balls into the Spring River while he played for the Whiz Kids in the early 1950s. It was while playing ball here that he was noticed by a Yankee scout. Mantle signed his first baseball contract (in a rainstorm) immediately following the game.

The Baxter Springs Heritage Center, 740 East Avenue (620–856–2385), has a full-scale replica of a lead and zinc mine, 1800s and 1900s boardwalks, a circa 1910 farmhouse, and Civil War history. This outstanding museum has 13,000 square feet of climate-controlled displays on two floors. The History Room tells the interesting history of the town.

Trivia

Old Route 66 cuts through the corner of Kansas from Galena to Riverton. It's a very short stretch, but you can still "get your kicks on Route 66" right here if you hurry. Kansas is the only state not mentioned along the route in the song of the same name. Trivia question: How many cities are mentioned in the song?

There is a sculpted frieze on the south side of the American Bank that can be seen from Thirteenth and Military. (The bank is at Twelfth and Military.) Artist Paula Collins created the frieze depicting the city's history. She used terra-cotta clay and sculpted the

Trivia

The song about Route 66 mentions twelve cities. (You missed it by two, didn't you? Sing it again, only this time pay attention.) Remember: It "winds from Chicago to L.A. . . ."

scenes in individual blocks that were fired and then fitted together. It is a very impressive work.

Highway 166 crosses the Spring River on the eastern boundary of Baxter Springs, at the western edge of the Ozark Plateau. The soil here is thin and rocky. Hardwood forests cover most of the hillsides. Sassafras and mistletoe grow in this part of Kansas, although they are not found anywhere else in the state.

Here the climate and vegetation are very different from the rest of the state; there are animals unique to this region. Caves and springs provide a wet habitat for unusual breeds of salamanders and frogs, some of which are endangered species. The area receives more than 40 inches of rain a year. Caverns fill and water percolates through the joints and fractures of rocks, creating caves and feeding springs. The springs, in turn, drain into clear streams that flow over gravel beds in steep-walled valleys, creating small waterfalls.

Lake Country

C *offeyville* lies just north of the Oklahoma line on Highway 166. Low hills surround this sandy basin on the west and south; the Verdigris River borders it on the east and north. Once this was a cow town, with teams of oxen loaded with supplies to sell to the cattlemen, cowboys, Native Americans, and soldiers who came to trade.

Coming into Coffeyville from Highway 166, turn north a block and stop to see a vision of the past. The vision is part of a mural on the Center for the Arts at Ninth and Walnut Streets. It features the Condon Bank's triangular building in 1892, the year the Dalton Gang was admiring bank buildings, too. Coffeyville artist Don Sprague has transformed the sides of the buildings in town into reflections of the past, known as the *Coffeyville Murals.*

The Dalton Gang lasted less than a year and a half but became part of western legend on October 5, 1892, when its members tried to hold up two banks at once in Coffeyville. Bob, Emmet, and Grat Dalton, Bill Powers, and Dick Broadwell hitched their horses in an alley and approached both banks. Citizens spotted them and spread the alarm. The cashier of the first bank lied about the safe, saying it was on a time lock, creating several minutes' delay in the robbery.

Townspeople opened fire through the bank windows. Bob and Emmet rushed out of the other bank and opened fire on the citizens, killing three. Marshall Charles Connelly tried to cut them off, and Grat dropped him. Stable owner John Kloeher, "the best shot in town," got Bob, Grat, and Bill; when Emmet was foolish enough to turn back to retrieve his brother's body, he too fell. Broadwell escaped on horseback, but was found less than a mile away. When the smoke cleared, eight men were dead.

You will see the Dalton Gang laid out in a row on the sidewalk, as the men were placed for viewing after the shoot-out. The paintings on the buildings are designed to be viewed from across the street, or about 50 to 100 feet away. From the sidewalk, 3 or 4 feet away, the perspective is lost.

There are freestanding paintings inside some windows, and all of the paintings are within blocks of each other, so you can see them all on a comfortable walk. They include Colonel Coffey's Trading Post, a turn-of-the-twentieth-century streetcar, and the Natatorium, a huge bathhouse built in 1906 on the site of a natural spring.

You can pick up a list of mural locations and information about other interesting spots in town by stopping at the Tourist Information Station at 2108 Walnut Street or by calling (316) 251–1194.

The Dalton Defenders Museum at 113 East Eighth Street (316–251–5944) honors the memory of the four men who died on the side of the law in the Dalton Raid on Coffeyville made by the Dalton family of desperadoes. The men were just average Coffeyville citizens—shoemakers and store clerks—as young as twenty-three years old. The museum is open daily from 9:00 A.M. to 5:00 P.M. (to 7:00 P.M. June through August) to give you the rest of the story. Admission is $3.00 for adults, $2.00 for teens, or purchase a combination ticket also good at the Brown Mansion for $5.00 (adults) or $3.00 (teens). Children age twelve and younger are free. Dalton Days re-creates the shoot-out the first weekend in October every year.

Enjoy good home cooking in the historic downtown area at *Mike & Barb's Diner,* 111 West Ninth (620–251–8255), open for breakfast and lunch. Mike and Barb Baker roll out of bed really early every day but Sunday to open at 5:00 A.M. They serve breakfast each morning to the hungry early birds in Coffeyville and then bring out lunch until 2:00 P.M. It is genuine home cooking. Not just fried chicken and chicken-fried steak, which are simply wonderful, but an assortment of other like-Mama-made dinners, such as chicken and homemade noodles, sausage casserole, and ham and beans. On Saturday, only breakfast is served to 11:00 A.M.

SOUTHEAST KANSAS

Trivia

The Military Road, built in the early 1800s, connected all the forts from Fort Snelling in Minnesota to Fort Wachita on the Red River in Texas. Baxter Springs's main street, called Military Avenue, is on the old Military Road. Baxter Springs is one of three sites in Kansas where Civil War military engagements took place. During the war, when the town was known as Fort Blair, it was attacked by the Confederate guerillas under William Quantrill and 400 men who rode with him. The fort was successfully defended, but Quantrill then attacked a large contingent of men from Fort Scott as they approached Fort Blair, which resulted in a total massacre of the Fort Scott troops.

In downtown Coffeyville, you will also find the **Bowser Bed & Breakfast,** 612 Elm (620–251–0933), an early-twentieth-century home decorated with oil paintings and period lace curtains and wallpaper. Innkeeper Marjorie Bowser invites you to experience this lovely old Victorian. The house has been completely restored over the past twenty years, enhancing the beauty of the original stained-glass windows and decorative oak woodwork.

While the morning sunshine streams through the south windows, enjoy a delicious continental breakfast, served in a beautiful formal dining room. Cards, including bridge, can be arranged by appointment. Your games will be played in the turret alcove of the grand living room. Upon your arrival hot or cold drinks are available. Taste Marge Bowser's Fruit Juice Slush and know good things are waiting for you. You will love your stay at this three-story Victorian home with a parlor for guests. Accommodations include three large bedrooms with private bath, air-conditioning, and your own refrigerator. Rooms are $59 to $69. Call (800) 627–4341.

The magnificent **Brown Mansion**, located at 2109 South Walnut Street, was completed in 1906; it remains as it was, the ultimate in grandeur. The porte cochere is topped with an ornate portico, and each room has a fireplace of different design. The full basement housed the butler's quarters, laundry, and walk-in icebox. The sixteen-room mansion has 20-inch-thick brick-and-concrete walls to serve as insulation for the gas heating system. Much of the original hand-carved furniture is still in use. There is a signed Tiffany chandelier in the dining room, believed to have been hung personally by the designer. Hours are changing, so call (620) 251–0431 for times. Admission is $4.00 for adults, $2.00 for teens. Children ages seven to twelve are $1.00. Children under age seven are free with an adult. You can also purchase a combination ticket good at the Dalton Defenders Museum.

Highway 75 will take you to the town of **Caney** and the privately owned **Safari Zoological Park,** 1.5 miles east of Highway 75 on old Highway 166. The park has about one hundred animals, including white tigers, bears, wolves, and reptiles. Admission for a tour only is $6.00 for adults,

$5.50 for seniors, and $5.00 for children. Additional fees apply for extended, daylong, or overnight stays. Facilities in the park include a swimming pool, picnic area with gas grills, camping areas for tents and RVs, and an air-conditioned cabin. Park hours are Monday through Saturday from 10:00 A.M. to 5:00 P.M., Sunday from noon to 5:00 P.M. For more information, call (620) 879–2885, or check the Web site at www.safaripark.org.

Independence is the birthplace of former Governor Alfred M. Landon, Republican candidate for president in 1936 against Franklin D. Roosevelt. "Alf" lost the election by one of the greatest margins in American political history. His daughter is former Republican Senator Nancy Landon Kassebaum.

Favorite son and playwright William Inge (*Come Back, Little Sheba* and *Bus Stop*) is honored in the annual William Inge Festival each April. His Pulitzer Prize–winning *Picnic* and Academy Award–winning *Splendor in the Grass* depict small-town life in the Midwest. Call (620) 331–4100 for information, or visit the Web site at www.indkschamber.org.

Riverside Park is a fine example of Kansas fun. Carousel rides are still just a nickel. The Ralph Mitchell Zoo (cheaper than a nickel, it's free!) was home to Miss Able, the first monkey in space. She resided at Monkey Island until her blastoff in 1960. Peacocks wander the park at will, but the bears, cougars, and monkeys do not. A train will carry you around the park and to the miniature golf course called "A Path Through the Past," where you can play through the history of the town for only a buck. The park is open year-round from 8:00 A.M. to midnight.

The *Independence Science and Technology Center,* 125 South Penn Avenue, invites visitors to mess around with echo tubes (tubes tubes tubes), an antigravity simulator (a great ride!), and the Van de Graaff generator (a hair-raising experience!). All for only $1.50. Hours are Monday through Saturday from 1:00 to 5:00 P.M. Call (620) 331–1999.

The population of Independence swells from 11,000 to more than 80,000 for the Neewollah* Festival in October when top performers in the entertainment world join street acts, concessions, and an artists' alley. Yes, top performers. We are talking the Nitty Gritty Dirt Band, Blood Sweat and Tears, REO Speedwagon, and Patty Loveless here. Then there is the parade, one of the biggest and grandest parades you have ever seen, a two-hour festival of music and pageantry. Look at the Web site at www.indkschamber.org.

*If you didn't guess, it's Halloween spelled backwards.

On the northern edge of Independence, just off Highway 75, is a private drive (marked with a sign) leading to a little piece of heaven, **Glencliff Farm Bed, Breakfast, and Spa.** This stately Tudor-style home, built in the 1920s, sits on 250 acres of countryside overlooking a valley. Relax in the cliffside, heated outdoor pool or follow one of the walking trails, where you may spot wild turkey or deer. Future plans include equestrian trails as well.

Choose from two suites with private baths, two rooms with shared baths, or two family cottages (one used to be a milk barn). Spa treatments including massage, wraps, and masks are available on-site. Your hosts, the Johnsons, can also arrange romantic extras such as candlelight dinners for two, wine, flowers, and chocolates. Rates range from $79 to $180 per night; spa treatments and romance packages are extra. For more information, call (620) 877–1277 or (877) 334–1277, or check the Web site at www.glencliff.com. Rates range from $79 to $189 per night.

Thirteen miles southwest of Independence on Highway 75 is a reproduction of the cabin made famous by Laura Ingalls Wilder's children's books and the television show based on them, **Little House on the**

Little House on the Prairie—the True Story

*A*lthough author Laura Ingalls Wilder based her Little House books on her own life, she did make a few changes. The Ingalls family actually came to Kansas in 1869, lured by the Homestead Act, which offered 160 acres of free land to farmers. That means little Laura was just two years old, not eight or so, as in the book. And the homestead isn't 40 miles from Independence, but 12 or 13. But Pa Ingalls really did build a house and stable here with the help of Mr. Edwards. Other events described in the books are also documented: The Ingalls family encountered wolves, some tense moments with Native Americans, and survived a prairie fire and malaria. They were treated by Dr. Tann, an African-American physician

later buried in an Independence cemetery. The Ingalls family left Kansas a year or two later, after hearing that the government had changed its mind about allowing homesteaders here.

The site is owned by Bill Kurtis, a television news reporter most recently seen on A&E's Investigative Reports, and his sister, Jean Schodorf. The historic homesite was purchased by their grandfather in the 1920s, and Kurtis has bought about 2,000 acres surrounding it, with the dream of restoring it to prairie like that described by Wilder in Little House on the Prairie. Future plans also include horse-drawn wagon rides, a herd of buffalo, an Osage Indian village, and period farmsteads where visitors can spend the night.

That's One Big Cat!

*T*he state has always been proud of its big-cat population. Big catfish, that is. Fishermen used to talk about fish that were bigger than they were—with faded photographs to prove it. And scuba divers will tell you about spotting "cats" of terrifying size.

Well, fishing at Elk City Reservoir, northwest of Independence, is more exciting now since Ken Paulie caught a record 121-pound catfish in 1998. Think about that! That is a monster fish, and there might be some bigger ones lurking about. Before Paulie's catch, the previous record holder was a fisherman in Texas who caught a puny 92 pounder. Experts say that the Elk City Reservoir has become an old-age home for catfish, and once a cat reaches 15 pounds, the lake is its smorgasbord and it is rarely hooked and even more rarely landed. Paulie caught his by accident. He was fishing for crappie with a minnow.

Prairie. Much research has been done to prove that the Ingalls family actually lived in a one-room cabin on this site from 1869 to 1871. An old post office and a one-room country schoolhouse have been relocated here. They are open May 15 through September 1, Monday through Saturday from 10:00 A.M. to 5:00 P.M. and Sunday from 1:00 to 5:00 P.M. For more information, check the Web site at www.littlehouseonprairie.com.

This is oil country. In 1891 several prominent citizens of **Neodesha** (pronounced "Nee-O-da-shay," an Osage Indian word meaning "the meeting of the waters") on Highway 75 invited an oilman to drill wells here in the hope of providing the city with a natural gas supply. The drilling revealed a treasure more valuable than the gold the conquistadores had searched for centuries before, and it changed the pastoral life of this part of the state forever. The Mid-Continent Field was producing more than half the nation's oil supply into the 1930s. It is now considered a National Historic Landmark. A replica of the first successful commercial oil well west of the Mississippi stands 67 feet high and has a 22-foot-square base. It is called simply **Norman No. 1** and sits at First and Mill in Neodesha. It is open Tuesday through Saturday from 10:00 A.M. to 5:00 P.M.

Fredonia, near the Chautauqua Hills at the junction of U.S. Highways 400 and 39 and Kansas State Highway 47, is about 20 miles from five lakes. The Clock Tower was built in 1886, and the time has rung out across the town every half hour ever since. A farmers' market opens Tuesday afternoons from June 15 through October 15 (and everything goes fast).

There's a B&B in Fredonia with the unlikely name of the **D. A. Loomis**

Bed & Breakfast. It is situated at 105 North Fifth Street, where Mr. Loomis built this large, comfortable house with sunny windows and pine woodwork at the turn of the twentieth century. It is now the home of owners Rose and Gene Benefiel. There are three guest rooms with private or shared baths. Rooms begin at $60 and include breakfast. Call (316) 378–3267/4492, e-mail at loomis@terraworld.net, or visit the Web site at www.terraworld.net/loomis.

Just 1 mile south on U.S. Highway 39 and 1 mile west of Fredonia is the old *Otto Grain Mill*, which was powered by the Fall River. Below the dam is a low-water bridge where canoeing buffs can begin an easy 4-mile trip to an oxbow bend with shaded picnic tables. Locals caution that the water can be very fast following a heavy rain.

The Martin and Osa Johnson Safari Museum, at 111 North Lincoln, is in *Chanute*'s beautifully renovated Santa Fe Depot. The museum contains the pictures and memorabilia of these world-famous photographers and explorers. It allows you to follow them from the South Seas through Africa, showing terrain untouched by civilization as well as animals now on the endangered list.

A re-created safari camp is only one of many unusual exhibits in the museum's *Imperato African Gallery.* There are ceremonial masks, swords, carved figures, textiles, musical instruments, and jewelry from four regions of West Africa. The gallery features the art and artifacts of more than sixty ethnic groups along with a dramatic, life-size Tyi Wara dance diorama. The Johnsons' feature films can be viewed in a thirty-seat theater.

The museum's *Selsor Art Gallery* is filled with original watercolors, oils, sketches, and lithographs by leading natural-history artists.

The museum's *Stott Explorers Library* (open by appointment only) has 10,000 books, journals, and manuscripts that form one of the country's foremost natural-history libraries. This research library specializes in early African exploration, ornithology, and primatology.

The Museum Shop offers art and crafts from Africa along with the Johnsons' original books and videos of their movies. The museum is open Monday through Saturday from 10:00 A.M. to 5:00 P.M., Sunday from 1:00 to 5:00 P.M. Fees are $4.00 for adults, $3.00 for seniors and students, $2.00 for children six to twelve years old. Call (620) 431–2730. Check the museum's Web site at www.safarimuseum.com, or e-mail the staff at osajohns@safarimuseum.com.

Chanute is filled with gracious houses and stately mansions of Queen

Anne, Italianate, and other styles of architecture, especially on Highland and Evergreen Streets. These are all private homes, but they deserve a drive-by.

The *Chanute Art Gallery*, at 17 North Lincoln (620–431–7807), is an art museum known for its works by Kansas and regional artists. Among the permanent collection of 600 works are many by the Kansas Prairie Printmakers, a group of Depression-era lithographers. There are also changing monthly exhibits in the more than 1,500 square feet of gallery space, plus a classroom, library, and excellent gift shop featuring work by Kansas artisans. Hours are Monday through Saturday from 10:00 A.M. to 4:00 P.M. Admission is free, but donations are welcome.

Gary Hawk is a well-known watercolor artist whose western and wildlife paintings have been reproduced on everything from plates and Christmas ornaments to pewter and brass belt buckles. The *Hawk Designs Inc.* studio, 1415 North Kentucky, Iola, displays his rural, western, and wildlife art. Original paintings are sold here. His limited-edition prints, along with a complete line of products bearing his designs, are sold at *Old Country Classy Attic* at 20 West Jackson. Call (620) 365–5343 for information. The studio is open by appointment. The Attic is open from 10:00 A.M. to 5:30 P.M. weekdays (until 8:00 P.M. Thursday) and from 9:00 A.M. to 5:00 P.M. Saturday. Call (620) 365–2440.

Iola boasts the oldest continuously performing community band in the state. The band performs nine summer evening concerts in the public bandstand downtown. The Allen County Courthouse, the *Old Jail Museum,* circa 1869, at 203 North Jefferson, and the *Historical Museum Gallery* at 207 North Jefferson are here. The museums are open May 1 through September 1 from 1:00 to 4:00 P.M. Tuesday through Saturday. Admission is free. While you're here, visit the Maj. Gen. Frederick Funston Boyhood Home at 14 South Washington Avenue. Take in performing-arts programs at the *Bowlus Fine Arts Center* at 205 East Madison. It's open August 15 to June 15, Monday through Friday from 8:00 A.M. to 4:00 P.M.; closed June 16 to August 16. Call (620) 365–3051. Iola has a handful of antiques shops, too.

West of Iola on Highway 54 is *Moran,* and just outside Moran is *Hedgeapple Acres Bed and Breakfast* (4430 Highway 54), where you can discover the simple joys of country living. You can cast a line into two stocked ponds or take a peaceful stroll around the eighty acres. After a home-cooked supper, you can enjoy a cup of cocoa in front of the fireplace. A satisfying country breakfast will be waiting for you in the morning. All four guest rooms have private baths. They are $65 to $85, including both breakfast and dinner. Call hosts Jack and Ann Donaldson (620–237–4646) for reservations and directions or e-mail at hedgeapple @aceks.com. Visit their Web site at aceks.com/hedgeapple.

While passing through *Piqua,* search out *St. Martin's Catholic Church,* built in 1884. It has beckoned pioneers and brought comfort to weary travelers for more than 125 years.

At the crossroads of Highways 54 and 75 is *Yates Center,* called the prairie hay capital of the world. The rich grasslands need no irrigation and provide the best grazing for the livestock raised here. The town square surrounds the majestic three-story *Woodson County Courthouse*, built in 1895, and still has its original brick streets. The Historic Town Square is listed on the National Register of Historic Districts. It showcases examples of restored Victorian architecture. A guided walking tour of the district is available.

If you happen to be in Yates Center at lunchtime, look for a place called *Frannie's* upstairs over the old Light's Hardware building (which isn't a hardware store anymore) on the southeast corner of the square. The daily menu is at the bottom of the stairs; everyone gets the same meal, but dessert takes some choosing—Frannie bakes fifteen to twenty different kinds of pie every day. Weekdays at lunchtime Frannie's is usually packed. Frannie serves up to 150 people a day in the winter and twice that in summer.

What's really interesting about Frannie's is the owner, Frannie Ward, who trusts all who eat at her place to ring up their own meal at the self-service cash register by the door. Just punch in the price of the meal and the state sales tax, leave your money, and out you go.

Frannie's philosophy is that it's silly to worry about stealing; folks around here wouldn't do that (and if they did, they probably need it and so are welcome to it). But her Golden Rule attitude goes further than that. For a dollar she delivers food to senior citizens who can't get out, and to the local factory, too.

The price of any meal is easy to figure. It's $1.00.

A Star Is Born

Just west of Iola on Highway 54 is Piqua (pronounced "pick-way"), the birthplace of silent-film star Buster Keaton. His mother was passing through with a vaudeville team on October 4, 1895, when Keaton was born. Now there is a free Keaton fest in Iola every year to celebrate his birth. Keaton fans descend upon the town from as far away as New York and California to pay homage to the great clown of silent comedy. The festival is held the last weekend of September each year, and includes film showings and speakers from the filmmaking industry.

One thin greenback for the daily special and a beverage; another dollar for a slice of pie. Twelve cents sales tax. And the food is very good. If you don't believe it, find Frannie's and see. She has no telephone. Hours are from about 7:30 A.M. to 5:00 P.M. Monday through Friday.

Kansas gardeners drive from as far as Wichita, Topeka, and Olathe to shop *Arnold's Greenhouse*, 1430 Highway 57 southeast, 4.5 miles west of *LeRoy*. What started as a hobby in 1977 when George and Rita Arnold built a 10-by-16-foot greenhouse in the backyard has mushroomed into a full-time business. You can't miss the huge display garden at the entrance, the 4,800-square-foot garden center, or the twenty-one greenhouses (covering a total of 80,000 square feet), one of which has a retractable roof. Arnold's carries about 3,500 different varieties of plants and is known for its unusual perennials and exotic annuals that thrive in Kansas's hot summer weather. Hours reflect Kansas gardening seasons: March, April, and May, Arnold's is open Monday through Saturday from 8:00 A.M. to dark; from June 1 through August, it's open Friday and Saturday from 8:00 A.M. to 6:00 P.M. and Monday through Thursday by appointment. In September and October, it's open Monday through Saturday from 8:00 A.M. to 6:00 P.M. Call (620) 964–2463 or (620) 964–2423 to request a catalog, or visit the Web site at www.arnoldsgreen house.com or e-mail at retail@arnoldsgreenhouse.com.

Luther's Smokehouse is the place to find barbecue in this area. Martin Luther calls himself a "jerky-holic" because he smokes about 1,500 pounds of beef, ostrich, turkey, and even emu jerky a week. Some are flavored with teriyaki or jalapeño seasonings, and all can be mail-ordered for $13.99 a pound, plus shipping. Martin and his wife, Shirlee, have a sense of humor that shows in this restaurant's decor: a lamp made of half a mannequin—her lower half, but decorously dressed in a skirt, booths made of hay bales, and a table with stuffed blue-jean legs. There's a dinner show at 7:00 P.M. on Saturday. To order jerky, call (800) 322–0868, visit the Web site at www.jerkyUSA.com, or write Luther's at Route 1, Box 2, LeRoy, Kansas 66857. The place opens at 8:00 A.M. daily with huge cinnamon rolls and stays open to 8:00 P.M. (5:30 P.M. on Sunday). Call (620) 964–2400.

Seventeen miles southwest of Yates Center on Highways 54 and 105 is *Toronto Lake*, which contains some of the biggest white bass in the state. The state park here offers not only fishing but also swimming, RV camping (by reservation), and hunting (in season). The lush foliage attracts plenty of insects, so bring bug repellant. A vehicle permit is required; fee for camping. Call (620) 637–2213 for information.

The city of **Toronto** is on the east bank of the Verdigris River and the eastern edge of the bluestem region of the Flint Hills. It was called "the green city" because of the trees and grasses that grow abundantly around it. It was settled by farmers from Canada in 1869. A prehistoric cave containing pictographs was discovered in 1858 and is located about 12 miles north of town. You can head north on Highway 75 to John Redmond Lake or Burlington.

If you like live music, check out **The Music Box** at 404 Neosho in downtown **Burlington** and enjoy a Branson (Missouri)-style show every Saturday at 8:00 P.M. Adult admission is $10. For reservations, call (620) 364–3036.

Four miles north of Burlington on Highway 75 is **John Redmond Lake,** where you will find more camping areas. You can also swim, hike, bird-watch, and hunt in season. Call (620) 364–8614 for information.

At the upstream end of the reservoir, 18,500 acres are reserved for the **Flint Hills National Wildlife Refuge** (620–392–5553). Native grassland and hardwood timber with shallow marshes and flooded sloughs wait in the broad, flat Neosho River Valley, where native grasses ripple in the wind.

Northwest of Burlington and John Redmond Lake, the **Fall River State Park and Wildlife Area** (620–637–2213) stretches across Greenwood County. There are both primitive camping and RV hookups available. You can rent canoes in nearby Eureka or hike. The area is much as it was

Flint Hills Scenic Byways Etiquette

*T*he state of Kansas asks that travelers on the scenic byways not pick flowers and native grasses or stray on to private land. The residents welcome visitors, so respect their privacy. Don't photograph the cowboys or their families, and stay out of the way of cattle drives (yes, they still have them). Climbing on fences or gates will not win you the love of the men and women who have to fix them. And it goes without saying: Don't litter the roadways or quiet little picnic spots you find. Speaking of roadways, it's best to obey the speed limits posted. Though it looks like a country mile of flat highway ahead of you, deer suddenly appear, and in the case of auto vs. deer, there is no winner. Death can, and has, come to both the deer and the driver. And, of course, the Kansas Highway Patrol is ever vigilant and sometimes hiding behind whatever is taller than the patrol car. The scenery is magnificent—enjoy it.

when the Wichita and Osage people hunted in the floodplains and upland areas surrounding Fall River.

Tucked between the timber area of the Chautauqua Hills to the east and the grasslands of the Flint Hills to the west, this area has open savannah scattered with black-jack oak and tallgrass prairies with an amazing diversity of plant and animal life. It is primarily designed for hiking, fishing, and hunting. If you prefer to shoot with a camera, visit the waterfowl observation blind, which has been constructed for people who want to observe and photograph the waterfowl that frequent the region's wetlands.

Hardwood forests are interspersed with shallow marshes and grasslands, creating a refuge for migratory waterfowl and dozens of other species as well. In the winter, golden and bald eagles ride the air currents over the marshes. Blue-winged teal, green herons, and wood ducks nest on the shores. In the fall, canvasbacks, redheads, and pelicans arrive to join the regular residents, the quail. The Wildlife Refuge office hours are from 8:00 A.M. to 4:30 P.M. Monday through Friday. A vehicle permit is required at the state park; camping is extra.

Lands of the Ottawa People

F ounded in 1857 by a free-state colony from Kentucky, *Garnett* has several buildings from the 1880s (constructed with locally manufactured bricks) on the downtown square. West Fourth Street is called "The White Way" because of its lovely old ornamental streetlights.

Many of the town's prominent homes line the street. Two buildings on the National Register of Historic Buildings are the Harris House and the Anderson County Courthouse, completed in 1902. Of Romanesque design with redbrick and white limestone, both were designed by George P.

A Famous Outlaw Hides Out Near Garnett

D uring the Civil War, two cattle buyers named Mr. Howard and Mr. Woodson were known to stay at the John Rutledge ranch 6 miles southeast of Garnett. Their true identities, however, were Jesse James and his brother Frank. The boys belonged to William Quantrill's guerrilla band, and they used the ranch as a hideout during the Civil War. A detective, who was no doubt hot on their trail, was found shot and burned in a haystack. The James boys, as usual, got the blame.

Trivia

Edgar Lee Masters (1868–1950), a great American poet and the author of Spoon River Anthology, *was born in Garnett. A U.S. stamp was issued to commemorate him*

Washburn, a noted Kansas architect of the period. Garnett's **North Lake Park** is a 255-acre park with a 55-acre lake. The Garnett Water Reservoir is located 5 miles to the southwest and has fishing, boating, and camping. Be alert—you may see Amish driving horse-drawn buggies along the roadways. The city Web site is www.garnettks.net.

There are six antiques shops in Garnett, including **Goodies Antiques** (785–448–6712) on the downtown square, where three floors of vintage goods await you.

Maloan's Restaurant and Bar (785–448–2616) at 101 West Fourth Avenue is housed in an 1883 building that was originally a bank. The menu features grilled steaks, seafood, chicken, and pork. A wonderful buffet brunch is served on Sunday. Weather permitting, eat outside on the second-floor deck. Restaurant hours are Monday through Friday from 11:00 A.M. to 1:30 P.M., Friday and Saturday from 5:00 to 9:00 P.M., and Sunday from 10:00 A.M. to 1:00 P.M.

Kirk House Bran Muffins

A recipe from Robert Logan's kitchen.

2 cups All-Bran

2 cups boiling water

1½ cups butter (3 sticks)

3 cups sugar

4 eggs, beaten

1 quart buttermilk

5 cups flour

5 teaspoons baking soda

1 teaspoon salt

4 cups 40% Bran Flakes

2 tablespoons molasses

2 cups raisins

1. Soak All-Bran in boiling water.

2. Cream together butter, sugar, eggs, and buttermilk. Add All-Bran to creamed mixture, and let stand one minute.

3. Beat in flour, baking soda, salt, Bran Flakes, and molasses. Stir in raisins.

4. Mix thoroughly, but do not stir again. Store in refrigerator.

5. Use only what you need for each baking. Fill prepared muffin pans so that each cup is half full. Bake in a 400° preheated oven for twenty minutes. Use big muffin tins for plump, soft muffins. The mix will keep in the refrigerator for six weeks.

Upstairs you'll find the spacious bar. The original brick walls and large windows provide a pleasant atmosphere. A new outdoor deck that seats about thirty people has been added for when the weather is good. The bar is open Wednesday through Saturday evenings.

The Prairie Spirit Rail Trail follows the right-of-way of the Leavenworth, Lawrence, and Galveston Railroad Co. (LL&G), which was constructed as one of the first north-south rail lines in the state in the early 1860s. The trail travels from Ottawa to Welda and is 33 miles in length. (Plans call for it to eventually extend to Iola.) In Ottawa, the Prairie Spirit connects to the 115-mile Flint Hills Nature Trail from Osawatomie to Herrington. The 37-mile Landon Trail, which starts just south of Topeka, connects to the Flint Hills Nature Trail in Lomax.

The Kirk House (785–448–5813) at 145 West Fourth Avenue, is one of the largest homes in Garnett, a 12,000-square-foot Georgian Revival mansion designed by architect George Washburn in 1913. It's now owned by Robert Logan and Robert Cugno, art dealers from California, and their very social dog Gar. There are four bedrooms, two with private bath, two shared, on the third floor (where there is also a ballroom). The Craftsman-style interior features quartersawn oak woodwork, hard-wood floors, large pocket doors, and a Tiffany mosaic fireplace with a Rookwood hearth.

The rates are $135 for a double room and $100 for a single, and include an extended continental breakfast. There is a fine collection of contemporary and international folk art and crafts throughout the house. The bed-and-breakfast is open only September through June. E-mail The Kirk House at khmge@terraworld.net.

The Garnett Public Library at 125 West Fourth Avenue has a lot more than just books. It is also the home of the *Mary Bridget McAuliffe Walker Art Collection.* Nearly 110 works make up the collection begun in her honor in 1951 by her son, Maynard Walker, a New York art dealer who was born in Garnett and spent his childhood here.

Robert Logan, of The Kirk House, helped design the gallery and is the curator of the collection. He and Robert Cugno have done a great deal to bring this caliber of art to the state. The gallery is a little jewel box done with beauty and taste. There is a changing gallery with new art moving through it and a Community Gallery featuring Kansas artists. For more information about the collection, you can reach them at The Kirk House (785–448–5813).

Artists whose works may be seen here include some very famous names: John Steuart Curry, Édouard Manet, Jean-Baptiste Corot, George Grosz, and Henry Varnum Poor, with an emphasis on early-twentieth-century American artists. The collection was not given the attention it deserved until Logan and Cugno, who knew the value of artwork, moved to Garnett and took it on as a project. Lighting was improved, the paintings were displayed to advantage, and artwork was sent to Kansas City's Nelson-Atkins Museum to be cleaned and restored.

The Walker Art Collection Committee was formed, and the collection was appraised and catalogued. Contributors have added more than forty pieces to the collection, giving it breadth with many examples of different schools of art and different media. A gallery adjacent to the library holds it all.

Some of the artists represented are not so well known but are still highly accomplished, such as Luigi Lucioni and Van Dearing Perrine, a Garnett native who died in 1955 and whose works are sought by collectors in New York. The committee sees him as a source of pride and inspiration to young artists in the Midwest.

The Walker Art Collection may be seen from 10:00 A.M. to 8:00 P.M. Monday, Tuesday, and Thursday, from 10:00 A.M. to 5:30 P.M. Wednesday and Friday, and from 10:00 A.M. to 4:00 P.M. Saturday. The library is closed Sunday. For further information, call (785) 448–3388.

The John Brown Historic Site (913–755–4384) at John Brown Memorial Park, Tenth and Main Streets in *Osawatomie* (a combination of the names Osage and Potawatomi, two Native American tribes of the area)

Jayhawking? Where Does That Expression Come From?

*A*ccording to the legend, Pat Devilin, a Free State Irishman, rode into Osawatomie one morning in 1856, with his saddlebags laden with considerable goods. As he tied his horse in front of a store, one of the men standing nearby said to him, "Pat, it looks like you have been foraging."

Pat, as he mounted the steps, replied, "Yes, I have been over in Missouri jayhawking." When asked what he meant by the expression, he said that in the old country there was a bird that worried its prey before devouring it. He added that what he had been doing was jayhawking. This is the only known origin of the word.

on Highway 169, is the 1854 log cabin that served as the headquarters for the famous abolitionist when he was living in this free-state stronghold. In the spring of 1859, Brown planned a dramatic act that he believed would cause a general slave uprising. He and eighteen men (including his sons and five blacks) captured the federal arsenal at Harper's Ferry in Virginia. The expected uprising did not occur, and Brown was arrested and hanged in 1859. The cabin was originally built by squatters in 1854. It was dismantled and moved to its present site in 1912. Hours are Monday and Tuesday from 11:00 A.M. to 5:00 P.M. (if volunteers are available), Wednesday through Saturday from 11:00 A.M. to 5:00 P.M., and Sunday from 1:00 to 5:00 P.M. There is no admission fee, but donations are welcome.

The Creamery Bridge, built in 1930, which spans the Marais des Cygnes River at Eighth Street, is one of two Marsh arch–triple span bridges located in Osawatomie. The other spans the Potawatomi Creek at Sixth Street. Both are on the National Register of Historic Places. What makes these bridges unique is that they were designed and patented by James B. Marsh to expand and contract along with the bridge floor under varying conditions of moisture and temperature. The Creamery Bridge has a rainbow span reaching 140 feet into the air. Both bridges are open to traffic.

Trivia

The Osawatomie State Hospital, erected in 1866, was the first mental health hospital built west of the Mississippi River.

You may have noticed that the streets in Paola running east and west are named for Native American tribes.

If you want to cruise by an absolutely magnificent Queen Anne home, head east on Carr Avenue just short of First Street and take a look at the *Mills House,* circa 1902. It was built by the man who drilled the Norman No. 1 oil well in Neodesha. This private home is on the National Register of Historic Places.

Another architectural gem is downtown on Sixth Street, between Parker and Lincoln Avenues. The *Old Stone Church* was built in 1861 of native stone hauled from the hills around the city by the Reverend Samuel L. Adair and his son Charles. Adair was the brother-in-law of the radical abolitionist John Brown. The minister was a gentler abolitionist and mental health pioneer. The city Web site is www.osawatomie.ks.us.

Northeast of Osawatomie, you'll find *Paola,* a wonderful place to eat. *Beethoven's,* at 120 West Peoria (913–557–9880), serves great German and American food. Hours are Tuesday through Thursday from 11:00 A.M. to 8:30 P.M., Friday and Saturday to 9:00 P.M., and Sunday 10:00 A.M.

to 1:30 P.M. Across the street, at 119 West Peoria, **Emory's Steakhouse** serves pork tenderloin bigger than the plate and prime rib so tender you can cut it with a fork. Hours are Wednesday and Thursday 10:30 A.M. to 9:00 P.M., Friday and Saturday to 10:00 P.M. Call (913) 294–4148 for reservations.

If you're staying in Paola, book a room at **The Victorian Lady Bed and Breakfast,** at 402 South Pearl. Innkeepers Harry and Lue Ann Hellyer will offer you chocolates on your pillow and a gourmet breakfast in the morning. Guest rooms have queen-size beds and private baths. Rates are $115 to $135. Ask about their anniversary packages; your hosts can also arrange a horse-drawn carriage ride, massage, flowers, and gift baskets. Call (888) VICLADY or (913) 294– 4652.

There are a half-dozen antiques shops in Paola, including **Pigeon West,** 14 South Silver (913–294–9094), where hours are 10:00 A.M. to 5:00 P.M. Tuesday through Saturday and by appointment. Owners Jeff Harte and Ann Davis sometimes just "stick a note on the door" and go to auctions, but that's the antiques business in action. There is also **Lucy Lockets Antiques,** 25 West Wea (913–557– 5829), open from 10:30 A.M. to 6:00 P.M. Monday through Saturday and 1:00 to 5:00 P.M. Sunday.

After all that shopping, stop at the 1950s soda fountain at **Asher Pharmacy** (913–294–3516) on the square for something cool and sweet.

Ottawa, off Interstate 35 at Highway 59, lies in a saucer-shaped valley along the Marais des Cygnes River. There was a natural ford across the river at the site of Ottawa, and the land was given to many Native American tribes for reservations. In 1832 the Ottawa people gave their Ohio lands to the United States in return for 34,000 acres of what is now Franklin County and donated 20,000 acres of that land to a trust for the education of Native Americans; later, Ottawa University was formed. In 1867 a treaty was signed, moving the Ottawa to Oklahoma, and settlers flocked in. Ottawa University still offers scholarships to the dispersed Ottawa nation.

This area of rich farmland is known as the dairy capital of Kansas. Ottawa has a complete block of businesses listed on the National Register of Historic Places. The **Old Depot Museum** at 135 West Tecumseh near Main Street, housed in a former railroad depot built in 1888, features a "Bleeding Kansas" exhibit, Civil War displays, an old general store, period rooms, and an HO model railroad display. It is open Tuesday through Saturday from 10:00 A.M. to 4:00 P.M. Admission is $3.00 for adults, $1.00 for students. Call (785) 242–1250.

Ottawa also has ten antiques shops, at last count, a couple of good country restaurants, and a very good bakery and sandwich shop across from the courthouse. Pomona Lake is 16 miles west of Ottawa on Highway 368; and just 4 miles west on Highway 31, the Marais des Cygnes River valley becomes **Melvern Reservoir.** Adjoining the lake is 6,930-acre **Eisenhower State Park,** with a 12-mile equestrian trail and two nature trails.

Barbecue is almost a religion in Kansas City, and people there consider themselves experts on ribs and brisket. Fights can erupt during conversations about sauces (to be or not to be sweet—that is the question). A goodly number of these fanatics drive to **Williamsburg,** 15 miles west of Ottawa just off Interstate 35 (between Ottawa and Emporia) to eat at **Guy and Mae's** at 119 Williams Street, where the slab is served wrapped in foil and placed on newspaper. Plastic forks are presented for the cole slaw, potato salad, or beans (at 50 cents a serving). On a Kansas City country music radio show, the question was asked "Where's your favorite slab?" Guy and Mae's won hands down over all of the world-famous barbecue places in Kansas City. Hours are 11:00 A.M. to midnight Tuesday through Saturday. Owners Diana Macoubrie, Judy Simpson, and Steve Wilcoxson took it over from Judy and Diana's mother. It's been a well-known barbecue secret for years. The ribs are served with their secret sauce on the side. You can take some sauce home in a container, but it's not sold commercially. Call (785) 746–8830.

PLACES TO STAY IN SOUTHEAST KANSAS

BURLINGTON
Country Haven Inn,
207 Cross Street,
(913) 894–5631

CHANUTE
Holiday Park Motel and Restaurant,
3030 South Santa Fe,
(620) 431–0850 or
(800) 842–9910

Safari Inn,
3428 South Santa Fe,
(620) 431–9460 or
(800) 432–9460

COFFEYVILLE
Regal Inn,
1215 East Third Street,
(620) 251–1034

FORT SCOTT
First Interstate Inn,
2222 South Main Street,
(620) 223–5330

GARNETT
Old American Inn,
325 North Maple,
(785) 448–6816

Sherwood Inn,
235 North Maple,
(785) 448–6816

INDEPENDENCE
Appletree Inn,
Eighth & Laurel,
(620) 331–5500

Super 8 Motel,
2900 West Main,
(620) 331–8288

IOLA
Best Western Inn,
1315 North State Street,
(620) 365–5161 or
(800) 769–0007

OSAWATOMIE
Landmark Inn,
304 Eastgate Drive,
(913) 755–3051

OTTAWA
Villager Lodge,
2209 South Princeton,
(785) 242–7000 or
(888) 540–4024

PITTSBURG
The Extra Inn & Breakfast Bar,
4023 Parkview Drive,
(620) 232–2800

PLACES TO EAT IN SOUTHEAST KANSAS

BURLINGTON
C&B Bar & Grill,
119 North Third,
(620) 364–5436

CHANUTE
G. Willikers,
5 East Main Street,
(620) 431–1116

COFFEYVILLE
Cactus Grill,
602 Northeast Street,
(620) 251–4200

FORT SCOTT
Birght's Grill,
1411 East Wall,
(620) 223–4140

GIRARD
Chicken Annie's of Girard,
Highway 57, 4 miles
east of Girard,
(316) 724–4090

INDEPENDENCE
John's Kitchen & Pub,
119 West Main,
(620) 331–4747

Wood's Food & Spirits,
308 North Eight Street,
(620) 331–7960

IOLA
Greenery Restaurant,
1315 North State Street,
(620) 365–7743

NEODESHA
Neodesha Family
Restaurant,
210 East Main Street,
(620) 325–3929

OTTAWA
Poncho's Mexican Food,
429 South Main,
(785) 242–8227

PAOLA
Poncho's Mexican
Restaurant,
316/70 Old KC Road
Route 5,
(913) 294–5535

PARSONS
Parsonian Coffee Shop,
1725 Broadway,
(620) 421–4400

Selected Chambers of Commerce and Visitors Bureaus

Crawford County Convention and Visitors Bureau,
*117 West Fourth Street, Pittsburg 66762;
(620) 231–1212 or (800) 879–1112*

Independence Convention and Visitors Bureau,
P.O. Box 386, Independence 67301; (620) 331–1890

Franklin County Convention and Visitors Bureau,
*109 East Second, P.O. Box 580, Ottawa 66067;
(785) 242–1411*

Columbus Chamber of Commerce,
320 East Maple, Columbus 66725; (316) 429–1492

Chanute Office of Tourism, Depot Plaza,
*P.O. Box 907, Chanute 66720;
(620) 431–5229 or (800) 735–5229*

Coffey County Chamber of Commerce,
P.O. Box 423, Burlington 66839; (877) 364–2002

Coffeyville Convention and Visitors Bureau,
807 Walnut, Coffeyville 67337; (620) 251–1194

Linn County Economic Development,
P.O. Box 10, Mound City 66506; (913) 795–2074

Osawatomie Chamber of Commerce,
*526 Main Street, P.O. Box 338, Osawatomie 66064;
(913) 755–4114*

City of Garnett,
*131 West Fifth, P.O. Box H, Garnett 66032;
(785) 448–6767*

South Central Kansas

ush green fields of fall-planted winter wheat dot the landscape in central Kansas. Here cattle graze on the wheat until its winter dormancy, when intermittent snow insulates it from the cold. In early spring it once again colors the fields with startling splashes of green.

One-fourth of the nation's winter wheat grows here, a crop well suited to the state's mild winters, hot summers, and seasonal rainfall. September moisture is critical: Too much causes root rot, but there will be no germination if it is too dry. A wrong decision in timing the planting of seed can be costly.

Kansas is at its most vibrant during the growing season. From late winter's brilliant green to summer's mellow gold, the wheat season is life to farmers. The harvest begins along the southern edge of the state and moves north, with wheat ripening one day later for every 15 or so miles. A hailstorm can wipe out a year's crop, a rainstorm can make the fields too muddy to work. Everything depends on the weather in a place where an innocent, blue, morning sky can turn angry and destroy a season's crop in hours. During June harvests, crews and giant combines travel through the state. Only during the winter dormancy can the farmer rest.

The Mennonites introduced a new wheat to Kansas in 1874, the hard wheat favored for bread baking and able to withstand Kansas weather. Developed in Turkey and called "Turkey Red" wheat, the plant grew well on the dry steppes of Russia—but it's called "Red" because of its color, not its politics. Members of a German religious sect who had originally migrated from their native Germany to Russia in search of religious freedom, the Mennonites settled around Newton and McPherson. Here the "amber waves of grain" shimmer in the summer sun.

Flint Hills

nterstate 35 and the Kansas Turnpike follow the Old Chisholm Trail. Wichita lies where the Arkansas (pronounced "Ar-KANsas" in this state) River meets the Little Arkansas River. It is the center of the

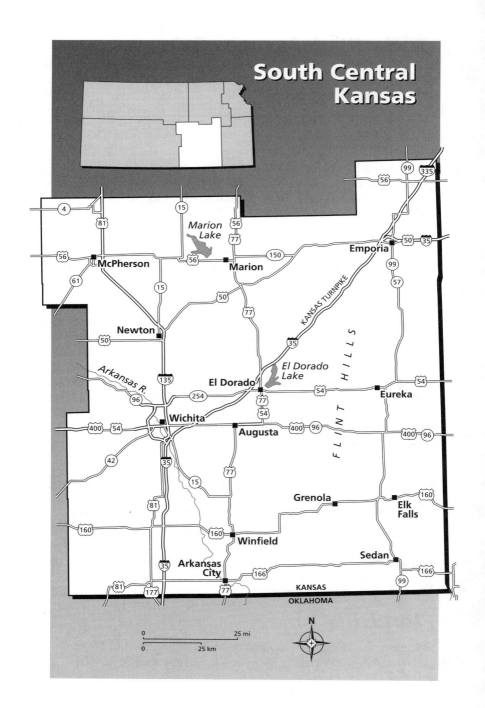

South Central Kansas

SOUTH CENTRAL KANSAS

aviation industry, the second-largest business in Kansas, and its industrial jet set makes the city fly.

On Saturdays, **Wichita**'s old-fashioned trolleys, trimmed in mahogany and brass, connect major downtown hotels, museums, the stadium, convention center, and Old Town. Call (316) 265–7221 for schedules. Wednesdays through Saturdays, from Memorial Day to Labor Day, trolleys with guides tour historic areas. Call for reservations.

The city shines brightest during its annual ten-day **River Festival** that begins the Friday before Mother's Day weekend. Attracting crowds that exceed 300,000, it has become one of the premier events of its kind in the country.

It begins with the Sundown Parade, led by the reigning Admiral Windwagon Smith. He was the legendary seafaring Edward T. Smith, who came to Wichita one day and, faced with the sea of flat plains, decided that sails on a wagon would provide an inexpensive means of transportation.

You don't see too many windwagons today; it was a great idea, but on the rough prairie trails not too successful. (Maybe we should try it again on the glass-smooth Kansas Turnpike—it has potential.) Throughout the following week the city is a kaleidoscope of events, from an antique bathtub race on the river to a pops concert with fireworks. For information, call (316) 267–2817, or visit the festival Web site at www.wichita riverfestival.org.

Just west of downtown, along the banks of the Arkansas River, are the Museums on the River, a group of adjoining attractions that includes Botanica—The Wichita Gardens, the Mid-America All-Indian Center, the Wichita Art Museum, and Old Cowtown, a living-history museum.

At 701 North Amidon is **Botanica—The Wichita Gardens,** a museum in bloom. The ten-acre botanical garden includes twenty themed areas ranging from the formal Shakespeare Garden to a riot of color in the Wildflower Garden. Sight-impaired visitors are invited to touch and smell plants in the Sally Stone Sensory Garden's living plant wall. Other areas not to be missed are the Margie Button Memorial Fountain and rose garden, the Woodland Walk, and the Butterfly Garden. In early summer, visit the Butterfly House, where more than 300 butterflies emerge from their chrysalises to fly freely among the flowers. Wear a bright color and stand still—one may alight on your shoulder. Be sure to bring a camera; the gardens offer many opportunities for photographers. A gift shop has unique ideas for plant lovers. The gardens are open from June through October, Monday through Saturday from 9:00 A.M. to 5:00 P.M., Sunday from 1:00 to 5:00 P.M.; closed weekends. Admission is $6.00 for adults, $5.00 for seniors, $3.00 for students; children under age five are free. A family rate of $12.00 includes one or two parents and minor-aged children. Call (316) 264–0448 for information, or visit the gardens' Web site at www.botanica.org.

The *"Keeper of the Plains,"* a 44-foot, five-ton sculpture, broods over the *Mid-America All-Indian Center,* at 650 North Seneca, overlooking the confluence of the Arkansas and Little Arkansas Rivers. Its sculptor, the late Blackbear Bosin, was known throughout the art world. The center is a nonprofit organization founded to serve the cultural and social needs of Native Americans, and it features a museum and gift shop. Native American tacos and fry bread are served on Tuesday from 11:00 A.M. to 2:00 P.M. and from 4:00 to 8:00 P.M. Powwows are held here several times a year; the public is welcome to watch the dancing, done in traditional dress. Hours are Tuesday through Saturday from 10:00 A.M. to 5:00 P.M. year-round and from 1:00 to 5:00 P.M. Sundays from May through December. Admission is $2.00 for adults, $1.00 for children ages six to twelve. Call (316) 262–5221, or visit the Web site at www.theindiancenter.com.

You can't miss the huge outdoor sculptures on the grounds of the *Wichita*

Will the Real Buffalo Bill Please Stand Up?

*O*n the highest point of the Pioneer Highland Cemetery, at 1001 North Hillside, rests an impressive monument. It is the final resting place of William Mathewson, also known as Buffalo Bill, the last of the old scouts. He spoke fourteen Native American languages, fought with Native Americans, and ultimately made peace with them. They knew the 6-foot-6-inch hero as Sinpah Zilbah, "the Long-Bearded Dangerous White Man." He is credited with a single-handed rescue of 155 men and a train of 144 wagons loaded with government guns and ammunition from a Native American attack. General Curtis said, "Nothing in the annals of history compares with the feats of bravery done by you." When a hard winter threatened settlers with starvation, he led buffalo-hunting expeditions. Grateful residents told of the sharpshooting skills of "Bill the Buffalo Killer." Thus the legend of Buffalo Bill was born.

Art Museum, 619 Stackman Drive. Titled *Dreamers Awake,* they are said to represent the universal struggles of the human experience. Judge for yourself. Due to expansion, the building will be closed for a while. For information, call (316) 268–4921.

Old Cowtown Museum, 1871 Sims Park Drive, brings back the feel of the Old West. Located in what was once Delano, a frontier cow town is re-created along the banks of the Arkansas River. More than forty authentically furnished buildings are on seventeen acres, including Wichita's first residence, the Munger House, and the city's first jail. Also featured are a general store, drugstore, saloon, one-room schoolhouse, blacksmith shop, livery stable, and a five-acre farm. Periodic living-history programs show how folks of the 1870s worked and played. Special events include an 1870s Independence Day, Frontier Days, an old-time county fair, and a prairie Victorian Christmas. Cowtown is open April 1 through October 31. Hours are from 10:00 A.M. to 5:00 P.M. Monday through Saturday, noon to 5:00 P.M. Sunday. Admission is $7.00 for adults, $6.50 for seniors, $5.00 for children ages twelve through seventeen, and $4.00 for children ages four through eleven. Call (316) 264–6398 for information, or visit the Web site at www.old-cowtown.org.

For a grand place to stay in the museum district and convenient to downtown, check into *The Castle Inn Riverside,* 1155 North River Boulevard. Known as the Campbell Castle, the building is listed on the National Register of Historic Places. It is a Scottish castle by a story-book river, yet it is close to the heart of the city. In this century-old castle, you can escape to the romance of another era. Sunlight shines through stained glass and glows on intricate woodwork and exquisite antiques. Twelve of its fourteen rooms have fireplaces. You can relax in the billiards room or explore the turret. A home-cooked breakfast awaits you in the dining room. As picturesque as it is, the hotel has all the amenities for modern travelers. The room rates are $125 to $295. Call (316) 263–9300 or (800) 580–1131, e-mail 1castle@gte.net, or visit the Web site at www.castleinnriverside.com.

The sweeping curves on Wichita's downtown riverfront skyline are the modernistic pavilions of its newest attraction, *Exploration Place,* 300 North McLean. Not just a children's museum, Exploration Place appeals to all ages. Tots love enjoying the laughing sunflowers, climbing inside a giant egg, and peeking through an enormous clock face. Older kids and adults are drawn to the flight pavilion, where a shimmering wind wall is in constant motion and trying out flight simulators is a popular activity. You can even walk a virtual dog in the health exhibit or play mini-golf. Live daily broadcasts are made from a local television station's weather lab inside the museum. In addition to a motion simulation theater (where the seats move in sync to the film), Exploration Place boasts a Cyberdome Theater, a cutting-edge use of interactive computer graphics. General admission is $8.00 for adults, $6.00 for children ages five to fifteen, and $3.00 for children ages two to four. Additional charge for mini-golf, Simulation Center, and Cyberdome Theater. Hours are noon to 5:00 P.M. Monday, 9:00 A.M. to 5:00 P.M. Tuesday through Sunday, with extended hours on weekends, some holidays, and in summer. Closed Mondays after Labor Day until Memorial Day. Call (316) 263–3373 or (877) 904–1444 or check out the Web site at www.exploration.org.

The Wichita–Sedgwick County Historical Museum, at 204 South Main Street, is housed in the old City Hall. The chiming of the clock in the tower of the 1892 limestone building can be heard for blocks. Inside is an 1880s Victorian home interior, a late-nineteenth-century drugstore, and an early auto repair shop with a Wichita-built 1917 Jones six auto. Hours are Tuesday through Friday from 11:00 A.M. to 4:00 P.M., Saturday and Sunday from 1:00 to 5:00 P.M. Call (316) 265–9314.

In the historic midtown you'll find Wichita's Calvary Baptist Church, at 601 North Water, now the home of the *Kansas African American*

Museum. Inside this large, brick building with beautiful wooden beams and stained-glass windows you can view artifacts and displays that provide insight into the history of blacks in Kansas.

The museum displays a collection of African and African-American artifacts and publications and changing exhibits about sports and entertainment personalities and black leaders in the fields of medicine, the military, and education. The museum is also the site of holiday caroling and spiritual assemblies that bring the old church alive with the power of gospel music.

The museum is open Tuesday through Friday from 10:00 A.M. to 5:00 P.M., Sunday from 2:00 to 6:00 P.M. Donations are encouraged. For more information, call (316) 262–7651.

There are some parts of town that are uniquely Wichita, so get off the main streets and head toward ***Wichita's Old Town District.*** The district is 6 blocks east of Wichita's present downtown center and extends about 0.5 mile east of the Arkansas River. It includes the 700 to 900 blocks of East Douglas Avenue. This revitalized century-old warehouse district has brick streets, boardwalks, and streetlamps. More than 200 businesses are concentrated here, including restaurants, antiques shops, nightclubs, and even dinner theater. There is plenty of free parking, and the trolley runs in this district.

The ***Farm and Art Market*** (316–262–3555) has three floors of curio and craft shops, clothing stores, artists' nooks, and food stalls at 835 East First Street. There is plenty of free parking, and walking is encouraged in this friendly, easygoing neighborhood. From May through October the outdoor plaza is the site of a farmers' market on Saturdays. Indoor shops are open Monday through Saturday from 10:00 A.M. to 6:00 P.M.; closed Sundays. Several big events are the St. Patrick's Day, Cinco de Mayo, Wichita River Festival, and Oktoberfest celebrations.

Step over to 234 North Mosley Street and enjoy the ***Mosley Street Melodrama,*** where villains abound and heros save the day. It's dinner and fun in one cozy little place. Call (316) 263–0222 for show times.

The Sunflower Shoppe at 607 West Douglas has nothing but Kansas products: wheat weavings, pottery, sunflowers, copper sculptures, and Wizard of Oz collectibles. Joan (say Jo Ann) Dodds is the owner of this unique shop. Open Monday through Saturday 10:00 A.M. to 5:30 P.M. Call (316) 265–0837, or visit the Web site, www.thesunflowershoppe.com.

Need some camping equipment? Visit the ***Coleman Factory Outlet Store and Museum*** at 235 North St. Francis, where you will find everything for the outdoors at this factory outlet for the Coleman Company. There is also a museum display of vintage Coleman products (the earliest lanterns are especially collectible). Hours are Monday through Friday from 9:00 A.M. to 6:00 P.M., Saturday from 9:00 A.M. to 1:00 P.M. Call (316) 264–0836.

If you like dinner theater, this town has another. The *Crown-Uptown Dinner Theatre*, at 3207 East Douglas, offers professional performances of Broadway shows each week, along with a buffet and bar. Dinner begins Thursday through Saturday at 6:30 P.M. and Sunday at 6:00 P.M. Performance follows. There is also a special children's matinee on Friday and Saturday at 11:00 A.M. Call (316) 681–1566 for information or reservations, or visit www.crownuptown.com.

For lodging that's close to downtown in an intimate setting, try the *Inn at the Park,* at 3751 East Douglas. This circa 1910 mansion has twelve suites, some with fireplaces. Rates are $114 to $164 on Friday and Saturday, or any suite for $89 Sunday through Thursday. A full breakfast is served. Call (316) 652–0500 or (800) 258–1951 for reservations, or visit the Web site at www.innatthepark.com.

The *Clifton Square Shopping Village* (3700 East Douglas), is a collection of shops in a nineteenth-century neighborhood. Shop for art, gifts, clothing, and collectibles. The stores are open Monday through Saturday 10:00 A.M. to 6:00 P.M., Sunday 1:00 to 5:00 P.M. Call (316) 686–2177 for tours.

Across the river from Old Town is the *Historic Delano District.* Period lighting, historic plaques, and walking tours are in the works for this area. Practically a local institution is retailer *Hatman Jack's,* 601 West Douglas. "The largest selection of hats in the state" is no idle boast; you can choose from western hats, derbies, golf hats, and caps of all kinds. Jack Kellogg is also one of about thirty custom hatters in the United States. Hours are 10:00 A.M. to 5:30 P.M. weekdays, except Thursday, when the store stays open until 6:00 P.M. Saturday hours are 10:00 A.M. to 5:30 P.M. Call (316) 264–4881 or visit the Web site at www.hatmanjacks.com.

For a closer look at the animal kingdom, visit *Sedgwick County Zoo,* 5555 Zoo Boulevard, just off I–235 on Wichita's west side. The 247-acre zoo is home to 2,700 animals from around the world. Exhibit areas include the African Veldt, Asian Steppes, Jungle, Australian Outback, and South American Pampas. The Pride of the Plains exhibit hosts African lions, meerkats, and warthogs, making it a favorite among young movie fans. Open every day except Christmas. Summer hours are 9:00 A.M. to 5:00 P.M.; opens an hour later in winter. Call (316) 942–2212, or visit the Web site at www.scz.org.

Old West Fades Away

*W*ichita was a cow town. It is said that at any one time there were as many as 100,000 head of longhorn cattle passing through. Since it took about fifteen cowboys to move a herd, that meant that there were large numbers of cowboys passing through. Of course, gamblers, "fancy ladies," and con artists also arrived. Wichita tried to keep the peace by outlawing guns and prostitution, so the action moved across the Arkansas River to the little town of Delano.

Delano was a wild and wide-open town. According to legend, on Sunday morning the "ladies" would have nude races to the river to entertain the cowboys. Rowdy Joe Lowe and his wife, Rowdy Kate, ran the most unruly saloon in town.

The town of Delano doesn't seem to exist anymore. It has been eaten up by Wichita. But people still remember Delano. Yes, indeed, they do.

The world's largest western store is at 6501 West Kellogg Drive, on the city's west side. ***Sheplers Western Wear*** has what you need for that Flint Hills trail ride. Boots by the zillions, jeans, and shirts—you name it, they've got it. Open Monday through Saturday from 10:00 A.M. to 9:00 P.M., Sunday from noon to 6:00 P.M. Call (316) 946–3600, or visit the Web site at www.sheplers.com.

The Inn at Willowbend (at 3939 Comotara, near the intersection of Thirty-seventh and Rock Road on Wichita's northeastern edge) overlooks the championship Willowbend Golf Course. Gary and Bernice Adamson opened the inn so that Gary could be on the golf course by noon every day. Golf is the theme of this sprawling stucco building. Complimentary drinks are served at cocktail hour, and breakfast specialties such as banana buckwheat pancakes are available in the morning. There are forty-four rooms, all with private bath. British decor throughout the inn and paintings of Scottish golf courses keep golf in mind, and the massive fireplace in the St. Andrews' Lounge makes you feel as though you are right in the ancient golf club itself. Rates are from $80 to $159, depending on room size and day of the week; breakfast is included. Call (316) 616–4032 or (800) 553–5775, or visit at www.theinn atwillowbend.net.

Red Barn Ostrich Farm Bed and Breakfast (6427 North Greenwich Road) offers guests an unusual setting 0.25 mile north of Highway 254. Early risers are rewarded by a view of 150 ostriches performing their sunrise ballet. And even if you don't get up early you can have a complete tour of Sue and Bob Johnson's farm. The Johnsons raise ostriches from eggs to yearlings. There are three guest rooms with private bath. For breakfast, steaming breads come straight from the oven every morning, and Sue's homemade jam and fresh fruits and juices are followed by a full specialty entree. Rooms are $75 per night. Call (316) 744–9800. Advance reservations are requested.

For modern fun, head for **Laser Quest** at 2120 North Woodlawn, also in the northeastern part of Wichita. Play in swirling fog accompanied by space-age music and lighting. Don your LQ pack, get a personalized scorecard, and go for it. Hours change seasonally. Call (316) 652–9500.

Wyldewood Cellars Winery (951 East 119th Street; 316–554–WINE or 316–554–9463) is south of Wichita, west of the turnpike (exit 33) in the town of **Peck.** It is the largest supplier of elderberry wine in the country. Take a guided tour and sample some of the delicious wine. The Marketplace features not only the wines but also other specialties, such as elderberry jelly and syrup and other Kansas products, including homemade fudge. You can send gift boxes home. The winery is open 10:00 A.M. to 6:00 P.M. Monday through Saturday, 1:00 to 5:00 P.M. Sunday. Visit the Web site at www.wyldewoodcellars.com, or order by calling (800) 711–9748.

The **Lake Afton Public Observatory,** 1845 Fairmount (316–978–7827), is 15 miles southwest of Wichita off Highway K–42. Far, far away from city lights, the observatory's telescopes offer marvelous views of the moon, planets, and galaxies from one large telescope and several small ones. See star clusters, double stars, and other celestial wonders. Photography night lets you bring your 35mm camera and some 200 or 400 ASA film and shoot the valleys and craters of the moon and the rings of Jupiter. The observatory also contains exhibits and displays. Drive west on Highway 54 (Kellogg Drive) to the Lake Afton sign. Go south 3 miles on Viola Road and 1 mile east on MacArthur Road. Follow the signs. There are programs on Friday and Saturday nights from approximately 7:30 until 10:00 P.M. (times change slightly each month as the days lengthen), and the observatory is open to the public Saturday and Sunday from 1:30 to 4:00 P.M. as well. There is an admission charge of $3.00 for adults, $2.00 for children ages six to twelve; children age six and younger are free. Call ahead for a recorded message of times and special events.

East of Wichita on Highway 54, the little town of **Augusta** features the **C. N. James Log Cabin** at 305 State Street. Built in 1868, the cabin was known as the Shamleffer and James General Store. It is 1½ stories tall and built of hand-hewn cottonwood logs from along the Walnut River. It is one of only two log cabins at their original site in the state. At one time it was Augusta's first school, with thirty-four students in the upper loft. It was the meeting place for the Baptist and Methodist churches and the Masonic Lodge. In the late 1870s, the loft was raised and it became a two-story cabin. Lap siding was added. Since then it has been a boardinghouse, residence, and woodworking shop. Now it is part of the *Augusta Historical Museum,* where you can also buy some of the top-selling books on Kansas. Museum hours are 11:00 A.M. to 3:00 P.M. Monday through Saturday. Call (316) 775–5655. There is no charge, but donations are accepted.

There is a multitude of attractions in Augusta, including an art gallery at 616 School Street (316–775–0705) operated by nationally known watercolorist Sandi Gore-Evans. The *Gore-Evans Gallery* has Christmas on its mind most of the year. The artist's Santa print series are very well known. There are ornaments, greeting cards, and figurines. Next door at 610 School Street is *Three French Hens Gift Shop* (316–775–5875), filled with beautiful items. Both shops are open from 10:00 A.M. to 5:30 P.M. Monday through Saturday.

Listed on the National Register of Historic Places is the *Augusta Theatre,* 523 State Street, built in 1935 and featuring an elaborate Art Deco interior. It is host to movies, live theater, and music sponsored by the Augusta Arts Council. Call (316) 775–3661 for events information.

One of the attractions in town is for the birds, literally. Tom Eckley, Sr., has anything your wild birds might need at *Early Bird,* 112 West Seventh (316–775–5029). You'll find birdhouses, feeders, and seed to fill them, and special feeders adapted for certain species. Hours are 10:00 A.M. to 6:00 P.M. Monday through Saturday.

Four miles east of Augusta on Highway 154 is a Spanish windmill. It serves no purpose other than as the quixotic target for a sharp, angular sculpture of a man on horseback.

If tilting at windmills piques your interest, you will want a closer look at the other unusual creations on *Henry's Sculpture Hill*. There are twenty-six welded-metal sculpture scenes created by Franklin Jensen.

There is Don Quixote, of course, followed by his companion, Sancho Panza. Next is a scene based on e.e. cummings's poem "Chanson Innocente"—Pan leading four children. Redbone, the running larger-than-life bison, is made of strips of redwood decking attached to an angled iron frame. From the highway you can see a 24-foot-long praying mantis, which weighs as much as a small truck, preparing to strike a grasshopper; Leo the Lion pawing the air; an eagle turning to catch the wind; and a boy walking a cow home. There are more than one hundred sculptures, most outside, but some inside the barn.

Henry's Sculpture Hill

All of this has evolved from Jensen's interest in literature and art (he was a high-school English teacher in Wichita). A few years ago he decided he needed more space and bought the twenty-eight acres. Although several sculptures are visible from the highway, most are seen only by people who take the time to look him up. Jensen spends a great deal of time researching the anatomy of each figure and often constructs scale models. Some can be seen by driving east about 5 miles and turning south on Boyer Road.

If you want to see the rest of the works or meet Jensen, call ahead for an appointment (316–775–5296).

East of Augusta, just south of Highway 96, is the town of **Beaumont,** a historic cow town. The **Old Frisco Water Tower** built in 1885 for the Frisco Railroad steam engines provided water for the railroad roundhouse and cattle-shipping operations. It is the last remaining railroad water tower in the state and is on the National Register of Historic Places. It is at Main and Eleventh Street.

East of Wichita 1 mile north of U.S. 54 (Kellogg Drive) on 159th Street in **Andover** is a golfer's dream: **Terradyne,** a Scottish-style eighteen-hole golf course at 1400 Terradyne Drive. This is a true Scottish course of rolling fairways with few trees and characteristic Scottish peaks, hills, and hidden bunkers. An experience every golfer should have until he or she can take that dream trip to St. Andrews (or Turnberry, or Royal Troon, or Murfield—dream on, golfers). The European-style clubhouse is reminiscent of St. Andrews with the Old World elegance of its marble floors and the dark rich woodwork. **The Greens** restaurant is quite good, too. This is a resort hotel and country club, so hotel guests can play there if you call ahead for tee times at (316) 733–2582; or visit www.terradyne-resort.com.

On a breezier note, the **Museum of the American Fan Collectors Association** is at 415 East Thirteenth Street, Andover. This may well be the world's most fan-tastic museum. It is located at the headquarters of Vornado, a fan manufacturer. The president of that business is quoted as saying, "Like the invention of the wheel, the invention of the fan is a milestone in the development of human civilization." On a hot August night, anyone would agree with that, and when you think about it, fans drive air-conditioning, heating, automobile cooling systems, computers, and many other necessities of life. The museum displays more than 350 fans dating from 1886, when the first electric fan was invented. Hours are 9:00 A.M. to 5:00 P.M. Monday through Friday. Call (316) 733–0035 or visit www.vornado.com/museum/html.

Northwest of Andover on Highway 254 is the town of **Kechi** (pronounced Keech-eye), birthplace of actress Kirstie Alley (her family operated Kechi Lumber) and the official antiques capital of Kansas. The town is filled with antiques shops, boutiques, food, fine arts, stained glass, and crafts of all kinds. Kechi was settled in 1865, and it still has a comfortable, small-town feeling. There's even summer theater in season. About a dozen shops are open all year, with independent hours as posted.

One of these shops is **Karg Art Glass** at 4535 East Sixty-first Street North (316–744–2442), where you can watch glassblowers work their magic. Rollin Karg studied hot glass at Emporia State University and he and his wife, Patti, decided to build their own furnace in Kechi. The large, open studio allows visitors to watch the blowers and learn how each piece is made. A gift gallery featuring sixty to eighty other artists has an exquisite collection of art glass. Glassblowers work Monday, Tuesday, Thursday, and Friday from 6:00 A.M. to 3:00 P.M. and Saturday from 6:00 A.M. to noon. The gallery is open Monday through Saturday from 8:00 A.M. to 4:30 P.M.

Other shops, all in cute little cottages or cabins, include **Primitive's Plus** at 127 Foreman Kechi Alley (316–744–1836). Hours are Tuesday through Saturday from 1:00 to 5:00 P.M. Here you can look at quilts, antiques, and furniture. **The Country Post** at 134-B East Kechi Road specializes in country primitive and garden decor. It's open Thursday from noon to 4:00 P.M., Friday from 11:00 A.M. to 4:00 P.M., and Saturday from noon to 5:00 P.M. For lunch you can stop in at **Creek House Kitchen** at 223 East Kechi

Road Tuesday through Saturday from 11:00 A.M. to 3:00 P.M., and Sunday from noon to 3:00 P.M. Other attractions are **Turkey Creek Weaving** and the **Kechi Playhouse** on North Oliver. Look at the town's Web site to get the full picture of what the town has to offer at www.kechikscoc.com, or call the chamber of commerce at (316) 744–1337.

For modern man, the beaten path is covered with asphalt. But for the pioneers, the deep grooves worn into the earth by wagon wheels and horses' hoofs offered a certain amount of security. Getting off the beaten path was not a good idea. Today the ruts, called "swales," can still be seen in many places where the Santa Fe Trail crossed the prairie. If you think you are ready to get on that beaten path, ready for an adventure unlike any other today, then join the **Flint Hills Overland Wagon Train Trips**, which leave about five times a year from Cassoday, off the Kansas Turnpike at the junction of Highway 177, for wagon-train trips across the central prairie.

Traveling away from modern roadways and through picturesque parts of the state, participants use horses, covered wagons, and coaches. Hearty meals (including coffee ground at the campsite and brewed in a sock— a clean one), evening entertainment (seasoned trail riders strumming guitars around the campfire, and maybe a tall tale or two), and a sunrise worship service are included in the tours. It is a once-in-a-lifetime adventure to see the glory of the Flint Hills "up close and personal."

The overnight trip is for nature lovers, for people who like to camp out and rough it, and who want to experience the life of the pioneers. If you are not ready for all of this, the abbreviated one-day trip is ideal. Call (316) 321–6300, or write Wagon Master Ervin Grant, Flint Hills Overland Wagon Train Trips, P.O. Box 1076, El Dorado 67042 for information. Reservations must be made and paid for twenty-one days in advance of the trip. The cost of the overnight trip—round-trip first class (1878 style)—is $150 for adults and $75 for kids ages four to twelve. Toddlers ride free (and love it). You can go along as a trail rider with your own horse for $75. There are assorted other rates for the one-day Saturday trip and for families, so call and check them out. Take a virtual trip at www.wagontrainskansas.com.

The **Kansas Oil Museum** is at 383 East Central in **El Dorado.** At the Texaco theater you can watch a video of one of the state's oil-drilling rigs in operation. There are also three working scale models of various rigs, and outdoors there is an oil field lease house furnished 1930s style. The house functions as a research facility and has extensive archives. The Teter Nature Trail is a 1.25-mile walking path through eight acres of wilderness with a diverse collection of plant and animal life. Visible from the path is a 100-foot steel oil derrick and rotary rig mast. Open from 9:00 A.M. to 5:00 P.M. Monday through Saturday, 1:00 to 5:00 P.M. on Sunday. Call (316) 321–9333.

The Coutts Memorial Museum of Art (316–321–1212) is in the Bluestem Building in downtown El Dorado and houses more than 1,000 original paintings, prints, drawings, and sculptures by such artists as Thomas Hart Benton and Frederic Remington. It is open from 1:00 to 5:00 P.M. Monday, Wednesday, and Friday, from 9:00 A.M. to 5:00 P.M. Tuesday and Thursday, and from noon to 4:00 P.M. Saturday.

El Dorado State Park and Wildlife Area is nearby, between Highway 177 and I–35, and has a well-stocked lake. Hunting and fishing are allowed in season.

The town of *Towanda* is 5 miles west of El Dorado on Interstate 35 (exit 71). The *Paradise Doll Museum,* at 119 South Sixth Street, Towanda (316–536–2678), is a repair facility for antique dolls. There are more than 3,000 examples on display, as well as regional craft items for sale. Owner Barbara Brush charges no admission. Her motto is "If I can fix it, I will," and she does—any kind of doll new or old. She lives nearby and will open by appointment. Official hours are Tuesday through Saturday from 1:00 to 5:00 P.M.

Trivia
Kansas ranks as the fourth-windiest state. Only Massachusetts, Montana, and Wyoming are windier.
There are 2.5 cows for each person in Kansas.

The town of *Cassoday*—the prairie chicken capital of the world—is on Highway 177, just off the Kansas Turnpike. From Towanda take Highway 254/54 east to Highway 177. There are cattle and horses in the pastures. There is nothing contrived or phony about Cassoday; this is a very real cow town. Beef and bread are the staples, and there are cowboys everywhere.

Does the idea of working on a ranch appeal to you? Say you are a career woman, say you don't know beans about cattle, say you never appear in public without makeup and a manicure, but all in all, the idea appeals to you. What to do? Head a little farther north on Highway 177 to *Matfield Green* and find Jane Koger's 6,000-acre working cattle ranch and join *Prairie Women Adventures and Retreat*, because there are no men here at the *Homestead Ranch.* Women can let their hair down and leave their makeup at home. You can get down and get dirty. In fact, you can roar through the pastures on an International Harvester tractor, with tires taller than you are. You can learn to use the hydraulic levers and gearshifts, and control 120 horsepower. Or you can control one horsepower, a quarter horse to be exact, and roam the 6,000 acres of prime grassland and 200 acres of cropland at the Homestead Ranch. (If you don't like horses, you can drive a four-wheeler out to the herd.)

What else to do? Well, care for and ride your horse, feed chickens and calves, if you want to take it easy. But if you want to be part of the real work, you can ride out for roundup and smell the burnt Hereford hair as you watch the Flying J brand appear out of white smoke on a calf's haunch during branding of the herd of 300 cows. You can be there for the birthing of calves in February and March and watch the newborn calf, wobbly and wet, with ears bigger than its head, search for its mother's milk for the first time.

Real work. That's what it is, and Jane and her female ranch hands do it all. In May, the women wield inch-long hypodermic needles for inoculations, scalpels for castration of the male calves, and branding irons. Weaning is in October, when calves are no longer cute and cuddly but weigh in at 550 pounds and are not at all anxious to leave their mothers' sides.

The Homestead Ranch provides public access to the Flint Hills and the six million acres of grassland there, all that is left of North America's tallgrass prairie. And so the ranch provides more than a chance for sore muscles, it offers a real opportunity to explore the last tallgrass prairie and experience the American frontier.

Newsweek magazine wrote about the ranch in an article entitled "Glad You Aren't Here," with the subtitle "No Husband, No Kids, and a Vacation to Remember." Articles about the ranch have also appeared in *Atlantic Monthly* and *Vogue* magazines. Come on, admit it, you have always wanted to try this. Right? Jane Koger is a feminist who believes her all-women crews are calmer and better for the cattle.

The Prickly Pear: Eat with Caution!

A surprise to most visitors is the common prickly pear cactus, which grows throughout the state in dry gravelly soil. Flowers of the prickly pear are yellow, orange, or even red. The fruit of this cactus is edible and quite sweet, but it contains many small seeds. The secret is to chew lightly and swallow the seeds whole. A food source for early Native Americans, the prickly pear is still harvested for its fruit, which is sold in grocery stores. Proceed with caution, though. As the name warns, the fruit has many nasty little prickles on its skin.

But all of the time spent at the ranch is not work time. Women are free to enjoy the serenity of the Flint Hills, spend weekends browsing through Jane's extensive library of women's literature, fish, hike, or picnic among the wildflowers.

There are two packages from which to choose. The first puts women to work in the maintenance of the 200-head cow/calf herd and 1,500 summer yearlings. The other is a "bare-bones" plan that requires guests to cook their own meals and do their own cleanup. Prices run $125 a night (less 20 percent for five nights or more).

Although the bunkhouses can accommodate twenty-four persons, only eight guests are permitted if the ranch hands are involved in heavy cattle work that could be dangerous to novices. Typical guests are professional women in their thirties and forties, but guests have ranged from ages eighteen to seventy-six, and a special weekend is set aside for women and their young daughters.

The special rate for groups of four to fifteen women is $35 per night; for sixteen to twenty-two women, the rate is $30 per night. Contact Prairie Women Adventures by writing P.O. Box 2, Matfield Green 66862, by calling (620) 753–3416, or by visiting the Web site at www. guestranches.com/homestead.

If you want to see bull riding—the real thing, western style—the **Sankey Ranch** (316–776–2592) is the place to go in **Rose Hill,** southeast of Wichita. Bud Sankey and his two sons, Lyle and Ike, will teach you how to ride a bull. Why would anyone want to learn to ride a bull, you might ask? (Bud says "for cash, why else would anyone do it?"). Well, maybe. But there are those who do it just for the excitement. For a mere $380 for four days, men come from all over the country to ride bulls. These are not wanna-be cowboys, they are professional men (doctors, lawyers, and CEOs), working men, young fellas who are looking at a career in rodeo, and the occasional woman; people who just have to try everything. Bud admits he discourages women because his bulls are "just too rough" for them. Ladies, do you hear a challenge, there?

Bud is justifiably proud of his sons. Lyle is the number-one instructor in the country and two-time National Finals Rodeo (NFR) Champion; four days in the arena with him will have you riding. With both indoor and outdoor arenas, there are no rain delays in this sport. Every ride is video-taped so riders can see what they are doing wrong (a souvenir you can play and replay for your friends back home).

Trivia

There is a Tourist Information Station in Belle Plaine on I–35/Kansas Turnpike at milepost 25.7.

Ike is the top contractor for the NFR and offers world-champion bucking horses. You are in good hands at Sankey Ranch. So are the bulls. Bud says the bulls are worth a lot of dollars and they take good care of them. They work an eight-second shift, then get time off. Bud has been ranching here for twenty-five years. It is a professionally run operation.

Not so sure about that bull-riding thrill? Well you can come to the ranch and just watch other people (who are braver than you) get flipped into the sawdust. Bud asks that you call ahead to arrange a time to watch, but you surely are welcome, he says.

Bud also has a full line of very good saddles and roping equipment for sale in the shop at the ranch. Call (316) 776–2592 and talk to Bud, then get on the next plane to Kansas.

To find Sankey Ranch, take the Andover exit from Interstate 35 West. Go right through Andover and cross Highway 54. Five miles south, turn east on 150th Street, then watch for signs leading to the ranch.

Rose Hill also has a bed-and-breakfast. **Queen Anne's Lace Bed and Breakfast**, at 15335 Southwest Queen Anne's Lace, is the pride of Jackie and Bob Collison. This peaceful country spot is on five wooded acres. Accommodations include full-size bed and private bath. Horses, goats, chickens, dogs, and cats are part of the landscape; in fact, certified "heater cats" are available on request. The den has a television, VCR, fireplace, and walk-out entry to the large patio with hot tub. A full breakfast is included in the $60 to $70 price. Bob and Jackie's specialties are unusual creations, such as stuffed French toast (filled with goat cheese) and oatmeal pancakes. Call (316) 733–4075.

For the past seventy-five-plus years, thousands of tourists have descended on **Belle Plaine,** south of Wichita, to see the **Bartlett Arboretum**, at Highway 55 and Line Street. This twenty-acre garden planted in 1910 by the Bartlett family is now a mature arboretum with trees, shrubs, flowers, and grasses from all over the world. Call (620) 488–3451.

The arboretum is unique in that it flowers in all growing seasons. In the spring, 30,000 tulips are bordered by 5,000 pansies. The garden contains fifteen varieties of flowering trees and shrubs. Summer annuals are planted in May. Along Euphrates Creek, thousands of yellow water iris are naturalized, adding sunny color to the display.

Shade trees line the pathways, a cool relief from the hot Kansas sun. In the fall a brilliant panorama of chrysanthemums and changing foliage compresses the color of the country into the arboretum. It is open April through November, daily from 9:00 A.M. to 6:00 P.M.

Along the peaceful western bank of the Arkansas River lies the small town of *Oxford,* southeast of Belle Plaine on Highway 160. It is filled with retirees and people who commute to nearby communities to work. The 113-year-old *Old Oxford Grist Mill* northeast of Oxford still processes grain with the power of the river; artists travel here to capture the picturesque mill. Oxford also contains the oldest building and church in the county. Visit the Web site at www.cjcconnection.com/oxford.htm.

Winfield's Vietnam War Memorial Wall grew from the twenty-fifth class reunion, in 1988, of a young man killed in that war. Hal McCoy found a friend's name on the Washington, D.C., memorial and went to his classmates with his idea for a replica of that memorial. It was originally intended to honor the casualties among classmates, family, and neighbors in Cowley County. The project grew, the cost grew, but the people of Winfield would not let it fail. Classmates of Gary Bannon raised nearly $100,000, and on Veterans Day 1989, McCoy presented the memorial honoring all servicemen and nurses from the state of Kansas who died in Southeast Asia on behalf of the Winfield High School Class of 1963. There are 778 names of servicemen and -women who were killed or missing in action. It's in Memorial Park between Ninth and Tenth Avenues, along with a central white cenotaph honoring all veterans.

The *Walnut Valley Festival* has been held at Cowley County Fairgrounds on Highway 160 on Winfield's west side the third week in September for more than thirty years. It is four days of toe-tapping, knee-slapping, hand-clapping music. This is a true all-acoustic bluegrass music festival, even though bluegrass is only one kind of music you will hear. If you are a fan of western, Irish, folk, blues, or Cajun music, this festival is for you, too. Winfield isn't called "the Pickers Paradise" for nothing. Locals say

How the Chisholm Trail Began

*T*he only cattle Jesse Chisholm ever drove were oxen yoked to a freight wagon. He was neither a cowboy nor a cattleman. Born in 1805, Chisholm was the son of a Scottish father and a Cherokee mother. He established a trading post where Wichita now stands and cut a trail south to Mexico through Indian Territory. While Chisholm set the trail as a trade route, the "Chisholm Trail" opened the way to the railheads in Kansas, and in turn the eastern markets, for the great herds of Texas longhorns.

it usually rains the weekend of the festival, and regulars come prepared. They say it is a must-do-at-least-once-in-your-lifetime event. Right up there with Woodstock. Once, the flooded Walnut River came up and lapped at the toes of those in the campground, but they unplugged their hookups and just kept on picking. Good thing the music is acoustic. Call (620) 221–3250.

The **Chisholm Trail Museum** is in nearby **Wellington.** In 1867 the Chisholm Trail, first marked by trader Jesse Chisholm for his wagons, wound from Abilene to San Antonio. It became a famous cattle trail, where more than a million head of Texas steers were driven to the shipping center of Abilene. Later, settlers moved in and fenced the land. The museum's collection has been donated by the descendants of those pioneers. Located at 502 North Washington Street, 4 blocks west of Highway 160, the museum is open weekends spring and fall, and weekday afternoons in summer. It is closed in the winter because the building is difficult to keep warm. Call (620) 326–3820 for the current schedule.

West on Highway 81 is **Caldwell,** dubbed the "Border Queen City" by cowboys on the Chisholm Trail. The **Border Queen Museum** and the **Cherokee Strip Center** retell the story of the Oklahoma Land Rush.

Caldwell is the home of **Wind, Earth and Sky,** Anna K. Petrik's gallery at 175 South Market. Anna has a large loom in the gallery, on which she weaves tapestries. The works of this fiber artist are inspired by the ever-changing southern Kansas landscape. Driving snow, blowing dust, wheat fields, and summer storms all contribute to designs that rise from the fabric's warp and weft in various textures. Anna uses her own thick, hand-spun yarns. She will create a piece especially for you, if you would like to commission one.

Eddie Morrison is a sculptor whose work is exhibited throughout the country. This Native American artist is the grandson of a Cherokee. He says he feels the presence of the Great Creator in every piece he makes. You can see an example of his work a half block off Main Street on Central entitled *Those Who Came Before,* a limestone relief depicting the cultures that have influenced this area. Call (620) 845–6666.

Another artist in Caldwell is the internationally acclaimed wilderness photographer Charles Phillips, who treks alone with a pack mule into remote regions of the American wilderness. His museum-quality photos possess a subtlety of tone and degree of detail that are more than the human eye can absorb. His studio, the **Charles Phillips Wilderness Fine Art Photography,** is at 13 South Main. Call (620) 845–6470 or (800) 353–3583, or e-mail cphillips@earthlink.net.

Other artists have left their mark in Caldwell. You can see *Cowboys Driving Cattle,* a 1941 mural by Kenneth Evett, a student of Thomas Hart Benton, on the south wall of the Caldwell post office at 14 North Main. Another mural is at the south side of Heritage Park at 102 South Main—a charming depiction of the historical progression of life on the plains by local artist Brenda Lebeda Almond.

One and a half miles south of Caldwell off Highway 81, watch for the **Ghost Riders of the Chisholm Trail.** These silhouettes are frozen in steel and concrete. The ghosts can be seen from Highway 81 on the windswept red bluff nearby. The life-size sculpture of a herd of longhorn cattle, a chuck wagon pulled by horses, and cowboys on horseback look startlingly real. So lifelike is the scene, observers are certain they have noticed both dust and sounds coming from the bluff.

This amazing piece of art has been named a Kansas Historical Attraction by the Kansas Historical Society. The ghosts will forever remind us of the great cattle drives of 1866–1886, when millions of Texas longhorn cattle passed here on their way to the other legendary railhead cow towns. Caldwell was the first stop on the trail after miles of Indian

More Than One Hundred Years of Testimony

*I*n the early twentieth century, passengers on the northbound Santa Fe out of Arkansas City could see the words CHRIST DIED FOR THE UNGODLY in large white stones. Then in smaller letters they could read the Bible citation from the Book of Romans, where these words are found. Today, the letters can be seen northbound on the U.S. 77 bypass.

One man was supposedly responsible. Fred Horton was a young dispatcher who came to Arkansas City with his bride when the Santa Fe line crossed into Oklahoma, just south of the town, in 1889. His daughter Ruth tells how at the end of the day her mother would hitch their horse to the phaeton, and they would drive down to the south yards to her father. Every evening he went to the north hills to work on his project. He did it almost single-handedly.

Horton rebuilt his quotation three times over a thirty-year period to get it the size and shape it is today. Each letter is 18 feet high, 12 feet wide, and 3 feet deep. The quotation is about 475 feet long and is built of stone from the hillside on which it stands.

For more than a hundred years the stones have testified to Horton's beliefs. The Auxiliary to the Brotherhood of Locomotive Engineers undertook the project of having the text set in cement. Currently, the Junior Chamber of Commerce keeps it weeded and washed.

Territory, and it was so rowdy that in six years the town went through sixteen marshals. Today a church steeple graces the top of Mount Lookout, but in those days, it was the "border queens" who excitedly watched for the cattle herds approaching the town and the eager cowboys who rode with them.

Eight and a half miles west of Arkansas City on Highway 166, at the *Post Musical Homestead* (620–442–4336), you won't believe what you see—and hear—in the one-hundred-plus-year-old barn and 1886 farmhouse, granary gallery, and chapel, owned by Bill and Orvaleen Post. There are murals and life-size fiberglass animals (a Jersey cow in the wooden stanchion, standing with her hind leg ready to kick again, and Old Jack, the mule), and original songs for you to sing along with are played in all five buildings. A most unusual, one-of-a-kind place, it lives up to the lyrics of the Bill Post song "Where in the World but Kansas?" Bill's music is even more famous than that: He made *Ripley's Believe It or Not* when another of his songs, the official state march, "Here's Kansas," was played by 6,000 high-school band members at the University of Kansas in 1993. You can enjoy the music from May through June and in September and October, Wednesday through Saturday from 9:00 A.M. to 5:30 P.M.

Arkansas City (pronounced "Ar-KAN-sas," remember?), east on Highway 166, was actually settled prior to 1870, but that was the year the sawmill and the flour and feed mills began operation. Nestled in a bluff at the confluence of the Arkansas and Walnut Rivers and at the north end of beautiful Kaw Lake, Ark City, as it is called locally, has played a vital role in the development of Indian lands to the south in Oklahoma.

Two of the most exciting races in the history of the country—the Run of 1889 and the renowned Cherokee Strip Run—began here; 100,000 people arrived months before the Cherokee Strip race to await the pistol shots signaling the start of the race at noon, September 16, 1893. Eager settlers lined up, jockeying for position in every kind of transport you can imagine—oxcarts, covered wagons, bicycles, and horses of every description. In addition, thousands walked, or ran, to find homesteads.

South on Highway 77 at Arkansas City you will find the *Cherokee Strip Land Rush Museum* on South Summit Street Road (620–442–6750). More than 7,000 artifacts telling the history of the strip from the 1880s to the 1920s are housed here. It's open April through August, Tuesday through Saturday from 10:00 A.M. to 5:00 P.M., Sunday from 1:00 to 5:00 P.M.; September through March, Tuesday through Saturday from 1:00 to 4:00 P.M., and Sunday 1:00 to 4:00 P.M. Admission is $3.50 for adults, $3.25 for seniors, and $1.50 for kids ages six through twelve.

The *Chaplin Nature Center,* Route 1, Arkansas City (620–442–4133), along the shores of the Arkansas River, combines 200 acres of magnificent woodlands, prairies, and streams into a beautiful preserve. Here you can see, smell, hear, and feel nature with discovery trails, guided nature walks, bird counts, and a naturalist on duty. It is open every weekend on Saturday from 9:00 A.M. to 5:00 P.M., Sunday from 1:00 to 5:00 P.M. Weekday hours are seasonal. From March through June the hours are 9:00 A.M. to 5:00 P.M., July through August, 8:00 A.M. to midnight, and from September through November, 9:00 A.M. to 5:00 P.M. It is closed from the end of November to March, but the natural trails are open from sunrise to sunset every day of the year.

Henry's "Better Made" Candies (620–876–5423) is in its fourth generation of candy making in *Dexter,* northeast of Arkansas City on Highway 15. Evelyn Pudden and her daughters currently run the business, started in 1890 when Tom Henry began work in a candy shop in Boston at the age of ten. He was the inventor of the original Oh, Henry! candy bar. Now an average of 65,000 pounds of candy, more than one hundred different kinds (including taffy, fudge, and sugar-free candies) are made annually. The shop is open to the public seven days a week. Evelyn has been in this sweet business her whole life—she loves it. Look for a big red-and-white building on Highway 15. Hours are from 8:00 A.M. to 5:00 P.M. seven days a week. There are candy-making demos at 1:00 and 2:30 P.M. on Sundays.

Dexter is in the southern part of the Flint Hills; every spring there is a redbud tour from Cedar Vale to Sedan that runs over backcountry roads beside stone fences and clear creeks. It is an even prettier drive in the fall, when the oak trees turn russet.

Scott's Museum (620–442–1070) at 906 Mill Road is another must-see place. You could easily spend hours here in the two buildings filled with turn-of-the-last-century memorabilia. There are objects and replicas of items you would expect to find in a parlor, kitchen, drugstore, grocery, and dentist and doctor's offices as well as a barber shop. An 1890 Montgomery Ward surrey with a fringe on top, a horse-drawn hearse, a sleigh, and many old cars await the vehicle buff. There's even a one-room schoolhouse. Groups are welcome at no charge.

Oops! Need something to fix that with? A part? A tool? Well you're in luck at *Bryant's Hardware* at 102 South Summit, where the motto is "Yes, we have it!" Call (620) 442–0030 and ask. The fourth generation of Bryants now run the store.

Grouse Creek, near *Silverdale,* is a lively stream with clear water. It runs through the *Kaw Wildlife Area.* There are no official campgrounds, but gravel bars provide good campsites. If the first riffle at the put-in is navigable, the entire stream may be floated without difficulty. If you follow Grouse Creek as it twists and turns beside the country roads, you will pass old ranches with stone houses and barns, limestone cliffs, and even a waterfall before you reach Oklahoma. Be sure to get landowners' permission if canoeing outside the public lands.

The town of *Sedan,* at the junction of Highways 166 and 99, is the hometown of "Weary Willy," probably the world's most famous clown. Behind the greasepaint was Sedan native Emmett Kelly. A museum in his honor has been created in an 1896 opera house on Main Street. *The Emmett Kelly Museum* houses memorabilia of the famous clown and his son Emmett, Jr. You'll also find exhibits connected with D. W. Washburn, also known as Sparky the Clown. Washburn was a juggler, ventriloquist, magician, and pantomimist born in Chanute. Hours are Sunday from 1:00 to 5:00 P.M., Tuesday through Saturday from 9:00 A.M. to noon and 1:00 to 5:00 P.M. Closed Monday. Admission is free, but donations are welcome. Call (620) 725–3470.

Sedan is also the home of the *Yellow Brick Road* (150 East Main Street), where you can put your name on an 8-by-10-inch brick in the Main Street sidewalk downtown. The road now has 10,000-plus bricks, with names from every state of the union and twenty-eight foreign countries, and a special brick from sister city, Sedan, France.

One of the more unusual places to visit is *Jones World* (620–725–5633) at 150 East Main Street, where you can see the world's smallest castle and the world's largest sunflower (20 feet from petal to petal). You can follow another yellow brick road and meet Dorothy, the Scarecrow, Tinman,

It's a Gas

*D*exter is the self-proclaimed "Wind Gas Capital of the World." Around 1903, in the heyday of wildcatting, folks here drilled for oil. They planned a celebration when the well came in, including a torch lighting. The well came in and grand torches were brought to ignite the gas, but the gas blew the torches out. The process was repeated with the same results.

The oil folks were disappointed until some time later, when it was discovered that the "wind gas" was natural helium. It was the first discovery of helium in the United States. Soon the Navy began bringing dirigibles from the Olathe Naval Air Station and refueling virtually right out of the ground. Later the helium was used as a coolant in various nuclear projects.

Lion, and the Wicked Witch. There are wildlife exhibits, and you can even watch candy being made right there in the Jones World candy kitchens. Open Monday through Thursday from 9:00 A.M. to 5:00 P.M., and Friday and Saturday to 8:00 P.M.

There is now a restaurant inside, too. J.W.'s is the name and it has a prairie theme. In fact, you have your choice: There's the Little Prairie House room, the Teepee room, or you can go straight to jail (do not pass go) and head for the Jail House room. Hours are from 11:00 A.M. to 4:00 P.M. Monday though Thursday, and until 8:00 P.M. on Friday and Saturday.

The *Chautauqua Hills Jelly Company,* on Main Street, was founded when a group of thirty-three Kansans came together to help revitalize their community by beginning a new industry. The beautifully restored limestone building is open for tours (call ahead to make arrangements); you can watch the fresh fruit being made into gourmet jams, jellies, and sauces, all of which are available separately or in gift boxes.

This storefront jelly kitchen is the biggest jelly and jam company in the state. The glass-enclosed assembly line is visible to customers. The additive-free jams and sauces are shipped everywhere. If you're there, though, you will enjoy the old-fashioned ice-cream parlor out front, where you can sample some of the tasty fruit sauces over your favorite flavor of ice cream.

Old hardware stores are a piece of Americana and *Ackarman's* has been a downtown gathering place since 1897.

Enjoy upscale shopping at *The Red Buffalo* on Main Street. You'll find prairie chic in the heart of the prairie and something for everyone on your list. The shop has books, jewelry, and gourmet foods. Top off the experience with a latte as good as any in the big cities. Then discover *Cousins Antiques* on Main Street, where you will find pine, walnut, and oak furniture, as well as painted primitives, folk art, and other "needful" things. Enjoy browsing in this one of many unique single-owner shops. It's well worth the drive. Call (620) 725–3551.

You can ride wagons through the incredible tallgrass country or walk the miles of nature trails at Bill Kurtis's *Red Buffalo Ranch.* A delicious chuck-wagon dinner and old-fashioned entertainment will top off your evening. Get in on the excitement of the Chautauqua Hills annual Chuck Wagon races. Like nothing you've ever experienced. You can schedule your own adventure by calling the ranch at (620) 725–5500. Red Buffalo is the Osage name for fire on the prairie—it comes like a red buffalo over the hills—and although burning is necessary for the prairie to survive, the winds can catch the flames and create a wall of flame 30 feet high.

Next stop is **Elk Falls,** where you can walk on the 1893 Iron Truss Bridge and have a wonderful view of the natural waterfalls. The bridge is a National Historic Register site.

Tucked in the rolling landscape of the Flint Hills along Highway 160, Elk Falls is a natural limestone formation that can be seen from the old bridge that is closed to vehicles but open to walkers. The slow-running river picks up speed as it flows through shallow, rocky flats and down a slight decline, where it slows again before its sudden, powerful drop off the sharp limestone bedrock. Artists, craftspeople, and photographers come to the area to capture the beauty of this phenomenon. The falls can make an impressive roar, and impressive, too, is the deep boulder-strewn river canyon in which it is located. But this is Kansas—it is called Elk Trickle in dry years.

The town of Elk Falls calls itself a "living ghost town" and, like Sedan, offers you immortality on its own famous road: You can write your name on a piece of gravel with a permanent marker and become part of history. The sense of humor displayed in their brochure makes you want to find the town and see just what kind of people live here. This is a beautiful little community in the Kansas Ozarks, with a population of about 120, so you can ask for directions anywhere. There are no addresses or street signs.

The center of the artistic community seems to be the **Elk Falls Pottery Works** (620–329–4425), operated by Steve and Jane Fry, who were drawn here not only because of the area's natural beauty but also for the excellent earthenware clay in the Elk River. For stoneware clay, they travel to Barton County. The Frys use a potter's wheel with a foot-powered wooden treadle wheel. Someone's there every day except Sunday.

Jane designs jewelry at the **Elk Falls Piecemakers**—tiny, 1½-inch square pins of porcelain with old-fashioned quilt patterns.

This energetic couple has also opened the **Sherman House Bed and Breakfast** a few blocks away. This lovingly restored 1870s building was a popular stop for passenger trains passing through Elk Falls in 1879. The spacious rooms offer visitors their own secluded guest house for exploring rural Kansas. (The owners live nearby.) The large, upstairs Bunkhouse Room is great for families with children—it sleeps six and is provided with games and "family-friendly" videos. The Bunkhouse has a queen-size, rustic pole bed for the grown-ups, and the kid-size tack room and tepee have a campfire night-light—they're gonna love it. The skylight in the Prairie Flower Suite lets you look at the stars. You can visit potters Steve and Jane Fry in their studio. Rooms are $55 for two people, $10 extra for each additional person, and come with a full breakfast. Call (620) 329–4425.

Next door to Sherman House is Edie Baker's *Quilts and More,* at 105 North Tenth Street. Edie has quilt fabrics and beautiful quilts to show off. Hours are 10:00 A.M. to 5:30 P.M. Monday through Friday, 10:00 A.M. to 4:00 P.M. Saturday. Call (620) 329–4440, or e-mail quiltsandmore@sktc.net.

Elk Falls is a good place for a stroll. Look for the 1880 Little White Church, still in use, or the 1872 O'Keefe Homestead, open by appointment. Call (620) 374–2438.

Hungry? Stop at the *Cottage Café,* 1 block east of Sherman House, and enjoy some "down-home" cooking and freshly baked bread and pie. Barry Pagel makes gourmet desserts and daily specials that change weekly. On Wednesday evenings he has a dinner buffet, and he does a breakfast buffet on Saturday mornings. This is everyone's favorite hangout. Hours are from 9:00 A.M. to 9:00 P.M. Wednesday through Saturday. Call (620) 329–4300.

A side trip north on Highway 99 from Elk Falls will take you to *Howard,* where you can find whimsical outdoor sculptures made from cast-offs. *Hubbell's Rubble People* are sure to bring a smile to your face. Just 4 blocks west of Highway 99 on Elk Street are dolls! dolls! and more dolls! *Bertha's Dolls* are upstairs, downstairs, and in all the cupboards. But they're just for looking, not for sale. Open by appointment. Call (620) 374–2636.

While in Howard, you'll want to stop at *Batson's Drug Store,* 102 North Wabash. Sit down at the counter in front of a '50s-vintage soda fountain and enjoy ice cream for 40 cents a scoop, sodas, sundaes, and old-fashioned limeades. Call (620) 374–2265.

"Here Lies Prudence Crandall and Her Brother Hezekiah"

*T*he Elk Falls Cemetery is interesting to history buffs. The cemetery was started before Elk Falls became a town, when a party of the famous "Buffalo Soldiers" camped in the vicinity. Several fell ill and died and were buried here. In the northwest corner of the cemetery there are simple markers inscribed A SOLDIER. Several Union soldiers and one Confederate soldier also rest here. So do Prudence Crandall—shunned in Connecticut for opening a school for black girls, she homesteaded in Kansas—and one of America's first women mayors, America L. King.

Lodging is available at the **Cattle Baron Inn,** 516 East Randolph, a 1910 Victorian with beautiful woodwork and stained glass and furnished with antiques. Innkeepers Dr. Robert Black, a veterinarian, and his wife, Shirley, also own some acreage with a lake about 7 miles from their home and invite guests to ride up there on four-wheelers and enjoy the countryside. The Blacks also have horses to ride some of the time, and other times, mares and new colts to visit. A nearby blueberry farm keeps the kitchen supplied, so there are always blueberry pancakes or muffins for breakfast. Rooms are $65 to $90. Call (620) 374–2503.

You can call (620) 374–2142 for an appointment to see a **Country School-house and Teacher's Quarters,** for a nostalgic look at the "3Rs" of the 1800s. Stop at **The Gragg Memorial Building** of antique farm implements or the **Benson Museum** on South Wabash for a look at Elk County's heritage.

There's more to do in this tiny town of 750 people. You can eat at **Poplar Pizza,** which has a varied menu, not just pizza, at 202 South Wabash (620–374–2525), or if you are in a hurry, there's **Toots** (620–374–2345), a drive-in on Highway 99 with window (or inside) service for a quick burger.

Take that burger for a serendipity picnic: Coming from the north on Highway 99, turn left at the south end of town (there is a sign, it's by the vet's office) and follow the gravel road as it goes down a hill, crosses a creek, and climbs back up again leading to Polk-Daniels Lake, a pretty little sixty-five-acre lake surrounded by stone bluffs. This quiet little spot was a 1936 WPA project, and like most WPA projects, there are handcrafted natural rock shelters and birdbaths. A permit is needed to fish or boat on the lake, but it's the perfect place for a picnic. Oddly, a person can water ski on the lake, but swimming is not permitted. I guess you have to be pretty good to attempt that.

If you're headed back west on Highway 160 from Elk Falls, the next stop will be **Moline** to see one of the oldest suspension bridges in the state. It was built at the turn of the twentieth century to give a view of the Wildcat Creek and stair-step cataract falls. You can walk out confidently, but cautiously, to enjoy the view yourself.

Nearly every community in the state has a landmark grain elevator, a necessity for farmers and ranchers as a place to sell grain or purchase feed. Some of the elevators in smaller communities have closed because of modern technology, and often they stand as a sad reminder of a declining economy.

The elevator at **Grenola,** the next stop on Highway 160 westbound, is one of those. Historical records show Grenola (the cities of Greenfield and Canola were merged) to have been a thriving community of more than 3,000 people. The grain elevator, built in 1909, stood next to the Santa Fe Railroad tracks. The Grenola Historical Society heard that the railroad was going to demolish the building, and it swung into action. The society had been looking for a permanent location for the **Grenola Museum** to display local historical artifacts, and so it bought the elevator for $200 at the sheriff's auction in 1989. The price was right and included the platform scales, the office safe, and other property at the site. What it didn't include was the land under the elevator.

The group raised the money to purchase the land, and cleaning and restoration of the elevator began. Removing the accumulated grain dust and grime was a major project, but by opening day in May 1990, the museum was ready.

Displays in the museum show the history of the area—a covered wagon, a surrey with a fringe on the top, an old grocery wagon, and an antique automobile all were donated. The museum's displays include an old country kitchen, a doctor's office, and a one-room schoolhouse with a

Grenola Museum

potbellied stove and original slate boards from other schoolhouses in the area. Old desks and a piano complete the theme. Most of the museum's collection is displayed in the long, feed-storage room that extends from the main elevator. Microfilm readers with reels containing newspapers dating from 1879 and Elk County census records, as well as old pictures and photographs, are found in the office. The museum is open from 10:00 A.M. to 4:00 P.M. Wednesday, Friday, and Saturday, 1:00 to 4:00 P.M. Sunday, and by appointment. Call (620) 358–2820.

Across the street from the elevator is a park with a gazebo of stone that came from old stone houses in the Flint Hills and a building dating from 1924 with a mural depicting a cattle drive and the railroad.

On the first Saturday in October, Grenola celebrates **Oktoberfest,** highlighted by a free "bean feed" that begins at 5:00 P.M. The beans, some 150 pounds of them, are cooked over an open fire in four huge cast-iron pots hanging on tripods. Locals fire up the pots in the park and help with the cooking, seasoning, and tasting of the beans, stirring with a long paddle or hoe. With the announcement "Beans are ready," people line up with bowls in hand. Cooks in the community supply plenty of corn bread to go with the beans. Hay bales serve as seating for those who do not bring lawn chairs.

There is a canoe trail at the Fall River Highway 99 Bridge to the Climax boat ramp. The length is 12 miles; it takes about six to eight hours to complete the trip.

Cattle Country

*H*awthorne Ranch, Rural Route 1, Box 161, Eureka, is about 8 miles north of **Eureka,** off Highway 54. Sally Hawthorne owns this 960-acre spread and invites you and the kids to try the **Hawthorne Ranch Trail Rides** (620–583–5887). She provides the horses and the tack, and even beginner riding lessons for $15. The ride lasts about two to two and a half hours; trips leave in the morning and again after noon. The ranch is on the edge of the Flint Hills, mostly grassland with ponds and creeks. Sally will point out "The Dome" (a trail marker for Indians), Turkey Knob, and other interesting trail sights. She always leads each trail ride, which is limited to fifteen persons. Primitive camping facilities, including a picnic table and an outhouse, are provided, and there is a pond for fishing and swimming.

Hamilton is the place to find, on Highway 99, if it's a hot day and an honest-to-goodness vanilla root beer sounds good. At **Holmes' Soda Fountain and Sundries,** 101 East Main, (620) 678–3341, Donita Edwards can make you a malt or a genuine cherry Coke. The drugstore has been at that spot since 1929. Hours are from 6:00 A.M. to 8:00 P.M. Monday through Saturday and from 7:00 A.M. to 2:00 P.M. Sunday.

While you're on the soda-fountain trail, stop in **Madison** on Highway 99. *Pope's Rexall Drugs,* 115 North Third Street, is just your basic small-town drugstore with cards, cosmetics, and a pharmacy in the back. But the old-fashioned soda fountain makes it worth a little detour. People say it's the oldest drugstore in Kansas that's still operating in its original building. According to owner Candee Martin, over the past 119 years, there have only been about a half-dozen druggists in the building. Whiskey was made in the basement during Prohibition. Now you can get malts, sodas, and old-fashioned fountain drinks instead. Call (620) 437–2058. Hours are 9:00 A.M. to 6:00 P.M. Monday through Friday.

The Chicken House (620–475–3386) on 8 East Highway 99 in the town of *Olpe* is well known as having the finest fried chicken around. Owners Leonard and Theresa Coble have been frying chicken there for more than forty years. The brick building is newer than that, though, because in 1974 the restaurant was struck by lightning and burned to the ground. They rebuilt, and now the restaurant seats 320 people, who drive in from every town in a 50-mile radius for the fried chicken, the homemade onion rings, the famous sunny wheat, nut, and honey breads, and the homemade pies. The Chicken House is open Monday through Saturday from 11:00 A.M. to 9:00 P.M.; closed Sundays.

Emporia, on Interstate 35, lies on a low ridge between the Cottonwood and Neosho Rivers. This once-treeless plain is now a forest of maples. The surrounding valley is still blanketed with pastures of bluestem. The town is filled with beautifully preserved old homes. Unique to Emporia are the early houses built by the Welsh settlers in

Veterans Day—A Kansas Connection

Veterans Day has its origins in Emporia. In 1953, local citizen Alan J. King proposed that Armistice Day be changed to honor not only World War I veterans but also those who served in all wars and conflicts. Veterans Day was celebrated in Emporia that year.

The next year, Kansas Congressman Ed Rees took King's proposal to Washington. President Dwight D. Eisenhower, also a Kansan, signed the bill proclaiming November 11 as Veterans Day. The holiday was first observed nationwide on November 11, 1954.

the style they had known in Wales—simple, clean lines reminiscent of an earlier period. The Howe house on East Logan Avenue is a good example of this Welsh heritage. Other houses are Italianate, Queen Anne, and post–World War I bungalows.

At the **White Rose Inn Bed & Breakfast** at 901 Merchant, you'll begin your stay with afternoon tea. Later retire to a private suite with your own bathroom and sitting room. In the morning the scent of fresh-baked muffins, biscuits, or coffee cakes will lure you to the dining room, or you can have your breakfast in bed if that's your mood. Hosts Sam and Lisa Tosti are happy to pamper you totally. They can arrange a manicure, pedicure, or massage in the privacy of your room in this quiet Victorian home. Five suites are available, all with private bath. Doesn't a weekend alone (or not) sound just lovely? Rates are $45 to $75. Call (620) 343–6336 or (800) 288–6198, or e-mail whiterose@carrollsweb.com. There's also a Web site at www. innsite.com/inns/A000285.html.

Shop **Madelynn's Presents June Cleaver's,** 1015 Industrial Road (620–343–2040), for linens and gifts and enjoy the coffee and pastry bar (open 9:30 A.M. to 5:30 P.M. Monday through Friday, Wednesday to 7:00 P.M., and Sunday 1:00 to 5:00 PM.); **Second Love,** 706 Commercial Street (620–342–1819), a country store with handcrafted items made by accomplished artisans from all over the country (open 9:30 A.M. to 5:30 P.M. Monday through Saturday); and **Sunflower Nook,** 1923 West Sixth Avenue (620–343–3903), for Kansas collectibles (open 10:00 A.M. to 5:30 P.M. Monday through Saturday). Antiques lovers can try the **Flint Hills Antique Mall,** 329 Commercial Street (620–343–0057), or the **Dalton Gang Antique Mall,** 502 Commercial Street (620–342–9217). Hours are 11:00 A.M. to 6:30 P.M. Tuesday through Sunday.

If you work up an appetite shopping, stop for lunch nearby at **S'ghetti's,** 1015 Commercial Street (620–343–1823), or the **Commercial Street Diner,** 614 Commercial Street (620–343–9866).

Prairie Passage is a collection of stone sculptures designed by Richard Stauffer and produced by the 1992 Kansas Sculptors Association Team Carve. The design reflects the city's role as gateway to the Flint Hills. The pylons—made of cottonwood limestone quarried in Chase County—range from 10 to 15 feet high and weigh between five and nine tons. They are clustered in four pairs of "echoing images."

The sculptures are silhouettes with incised lines of varying depth and thickness done by feather wedging, chiseling, drilling, and masonry sawing. For more information, contact the Emporia Convention and

Visitors Bureau at (620) 342–1803 or (800) 279–3730.

You might enjoy browsing through **Cookie Jar Heaven** at 121 Mechanic. John and Charlotte Smith's collection of more than 2,050 cookie jars and 300 buttonhooks are on display. Call (620) 343–3317; the home is open by chance or appointment. The Smiths live nearby. The jars are not for sale, and there is no charge. You are just invited to wander through and enjoy the collections. Donations are accepted.

You can tour history in Emporia starting at the **Emporia Gazette,** 517 Merchant Street, and follow the literary and cultural heritage left by the famous editor William Allen White, well-known small-town sage. The memorial drive passes the White home and ends at the **William Allen White Library** at Emporia State University, Twelfth and Commercial Streets, which houses the world's largest collection of public and private memorabilia of this Pulitzer Prize winner. The memorial library is open year-round Monday through Friday from 8:00 A.M. to 5:00 P.M. and weekends and evenings while school is in session. Call (620) 341–5207.

Emporia also has a fine zoo at 75 Sodens Road, near South Commercial Street. Here you can see animals in their natural habitats, with nearly 400 specimens of birds, mammals, and reptiles, from your car or walk-through areas. You'll also see game native to Kansas prairies—bison, white-tailed deer, prairie dogs—as well as longhorn steers and other exotic species. The drive-by area is open year-round from dawn to dusk, the walk-through from 10:00 A.M. to 4:30 P.M. During summer months the walk-through section extends its hours to 8:30 P.M. Call (620) 342–6558.

The **Lyon County Historical Museum** (620–342–0933), at 118 East Sixth Avenue, is housed in the former 1904 Carnegie Library, with leaded-glass windows and an unusual water fountain in the foyer. Rich oak woodwork embellishes the main part of the building, now used for exhibits. A growing collection of archives is housed at 225 East Sixth Avenue. There is the Gallery of Gifts, where most items for sale are made by Kansas artists, craftspeople, and manufacturers. The museum is open Tuesday through Saturday from 1:00 to 5:00 P.M.; call for archive hours.

National Teachers Hall of Fame, at 1320 C of E Drive, annually recognizes five teachers who have demonstrated commitment to the profession. We all remember a special teacher who changed our lives. Now there is a way to memorialize these teachers. For more information, call (800) 96–TEACH. Hours are 8:00 A.M. to 4:00 P.M. Monday through Friday.

The Flint Hills Rodeo has been coming to **Strong City,** west of Emporia on Highway 50, since 1937 and is the oldest consecutive rodeo in the state. The first full weekend of June draws cowboys and cowgirls from near and far to try to qualify for the National Finals Rodeo. From barrel racing to bareback broncs to bull riding, events at the Flint Hills Rodeo generate a lot of excitement.

The Rodeo Parade begins in Cottonwood Falls and ends in Strong City at the rodeo grounds. For more information, call Chase County Convention and Visitors Bureau at (800) 431–6344.

South of Strong City on Highway 57 is tiny **Cottonwood Falls,** where you can bed down for the night in comfort at the **Grand Central Hotel** (215 Broadway). The two-story hotel, built in 1884, has undergone a major renovation but still has a western flair. The ten large suites upstairs—named for the surrounding ranches—are not just comfortable but "cushy," complete with concierge service. Iron beds with thick down comforters and white terry robes give you the feeling that you are at a spa. You'll be very pampered here. The restaurant serves a big continental breakfast each morning. White linen covers the tables for elegant lunches and dinners. Prices are from $139 to $179. Call (620) 273–6763 or (800) 951–6763, or visit www.grandcentralhotel.com.

If that's too rich for you, **The 1874 Stonehouse,** Mulberry Hill, Route 1, Box 67A, Cottonwood Falls, might be more your style. This two-story limestone home is about 2 miles east of town. There are four upstairs guest rooms, with private bath, overlooking the surrounding sixty acres. On the grounds is a 1-mile walking trail. Guests are invited to use two rooms on the main floor—the parlor, where music or satellite TV is available, and the fireplace room, where you can curl up with a book. Breakfast is served here daily. Rates are $95 to $150 per night. Billie and Joe Altenhofen invite you to check their home page on the Web at www.stonehousebandb.com. Call (620) 273–8481, or e-mail tranquility@stonehousebandb.com.

The **Chase County Courthouse** in Cottonwood Falls holds the distinction of being the oldest in the state still in use. The French Renaissance–style limestone structure was completed in 1873 and is especially noted for its walnut spiral staircase stretching from the first to the third floors. Tours are offered. For information, call (800) 431–6344.

The **Roniger Native-American Artifacts Museum** (620–273–6310), behind the impressive courthouse at 315 Union Street, was a gift from

George and Frank Roniger, who had a fine collection of Native American artifacts. There's a story behind the museum: When the brothers offered their collection to the Smithsonian, that institution wanted a large amount of money to mount and display it, so the brothers decided to spend the money to build a museum for Chase County instead. It is open from 1:00 to 5:00 P.M. every day and by appointment. Admission is free; donations are welcome.

Shop *The Gallery at Cottonwood Falls,* 313 Broadway (620–273–6100), for art, glassware, pottery, Navajo and Hopi crafts, homespun wool sweaters, and antiques.

Two miles north of Strong City on Highway 177 is the historic *Z-Bar/Spring Hill Ranch,* the crowning achievement of cattleman Stephen Jones. Built in the 1880s with hand-cut native limestone, the eleven-room house is Second Empire style of the nineteenth century. The massive, three-story barn is impressive in its own right. You can see the Lower Fox Creek School, a one-room schoolhouse located on a nearby hilltop. Water to the house was provided by a spring on the hillside; thus the name Spring Hill Ranch. It is a National Historic Landmark.

The former ranch lands, now the *Tallgrass Prairie National Preserve,* were once the hunting grounds of the Kansa and Osage. The hills and prairie streams are home still to thirty-one species of mammals and nearly 400 species of plants, 130 kinds of birds, and numerous reptiles and amphibians. The National Park Trust purchased the 10,894-acre remnant of tallgrass prairie to preserve it for future generations.

There currently are no picnicking, camping facilities, flush toilets, or potable water here. It is recommended that you wear comfortable outdoor clothing as well as shoes suitable for negotiating uneven walkways, steep stairs, and unpaved footpaths. Your reward will be a close-up look at a prairie ecosystem. The trail winds across rolling hills, over a spring-fed stream lined with cottonwood and hackberry trees, and through a fascinating array of grasses and flowers. Be prepared for tiny insects and small animals that make the prairie their home. The historic ranch headquarters and Southwind Nature Trail are open daily except holidays 9:00 A.M. to 4:00 P.M. Fees are $2.00 per adult, $1.00 per child age eighteen and younger. Visitor information is available on the back porch of the ranch-house headquarters, including a ten-minute orientation video. Guided tours through the house are hourly on Saturday and Sunday from 10:30 A.M. to 3:30 P.M.

A 7-mile bus tour led by National Park Service rangers will take you through the backcountry, where you will learn about the prairie's intricate system of plants and animals and the geological history of the Flint Hills. From mid-April through the end of October, a one-hour-and-forty-five-minute tour is available every day of the week at 11:00 A.M., 1:00 P.M., and 3:00 P.M. The cost is $5.00 for adults and $3.00 for children under age eighteen. Advance reservations are recommended, but arrangements can be made the day of your visit if space is available. For more information or arrangements for wheelchair access, call (620) 273–8494, write to the park superintendent at P.O. Box 585, Cottonwood Falls 66845, or visit the Web site at www.nps.gov/tapr.

The town of **Elmdale** is west of Strong City on Highway 50. Nearby, **The Clover Cliff Ranch** is a beautiful, old, two-story native limestone house in the center of 4,500 acres of Kansas farmland. "Clover Cliff isn't just a ranch," owner Jim Donahue told *Kansas* magazine. "It's a historic showplace." Now it is a bed-and-breakfast where guests can hike, fish in the ponds or nearby Cottonwood River, or just sit on the enclosed porch and enjoy the scenery. You can bring your own horse to ride, too. The main house, an expansion of a one-room log cabin built in 1860, burned down a few years ago. Jim and his wife, Joan (pronounced "Jo-Ann") rebuilt it, and it is once again one of the most beautiful homes in the Flint Hills. There are two other houses on the ranch, the Princess and the Gables. Both are lovely, old stone houses with more conveniences. Rates range from $85 to $115 for two people. Add $20 for each additional person. Price includes full breakfast. Groups can tour the ranch in a covered wagon or horse-drawn carriage. Call (800) 457–7406, or visit the Web site at www.clovercliff.com.

You hear a lot about the Harvey Girls in Kansas. When Frederick Harvey opened his first restaurant in Topeka to go on to become the first restaurant chain in America, everyone wanted to keep a bit of that fame at home. So it is in **Florence,** where Harvey opened his first restaurant and hotel, the Clifton Hotel. **The Harvey House Museum** was once a railroad stop; now it houses a unique museum/restaurant where the Florence Historical Society serves authentic dinners to parties of twelve or more. You can sample a five-course meal served the way the famed Harvey Girls would have served it, complete with costumes that replicate the uniforms. The people at Harvey House had to have everything ready when the train arrived, but "fast food" then meant vintage claret and quail in aspic—served in a setting that would rival restaurants anywhere—but served quickly so the train could depart on time. The museum is open to visitors from noon until 5:00 P.M. Wednesday through Saturday.

The comfortable atmosphere at *Shippy's Town and Country Café* on Highway 77 has a stream of loyal patrons who travel that roadway. Caroline Spencer, owner, offers specials every day and employs some of the best cooks in the area. All of the desserts are made on-site. Great pies and the Wednesday chicken-fried steak special is, indeed, special. The cafe is open from 6:00 A.M. to 2:00 P.M. Sunday and Monday, until 8:00 P.M. Tuesday through Thursday, and until 9:00 P.M. Friday and Saturday.

This region is the beginning of the Western Plains and buffalo country. The Santa Fe Trail crossed the county from east to west; the Chisholm Trail crossed it from southwest to northeast.

Nestled in the beautiful valley of the Cottonwood, Marion Lake is near the Cottonwood Crossing of the Santa Fe Trail; the deep wagon ruts can still be seen, although they are barely visible through the grass and prairie flowers. The lake is excellent for fishing, and there is hunting in public hunting areas, as well as picnicking, camping, boating, and hiking.

It's a very pleasant drive on Highway 56 west. The lake takes its name from the nearby town of *Marion,* settled in the 1860s in the fertile Cottonwood Valley at the western edge of the Flint Hills. The lake is surrounded by native hardwoods, wildflowers, and flowering shrubs. Here the seasons' colors change from spring redbud, flowering catalpa, and Osage orange to the beauty of the fall sumac. You can fish for largemouth bass, white bass, and walleye in well-stocked coves and hunt in specified areas for pheasant, mourning dove, and deer.

The *Marion Museum* is tucked into a century-plus-year-old church near Central Park. Built in 1887 as a Baptist worship house, the ornate wood ceilings and stained-glass windows reflect a time of hymns and sermons while telling the story of the history of Marion from the time when the first twenty-three settlers came into the area in five covered wagons. They stopped on a bluff above the park and saw Cottonwood Valley to the west. Soon after that, they discovered a fresh-water spring coming out of the bluff and decided that this was a fine place to stay. They lowered their wagons and horses down into what is now the park and the town of Marion grew from that camp. The museum is open Tuesday through Saturday from 10:00 A.M. to 2:00 P.M., and Sunday from noon to 2:00 P.M.

Kingfisher's Inn, 1725 North Upland Road (620–382–3755), offers family dining with a lakeside view. The specialty here is pan-fried chicken. It's open Wednesday through Saturday from 11:00 A.M. to 2:00 P.M. and 5:00 to 9:00 P.M. and Sunday from 11:00 A.M. to 9:00 P.M. The owners are Bob and Kathy Sprowls.

This is cattle country and truly the Heart of America—very friendly, easygoing, and welcoming to the many people who enjoy the lake in summer. Downtown Marion gets rave reviews from people passing through because of its pretty little park by the river; and because there is a lake on either side of the town, it's a popular summer spot.

A country home overlooking a private lake and the surrounding 480 acres of wildlife is a bed-and-breakfast owned by Kent and Alice Richmond. *Country Dreams Bed and Breakfast* has five guest rooms, and all have private connecting baths and queen-size beds. Guests are invited to use the family room and the native stone fireplace and satellite television system. A full country breakfast is served, and other meals may be arranged in advance. Rooms are $65 per night. Horses can be stabled in a nearby barn. Call (620) 382–2250 or (800) 570–0540 for rates. The home is 3 miles north of Highway 150 at the 7-mile marker. Visit their Web site at www.adport.com/sites/dreams.

Ernest Hett was the founder of *The Copper Shed,* 1832 East 140th Street, 5 miles south of Marion and 1.5 miles west on County Road 140. His daughter Julie Nelson's husband, Dwight Nelson, and Kent Nelson, his brother, make the russet-colored metal sculptures now. The shed and a barn nearby are worth a drive to visit. The smaller sculptures represent all that is beautiful about the state and are often mounted on parts from antique farm machinery. The windmill, for example, is mounted on the sickle section from an old hay cutter.

You can visit the barn and watch them work or just browse in the shed, where the Nelsons' works and the works of other Kansas artists are displayed among antiques and collectibles that are also for sale.

Not only metal sculptures, but wheat weaving and sprays, black walnut bears, driftwood Santas, and various kinds of fancywork are also for sale in the shed. Collectors can find bunnies, bears, geese, chickens, ducks, and handmade dolls. There are metal and wooden puzzles and painted skins and leaves. Kansas souvenirs, sunflowers, mugs, antique tools, and kitchen utensils are next to tole-painted cream cans and saw blades. It's all here.

The Copper Shed is open by chance or by appointment. Call ahead (620–382–2041).

Melting Pot

The town of **Hillsboro,** on Highway 56 west of Marion between Emporia and McPherson, is a Mennonite community and headquarters for the Mennonite Brethren of the United States. Tabor College, a private Mennonite school, is here.

A German feast awaits travelers on Highway 56 at the 1887 ***Olde Towne Restaurant*** (620–947–5446), 126 North Main Street, Hillsboro. The restored limestone building was built more than one hundred years ago in the heart of Deutsche country in Kansas. Owners Linden and Durene Thiessen want you to share in "the way things used to be." German and Russian settlers arrived here in the late 1800s and brought many recipes with them: cherry moos, zwieback, verenika, and homemade German sausages. The restaurant has a great Low German buffet on Saturday night.

The building has 20-inch-thick limestone walls and, because it was built originally as a bank, a vault in the basement. It later housed an egg business; depressions in the wood floor of the dining room indicate where women once stood to candle eggs. In the main dining room is a huge wooden door that once opened to a cold-storage area. The tin ceiling is original. There is local artwork on the walls. The basement is decorated with antique farm tools, and light comes from two chandeliers made from wooden wheels with canning jars attached. Remnants of the egg-factory days remain: Wooden egg cases decorate a corner of the basement, and a short strip of a wooden conveyor belt is attached to

Back from the Brink of Extinction

Before the 1800s, experts estimate the number of buffalo at 120 million. Buffalo were once the most numerous of any large mammal on earth. By the turn of the twentieth century, only twenty-two buffalo could be found in the United States. You read that right—twenty-two. A few conscientious ranchers took it upon themselves to save the animal from extinction. Buffalo have made a remarkable comeback and are now bred for their high-protein, low-fat meat (half the calories of beef). They are resistant to many of the diseases that plague the cattle industry and can endure the harshest of winters. They also tolerate the intense summers of the Midwest. Buffalo cows have been known to live for forty-two years and bear thirty-eight calves, which certainly makes breeding easier. These animals weigh in at about a ton and can run 35 miles an hour.

beams supporting the old freight elevator. Along a wall is a mural of the building. Hours are Tuesday through Thursday from 7:00 A.M. to 2:00 P.M., Friday and Saturday from 7:00 A.M. to 8:30 P.M.

While you are in town you might take a peek in **Boucher's Red Barn** at 201 North Main Street, a shop with "lots of pretty glass" (Royal Ruby, Wexford Crystal, Franciscan, Bubble Crystal) and more. There are marbles, old books, and all manner of collectibles and antiques. Hours are from 9:00 A.M. to 5:30 P.M. Tuesday through Saturday.

Carousel Bed and Breakfast at 312 East A Street is a 1910 Victorian. Innkeepers Jack and Betty Price have decorated it with lace curtains and antiques; the wraparound porch is the perfect place to enjoy the tranquility of the quiet Mennonite community in the wheat belt of southeast Kansas and only a block from Tabor College. Betty serves a full breakfast as well as complimentary snacks. There are walking trails and a nearby golf course, swimming pool, and lake. There are two rooms, both with private bath. Rates are $55. Call (620) 947–3503 for reservations.

The **Adobe House Museum** is the only adobe house that has been preserved. A team of people led by Emil Bartel built special tools and moved the delicate structure, made of mud and straw bricks, to the corner of D and Ash Streets where it now stands. The bricks were made by either horses or humans walking in the mud and straw mixture, which was then poured into wooden molds and set in the Kansas sun to bake. Most adobe houses had a standard floor plan with a grass-burning oven in the kitchen (yes, that's *grass,* not gas). There was a dining room, living room, parlor, and three bedrooms to house the large pioneer families.

Along with the adobe house and barn, the museum complex also contains the **Kreutziger Schoolhouse** (complete with iron bell and pot-bellied stove), which was moved to Hillsboro in 1965 from a small town in Canada.

The **Friesen Dutch Mill** was reconstructed from one original photo of the mill. Inside, the millstone grinds the flour and occasionally a decorative cloth bag of flour is available for purchase. Credit for the reconstruction goes to college professor Richard Wall, a handyman who became an amateur millwright during the project.

The **Ebenfeld Mennonite Brethren Church,** located 5 miles southeast of Hillsboro, is believed to be the first organized Mennonite Brethren congregation in North America, begun in 1874 when two Mennonite Brethren families immigrated from south Russia due to religious intolerance and set aside Sunday as a day of worship. The **His-**

toric *Mennonite Brethren Church,* built in 1893 and now located on the campus of Tabor College, is believed to be the oldest existing Mennonite Brethren church *structure* in North America. It is a simple, plain white church with a Roman-arched ceiling and Roman-arched windows.

The *William F. Schaeffler House,* at the corner of Grand and Lincoln Streets, was built in 1909. The house was very "modern" in its day and had features that still make it fascinating to visitors. There is a dumbwaiter from the kitchen to the basement for canned goods, fireplaces that are strictly decorative, inside bathrooms for use at night or when someone was ill, and carbide gas that ran to each room of the house for lighting. The dining room holds a twelve-place china set, and the library is filled with stackable oak shelving containing many valuable books. Call the Hillsboro Historical Society at (620) 947–3775 for an appointment for a tour.

The Mennonite Heritage Museum at 219 North Poplar in *Goessel,* on Highway 215, tells the history of the Mennonite immigration. These peace-loving settlers came to this area in 1874 seeking freedom to live their faith in the lifestyle they had chosen.

Lindsborg Is a Festival Town

*O*f all the places in the state I have visited, Lindsborg is at the top of the list as a family favorite. It is a perfect weekend trip from most urban areas, and whenever I visited, there was something there for everyone in my family.

The entire town is a tribute to the Swedish pioneers from Varmland, Sweden, who settled in the Smoky Valley in 1868. My favorite time to go is during one of the many festivals, when townspeople walk in the streets dressed in Swedish costumes and tourists become Swedish for the weekend. I end up buying brightly colored Dala horses that have become the symbol for this town.

It's a good idea to go hungry for a few days before arriving so that you can load up on potato sausage, meatballs, and Swedish tea ring while you watch the folkdanslag *(folk dancers)* perform to Swedish folk music. Lindsborg resembles Sweden as it was a century ago.

If you are interested in art, Lindsborg's many galleries will keep you busy any time. During the festivals, large tents located off Main Street are filled with wares made by area craftspeople. Midwestern baskets, paintings, pottery, wreaths, and wheat weavings are for sale.

Parades are another great part of festival weeks. Some comical floats celebrate silly things like lutfisk, *a dried stock fish eaten at Christmas. I've also seen a 30-foot motorized Viking ship, complete with fur-clad Vikings. Any of the festival weekends makes a perfect getaway.*

The Mennonite Immigrant Historical Foundation has constructed an eight-building museum complex with a Wheat Palace (which contains a full-scale replica of the Liberty Bell made entirely from Turkey Red wheat), Immigrant House, school, bank, barn, and other buildings. It is open March and April and October through December, Tuesday to Sunday from noon to 4:00 P.M.; May through September, Tuesday to Friday from 10:00 A.M. to 5:00 P.M. and Saturday and Sunday from 1:00 to 5:00 P.M.; January and February by appointment only. Admission is $3.00 for adults, $1.50 for children. Call (620) 367–8200.

Six miles north of **Canton** lies a 4,000-acre midgrass prairie, fenced to contain 200 bison and 50 elk. The preserve also contains a forty-six-acre fishing lake with campsites and a boat ramp. It is open year-round Monday through Friday from 8:00 A.M. to 5:00 P.M.

The Maxwell Wildlife Refuge, 2577 Pueblo Road, Canton, lets you see the prairie the way our ancestors might have seen it. Herds of buffalo and elk roam free. You can experience all the sights and sounds of the native Kansas prairie while riding in a modern version of a covered wagon—a tram, which departs from the visitors center and winds across a trail right into the territory of the buffalo herd. A tour guide recounts the region's history and points out prairie wildlife along the way. The best time is in the spring, when the buffalo calves are born among the wildflowers in the shade of the cottonwood trees.

This 2,500-acre prairie preserve has the largest buffalo herd on a refuge in the state. Admission is $7.00 for adults, $5.00 for kids under age twelve. Open weekends Memorial Day through October; weekends for groups by appointment. The preserve is situated 10 miles east of Highway 135 on Highway 56, then 7 miles north of Highway 56. Call (620) 628–4455.

Although **McPherson** does have a bagpipe band, its name has more to

The Wickedest City in the West

*L*ike all of the other cow towns on the Chisholm Trail, Newton was bloody and lawless, and it was nicknamed "the wickedest city in the West." Newton was the western terminus for the Atchison, Topeka, and Santa Fe Railroads, and the railhead brought a horde of gunslingers, gamblers, "soiled doves," cowboys, and railroad crews to town. Peace officers often worked both sides of the law. Bully Brooks was marshal of Newton in 1872. Two years later he was hanged as a horse thief at nearby Sumner County.

do with history than nationality. Civil War soldiers from this area served under General James "Birdseye" McPherson, killed in battle in Atlanta; the town is named in his honor.

Even if you can't stay two years to complete a degree in antique auto restoration at **McPherson College,** you can still get a tour of the program facility (Jay Leno is one of its supporters) by calling (620) 241–0731.

Vaniman Mansion is now the home of the **McPherson Museum** at 1130 East Euclid Street (620–241–8464), on Highway 56. This elegant three-story home is furnished in 1920s style with hand-crocheted lace-edged curtains. Among the numerous exhibits are the very rare skeleton of a prehistoric giant ground sloth, the largest collection of Indian pottery outside the Smithsonian, and the world's first man-made diamond. Mr. Vaniman's collection of mounted birds and animals are on display. The museum is open from 1:00 to 5:00 P.M. daily except Monday and legal holidays. Admission is free.

In 1868 a group of Swedish immigrants made a new home in America's heartland, in the valley of the Smoky Hill River. The result is **Lindsborg,** off Interstate 35 on Highway 4. It is a community that calls itself "Little Sweden, U.S.A."

Old World facades adorn every building, and bright red, wooden Dala horses (pronounced "daw-la") are prominently displayed in front of most residences. You must buy yourself a Dala horse (Dalahäst) when you visit Lindsborg. It is one of the most traditional Swedish items, passed on from generation to generation.

You can stay right smack downtown at the **Brunswick Hotel,** at 202 South Main Street (877–384–6835). Innkeepers Dennis and Charlotte Much will welcome you to this 1887 beauty. Arched, stained-glass windows in the dining room bathe you in morning light. Dennis creates bountiful breakfasts of Swedish pancakes with raspberry sauce and French "featherbed" eggs. Fine dinners are also the rule, accompanied by a good wine selection. There are five rooms and two suites with queen-size sleeper sofas; one has a wood-burning fireplace. Rooms are $49.50 to $75.00. Call (785) 227–2903, or e-mail hotel@midusa.net; the Web site is www. brunswickhotelkansas.com.

The **Swedish Country Inn** (785–227–2985 or 800–231–0266) at 112 West Lincoln is in the former Carlton Hotel, now an authentic Swedish bed-and-breakfast; Becky Anderson is the innkeeper. The cream and baby blue, two-story brick building a half block from downtown is

Lindsborg horse

trimmed in copper accents. There are nineteen rooms, and all have private baths. A truly Scandinavian feature is the redwood sauna in the lower level. The pine furniture and accessories are imported from Sweden, and hand-quilted spreads adorn every room. A typical Scandinavian buffet breakfast of specialty breads, pastries, cheese, and meats is served every morning. This scrumptious buffet is open to the public Monday through Friday from 7:00 to 10:00 A.M., Saturday and Sunday from 7:00 to 11:00 A.M. Breakfast is included in room price for hotel guests. Rooms are from $49.50 to $96.00 (for a suite sleeping six people). The building is air-conditioned, and bicycles (including two tandem bikes) are available for guests to tour the town. Visit their Web site at www.swedishcountryinn.com.

The *Smoky Valley Bed & Breakfast* at 130 Second State Street (785–227–4460 or 800–532–4407) is a redbrick circa 1880 home surrounded by a large garden. Three rooms have queen-size beds and private baths. Each is a corner room with views of grand old trees and gardens. Innkeeper JoAn Hamilton has used family heirlooms to make the house feel like home. A large circular staircase and unique ornate fireplace in the parlor lend an elegant look. A full breakfast in the dining parlor or in your room will be waiting for you each morning. Rooms are $65 to $95 March 15 through December 31; reduced rates apply the rest of the year. See their Web site at www.smokyvalleybnb.com, or e-mail to smokyvalleybnb@ks-usa.net.

There is no shortage of places to stay in Lindsborg, but it makes such a great day trip or weekend getaway that people flock here. The *Morning Mist Bed and Breakfast* is at 618 North Chestnut. Hosts Gary and JoAnn Mattson welcome guests to their charming circa 1907 home in a meadow setting a short walk from town. There are five rooms with private baths, whirlpools, and one with a fireplace. Breakfast is a culinary delight. Rates are $55 to $100. Look for their Web site at www.morningmistb-b.com. Call (888) 566–MIST, or e-mail lodging@morningmistb-b.com.

Hemslöjd, at 201 North Main Street (785–227–2053 or 800–779–3344), is a shop filled with custom-made Dala horses, Swedish candelabra, and etched glass. You can watch craftspeople work in the Dala Horse Factory, owned by Ken Sjogren and Ken Swisher. It is open from 8:00 A.M. to 5:30 P.M. Monday through Saturday (later in summer) and from 12:30 to 4:30 P.M. Sunday.

Lindsborg is best known for its three major festivals: In December it is Santa Lucia Day, honoring a Sicilian who, according to Swedish legend, brought food and drink to hungry Swedes during a famine in the Middle Ages; Midsommardag (Midsummer's Day) in June; and the Svensk Hyllningsfest in October every odd-numbered year.

You can step into the Old World charm of *The Courtyard* at 125 North Main Street and find mouth-watering pastries, antiques, and arts and crafts. The *Courtyard Bakery and Kafe* under the skylight is the spot for lunch, with home-baked Swedish delicacies, gourmet coffee, deli sandwiches, salads, soups, and anything from the bakery display— cookies, pastries, and breads baked daily. Hours are Sunday from noon to 4:00 P.M. and weekdays from 9:00 A.M. to 5:30 P.M. Call (785) 227–4233 or (877) 903–4233.

In the same building you'll find the *Courtyard Gallery* (785–227–3007), which features handblown glass paperweights by Rollin Karg, decoy ducks and carved songbirds by Eugene Fleharty, and paintings, sculpture, pottery, art glass, and woodcarving by Great Plains artists.

For some unusual clothing, look for *Elizabeth's Handwoven Fashions* (888–215–7329) at 110 North Main Street. The fabric is woven on three looms in the back of the store; choose your own yarn colors for a custom-made item. Hours are 10:00 A.M. to 5:00 P.M. Monday through Saturday. You can view Beth Walker's work at www.hand-woven.com.

The Olive Springs School House Gallery (785–254–7833) is the studio of Maleta Forsberg, whose love of all creatures great and small is evident in her art. She and numerous pets live next door to the gallery on 120 acres 10 miles southeast of Lindsborg. The gallery is a restored schoolhouse built in 1885. It is open by appointment; call for directions. It's 7 miles east of Lindsborg, Roxbury exit 72 on I–135, at the corner of Twenty-fourth Avenue and Smoky Valley Road.

Lindsborg has many, many galleries and artists in residence—far too many to list here—but you can pick up the *Lindsborg Visual Arts Directory* from the Lindsborg Arts Council at 101 North Main Street (785–227–3032). Listed are galleries and studios of artists who specialize not only in paintings but also in ceramics, fiber art, folk art, graphic art, photography, jewelry, metalsmithing, sculpture, stained glass, and woodcraft. Lindsborg is also a good place to forget your diet and enjoy the many eateries tucked around town. The **Swedish Crown Restaurant** will transport you thousands of miles across the world with the taste of fine Swedish foods and beverages. It is in a century-old building at 121 North Main Street and is open Monday through Saturday from 11:00 A.M. to 9:00 P.M. and Sunday from 10:30 A.M. to 8:00 P.M. Call (785) 227–2076.

The **Messiah Festival of Music and Art** has been an annual event at Bethany College in Lindsborg for one-hundred-plus years. Bethany's oratorio tradition began with the first *Messiah* in 1882. Through the years the festival has grown to international fame. It begins on Palm Sunday and continues through Easter Sunday. Tickets may be purchased by mail or phone (785–227–3311).

The **REO Auto Museum** at Lincoln and Harrison Streets, near Old Highway 81, specializes in REOs dating from 1908, but it also has other cars, bringing the total to forty. This is the private collection of Quintin and Florence Applequist. It is open daily from 1:00 to 4:00 P.M. A donation is requested. Call (785) 227–3252.

The **Old Mill Museum** (785–227–3595), in the park at 120 Mill Street, began on the first floor of the circa 1898 Smoky Valley Roller Mill, but the present complex consists of twelve buildings. They feature Native American artifacts as well as the Swedish culture of the town. The Swedish pavilion, which was brought to St. Louis from Sweden for the 1904 World's Fair, has a huge maypole standing in front of it. An 1870 log cabin, 1880 depot (and Santa Fe locomotive), and other nineteenth-century buildings are also here. It is open Monday through Saturday from 9:00 A.M. to 5:00 P.M., Sundays 1:00 to 5:00 P.M. Admission is $2.00 for adults, $1.00 for children six to twelve years old.

Take time to visit **Anderson Butik Scandinavian Shop** at 134 North

Main Street (785–227–2356). It is one of the leading suppliers of Swedish gifts and foods by mail in the country. Their Scandinavian tour office is in the Swedish timber cottage, at 125 North Second, transported to Lindsborg from Siljansnäs, Sweden. It is made of pine logs from Swedish forests. The joints that form the cross-sections were hand cut with an ax; the exterior surfaces of the timbers were cut by hand with a hatchet for the Old Country look. Wooden pegs were driven into the timbers to hold them tightly and give stability to the walls. After every log, door, and window was numbered, the cottage was dismantled and shipped to Lindsborg. Hours at the shop are 9:30 A.M. to 5:30 P.M. Monday through Saturday and 12:30 to 4:00 P.M. on Sunday.

West of Lindsborg on Highway 4 is *Marquette.* This 1880s town with its carefully restored Main Street is fun to visit. Do yourself a favor and find *Cookies, Etc.* at 109 North Washington and enjoy great cookies, cupcakes, or muffins with a cup of coffee. Phone (785) 546–2525. Hours are Monday, Thursday, and Friday 3:30 to 6:00 P.M., Tuesday 9:30 to 11:30 A.M. and Saturday 10:00 A.M. to 2:00 P.M. Or head across the street to *Marquette City Sundries* at 104 North Washington for ice cream served at an old-fashioned marble-topped soda fountain dating at least from 1901. Phone (785) 546–8801.

A few miles north of Lindsborg stands *Coronado Heights*, a butte with an incredible view from which the Spanish explorer Coronado looked over miles of prairie in 1541. It is believed that this part of the Smoky Hills is the northernmost point in Kansas that Coronado traveled. This hill stands alone on the prairie. In 1936 the Works Progress Administration (WPA) built a castle-like structure atop this point, from which you can see a tapestry of farmland, wildflowers, wheat fields, and lonely clusters of trees.

Inside the structure are an enormous stone fireplace and two large picnic tables. Stairs wind up through the tower to the open rooftop. A path leads down from the plateau of the butte to more picnic tables and heavy, stone fireplaces. The park is splashed with wildflowers, yuccas, soapweed, and prairie grass.

Newton lies amid gently rolling hills at the junction of Highway 50 and Interstate 135. There, an elegant, sixteen-room Victorian home is one of several attractions honoring the strong Mennonite heritage in the Newton area. The *Warkentin House* at 211 East First Street is open September through December, Saturday and Sunday from 1:00 to 4:30 P.M.; June, July, and August, Tuesday through Sunday, from 1:00 to 4:30 P.M.; April and May, Saturday and Sunday, from 1:00 to 4:30

Coronado Heights

P.M.; and January through March, by appointment. Admission is $3.00 for adults, $1.50 for children ages five through twelve.

Other buildings in town that appear on the National Register of Historic Places are the *Neal House,* at 301 East Fourth, and the *Bethel College Administration Building.* Bethel College, at North Main and Twenty-seventh Streets (in North Newton), is the oldest Mennonite school in America. It was chartered in 1887 and is the home of the *Kauffman Museum,* highlighting the strong Mennonite heritage here. The museum displays the culture of the Mennonite settlers. Other exhibits include the natural history of the Central Plains and the mammals and birds of North American prairies. The museum is surrounded by an award-winning "living prairie," which has more than one hundred species of prairie grasses and flowering plants, streamside woods, and a farmstead. It is open Tuesday through Friday from 9:30 A.M. to 4:30 P.M., Saturday and Sunday from 1:30 to 4:30 P.M. year-round. Admission is $2.00 for adults, $1.00 for children ages six to sixteen. Call (316) 283–1612.

The Old Parsonage Bed and Breakfast at 330 East Fourth (316–283–6808), in Newton's oldest neighborhood, was the parsonage for the First Mennonite Church. It is a cozy yet spacious home filled with family heirlooms and just a short walk from the Warkentin House.

Rates are $48 and include breakfast. Hosts Carl and Betty Friesen can direct you to nearby Bethel College to see the Kauffman Museum.

Here's an interesting way to get off the beaten path. At *Country Boys Carriage and Prairie Adventures* (office at 1504 South Rock Road, Newton), you can rent your own covered wagon, carriage, surrey, or hayrack. The Prairie Adventure features Flint Hills wagon-train trips ("Experience the pioneer life on a covered wagon without all the hardships!" they say) and group trail rides throughout the summer (bring your own horse). Cost is $45 per person. The overnight experience costs about $140 for adults, $75 for children ages five to twelve; it includes a steak dinner. (If your idea of camping out is a Motel 6, deduct 20 percent from the adult rate and come for one day, Saturday.) Trail riders are charged $80, to follow the wagons and camp overnight, but you must have your own horse and feed for the horse. Call (316) 283–2636 for reservations, or visit their Web site at www.kscoveredwagon.com.

The place to stop for a meal is *The Breadbasket* at 219 North Main Street (316–283–3811), where you can have a good old-fashioned Mennonite buffet on Friday and Saturday evenings. The bakers start at midnight, and by morning the bakery is filled with mouth-watering pies, muffins, breads, cookies, sweet rolls, and, of course, zwieback. Breakfast is an incredible choice of pastries, fruit, biscuits and gravy, pancakes, sausage, and on and on. Lunch sandwiches are on freshly baked buns. Hours are 6:30 A.M. to 5:30 P.M. Monday through Thursday, 6:30 A.M. to 8:00 P.M. Friday and Saturday; closed Sunday.

The High Street Company is a unique little gift and antiques shop at 315 North High Street. Vicki Stobbe will help you explore every nook and cranny of this former 1910 neighborhood grocery, filled with gifts, antiques, and collectibles. Hours are Monday to Friday from 10:00 A.M. to 5:30 P.M. and Saturday from 10:00 A.M. to 4:00 P.M. Call (316) 283–1080.

> ### Trivia
>
> *Stop by the Newton Convention and Visitors Bureau at 500 Main Place, Suite 101, and pick up a historical driving tour of the area, or check out the Web site at www.infonew tonks.com. Fax them at (316) 283–8732, or call (316) 283–7555 or (800) 899–0455. You certainly can't say they're not accessible.*

The *Carriage Factory Gallery* (316–284–2749) at 128 East Sixth Street is a 107-year-old stone building originally built for manufacturing carriages. It now shows a variety of art by twenty-two area artists, sponsored by the Newton Fine Arts Association. Hours are 11:00 A.M. to 4:00 P.M. Tuesday through Saturday; closed Sunday and Monday.

Going east on Highway 50 will bring you to downtown *Peabody*'s Walnut Street and it is like a visit to the past. It's not just the friendly atmosphere and nice little shops, but in addition, there is the **1881 Morgan House** at 212 North Walnut Street. It was the home of the first editor of the *Peabody Gazette,* W. H. Morgan. Hours are from Memorial Day through Labor Day, Wednesday through Saturday from 1:00 to 4:00 P.M., or by appointment by calling (620) 983–2174. Just south of the Morgan House is the **Printing Museum,** which displays printing equipment from the turn of the twentieth century, including that of the last paper in the state to print with "hot type." The equipment is all operational, which makes it one of a kind.

The small town of **Hesston** is a good spot to stop and stretch your legs. Spend some time at the **Dyck Arboretum** at 177 West Hickory Street at the south end of Main Street. In addition to 180 types of trees, shrubs, and woody plants, it features 380 types of flowers in perennial gardens and wildflower displays. There is also a bird-watching area and a pond with an island garden. Tours can be arranged. The visitors center is open from 9:00 A.M. to 4:00 P.M. Monday through Friday year-round and 1:00 to 4:00 P.M. Saturday and Sunday from May through October, but the park is open every day until sundown. Admission is $2.00 for adults, $1.00 for children age twelve and younger. Call (620) 327–8127.

At 100 North Main Street, Betsy Goertzen's **Sunflower Patch Gift Shop** is open from 9:00 A.M. to 5:00 P.M. every weekday and until 2:00 P.M. on Saturday. The shop has a nice collection of candles and other gift items; there is a bulk food store in the back room. Call (620) 327–2959.

The **Kansas Learning Center for Health** at 505 Main Street in **Halstead,** slightly south of Highway 50, is home to "Valeda," the talking, transparent woman. This place is fantastic! It contains about twenty-three exhibits depicting the normal, healthy human body and the way it functions. You can test your lung capacity with a breathometer, listen to your heartbeat on a heart monitor, and look into a giant mouth to inspect the taste buds. There are a giant tooth and an eye, with each part illuminated as it is described. An exhibit explains how chromosomes work and why boys and girls are different (and who decides the sex of a baby), and you can see the development of a child from egg and sperm to baby.

Admission is $2.00 for adults, $1.50 for children, with a cap of $5.00 for a family of any size. There are also senior-citizen and group rates. The center is open Monday through Friday from 10:00 A.M. to 4:00 P.M., Sunday from 1:00 to 5:00 P.M.; closed Saturday. Call (316) 835–2662 for more information; or visit www.learningcenter.org.

There's an interesting place to stay in Halstead. Dru Wranosky and her mother-in-law Kathelyn are hosts at **nee Murray way Bed and Breakfast**, 220 West Third Street. This enchanting Victorian house was built in 1911. The tree-covered front lawn has thirty varieties of trees from all over the world. In the foyer you'll find original leaded and beveled glass. A full breakfast is served in the formal dining room. All of the guest rooms have queen-size beds, some have private baths, two have sitting porches, and one has a fireplace. Rooms are $55 a night for two people. Call (316) 835–2027.

PLACES TO STAY IN SOUTH CENTRAL KANSAS

ARKANSAS CITY
LouAnn's Campgrounds,
County Road 12,
(620) 442–4458

Regency Court,
3232 North Summit,
(620) 442–7700

EL DORADO
Red Coach Inn,
2529 Central,
(620) 621–6900

ELK FALLS
Silver Bell Motel,
(Longton 6 miles east),
Trailer hookups,
(620) 642–6145

EMPORIA
Best Western
Hospitality House,
3021 West Highway 50,
(316) 342–7587 or
(800) 362–2036

Candlewood Suites,
2602 Candlewood Drive,
(620) 343–7756

Econo Lodge,
2511 West Eighteenth
Avenue,
(620) 343–7750

Emporia RV Park
& Campground,
4601 West Highway 50,
(620) 343–3422

Ramada,
2700 West Eighteenth
Avenue,
(620) 343–2200

HILLSBORO
Hill Crest Motel,
808 East "D,"
(785) 947–3154

LINDSBORG
Coronado Motel,
305 Harrison Street,
(800) 747–2793

Malm's RV Resort,
Highway 4/ Business 81,
(800) 467–6256

Viking Motel,
446 Harrison Street,
(785) 227–3336 or
(800) 326–8390

LONGTON
Silver Bell Motel
and RV hookups,
Highway 160,
(620) 642–6145

MARION
Marion Country Inn Motel,
1305 East Main,
(620) 382–2147

MCPHERSON
Mustang RV Park,
1909 Millers Lane,
(620) 241–0237

Red Coach Inn,
2111 East Kansas,
(620) 241–6960 or
(800) 362–0072

NEWTON
Best Western
Red Coach Inn,
1301 East First Street,
(620) 283–9120 or
(800) 777–9120

Newell Motel & Truck
Plaza,
200 Manchester,
(316) 283–4000

WICHITA
Candlewood Suites,
570 South Julia,
(316) 942–0400 or
(800) 946–6200

Comfort Inn East,
9525 East Corporate Hills,
(316) 686–2844 or
(800) 228–5150

Comfort Suites,
658 Westdale Drive,
(316) 945–2600 or
(800) 228–5150

The Kansas Inn,
1011 North Topeka,
(316) 269–9999 or
(888) 539–0123

LaQuinta Inn,
7700 East Kellogg Drive,
(316) 681–2881

Quality Inn Airport,
600 South Holland Drive,
(316) 722–2881 or
(800) 228–5151

WINFIELD
Comfort Inn,
Highway 27 at Quail Ridge,
(316) 221–7529 or
(800) 228–5150

**PLACES TO EAT IN
SOUTH CENTRAL KANSAS**

ARKANSAS CITY
Brick's Restaurant
301 South Summit
(620) 442–5390

BENTON
Prairie Rose Chuckwagon
Supper,
15231 Southwest Parallel
Road,
(316) 778–2121

BURNS
Burns Café & Bakery,
106 East Broadway,
(785) 726–5528

CALDWELL
Last Chance Bar & Grill,
30 South Main Street,
(620) 845–2434

DURHAM
Main Street Café,
517 Douglas,
(785) 732–2096

EL DORADO
Carl's Place,
127 North Main,
(620) 321–0855

EMPORIA
Bruff's,
22 East Sixth Street,
(620) 342–1223

FLORENCE
Chuck Wagon,
503 Main Street,
(785) 878–4382

Selected Chambers of Commerce and Visitors Bureaus

Emporia Convention and Visitors Bureau,
*427 Commercial Drive,
P.O. Box 417, Emporia 66801;
(620) 342–1803 or (800) 279–3730;
fax (620) 342–3223;
www.emporia.com*

Lindsborg Chamber of Commerce,
*104 East Lincoln Street, P.O. Box 191, Lindsborg 67456;
(785) 227–3706 or (888) 227–2227;
www.lindsborg.org*

Marion Chamber of Commerce,
*300 South Third Street, Marion 66861;
(620) 382–3425*

Arkansas City Convention and Visitors Bureau,
*P.O. Box 795, Arkansas City 67005;
(620) 442–0230; fax (620) 441–0048;
www.arkcityks.org*

Caldwell Chamber of Commerce,
P.O. Box 42, Caldwell 67022; (620) 845–6444

Hesston Chamber of Commerce,
*P.O. Box 669, Hesston 67062; (620) 327–4102;
www.southwind.net/hesston*

INMAN
Ruthie's Café,
Downtown Inman,
(620) 585–6925

LINCOLNVILLE
Tammy's Café,
Highway 77,
(620) 924–5410

LINDSBORG
Swedish Crown,
121 North Main Street,
(785) 227–2076

MARION
McGillicuddy's,
214 East Main,
(620) 382–3400

Stone City Cafe,
211 East Main,
(620) 382–2656

Wagon Wheel Express,
202 West Main,
(620) 382–3544

MCPHERSON
Sports Page of McPherson,
900 West Kansas,
(620) 241–1200

MOUNDRIDGE
Country Kitchen,
114 South Christian,
(620) 345–6459

NEWTON
Charlie's,
200 Manchester,
(620) 283–0790

Spear's Restaurant &
Pie Shop,
Third & Main Streets,
(316) 283–3510

PEABODY
Coneburg Inn,
904 North Peabody,
(785) 983–2602

RAMONA
Cheers II Restaurant
and Bar,
296 North "D,"
(785) 965–2686

TAMPA
Butch's Diner,
Main Street,
(785) 965–2230

WICHITA
The Grape,
550 North Rock Road,
(316) 634–0113

Old Chicago,
7700 East Kellogg Drive,
(316) 263–9711

Selected Chambers of Commerce and Visitors Bureaus

Hillsboro Chamber of Commerce,
109 South Main Street, Hillsboro 67063;
(620) 947–3506

Kechi Chamber of Commerce,
P.O. Box 578, Kechi 67067;
(620) 744–1337

Lindsborg Chamber of Commerce,
104 East Lincoln, P.O. Box 191, Lindsborg 67456;
(785) 227–3706;
www.lindsborg.org

Mulvane Chamber of Commerce,
P.O. Box 67, Mulvane 67110;
(620) 777–1144

Newton Chamber of Commerce,
P.O. Box 353, Newton 67114;
(316) 283–7555 or (800) 899–0455;
fax (316) 283–8732

Wichita Convention and Visitors Bureau,
100 South Main, Suite 100; (316) 265–2800;
www.wichita-cvb.org

Winfield Convention and Tourism,
P.O. Box 646, Winfield 67156; (620) 221–2421

Southwest Kansas

The crops growing in Kansas today reflect the prairies of yesterday. Strips of trees known as gallery forests grow along meandering rivers and creeks, much as they did long ago. The tallgrass prairies of eastern Kansas now grow tall corn. The midgrass prairies are sown in wheat, and in the western part of the state, the short-grass prairies have prevailed because there is not enough rain to support tall grasses. Today steers roam where buffalo once covered these grasslands for miles in every direction. The short-grass prairie has become pastureland with vast uninterrupted sweeps of sky, resembling a tranquil, waterless sea.

The buffalo herds dwindled because they interfered with the building of railroads and the settling of the western part of the state. A herd of four million was reported near Fort Larned as late as 1870, covering an area 50 miles long and 25 miles wide. During the 1880s almost all of these creatures were destroyed for sport as well as for the hides and meat. Folks going through the territory by train would even shoot from their windows, leaving the carcasses for the vultures. The Native Americans were gradually replaced by cattlemen. In dry grasslands elsewhere, several acres of land are needed to provide enough feed for one animal. But the big and little bluestem grasses of western Kansas are rich in nutrients; today over 300,000 head of cattle are brought here from southwestern states to fatten before being taken to market.

Cities such as Abilene, Dodge City, and Wichita sprang to life as great herds of longhorn steers were driven from Texas up the Chisholm and other trails to be shipped east to market on the new railroads. They were wild, disorderly cow towns before the farmers came to share the Great Plains with the cattlemen. Between Copeland and Sublette the road enters boundless level plains. During the summer months the mirage is a common phenomenon here; travelers often see large lakes in the distance, which vanish as they are approached. Before this country saw a plow, it was thickly covered with buffalo grass. Although it may resemble the "Great American Desert" that Zebulon Pike reported the Great Plains to be, this section of Kansas has the largest share of minerals and natural resources to be found in the state.

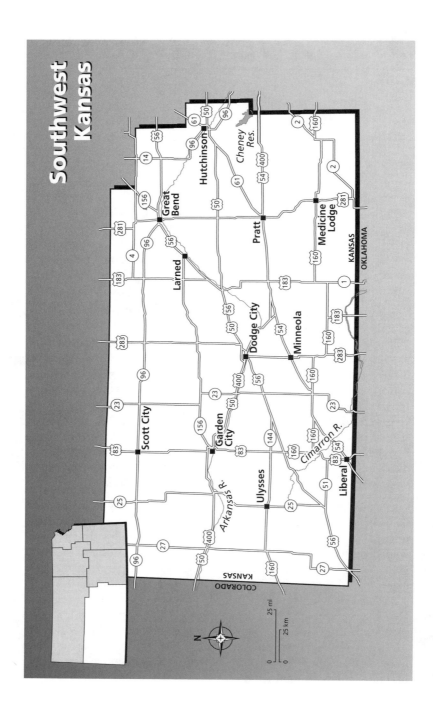

Southwest Kansas

The Great Plains owe their flatness to the erosion of the Rockies before and during the Ice Age, when streams deposited huge loads of sand and gravel as thick as 300 feet over western Kansas. Along with these deposits came large quantities of underground water, which can be used for irrigation of crops.

The Wild West and Chalk Hills

We begin our tour of southwest Kansas in **Dodge City,** the meanest, wildest town in the old Wild West. Dodge was called "Hell on the Plains," and with good reason. Gunslingers worked both sides of the law—occasionally at the same time. Marshal Henry Brown of Dodge City once rode with Billy the Kid.

The famous **Boot Hill Cemetery** was originally at Fourth and Spruce Streets, a bluff 100 feet above the Arkansas River. In 1872 two cowboys

> AUTHOR'S TOP TEN IN
> SOUTHWEST KANSAS
>
> *Dodge City*
> *Cynthia's Pizzeria*
> *Kansas Cosmosphere and Space Center*
> *Stauth Memorial Museum*
> *Stan Herd's earthwork*
> *Mid-America Air Museum*
> *Fort Larned National Historic Site*
> *Yoder*
> *Parman Brothers Limited Trail Rides*

Dodge City

<table><tr><td>Trivia</td></tr></table>

Dodge City, with an average daily wind speed of 14 miles per hour, is the windiest city in the United States.

had a gunfight while camping here. The dead man was unknown and, wrapped in his blanket, was buried where he fell, boots and all; thus Boot Hill was born. The frequent and sudden deaths of unknown cowboys and buffalo hunters filled the cemetery quickly. Historians say that the burial in 1878 of Alice Chambers, a dance-hall girl, was Boot Hill's last. In 1879 the bodies were moved to Prairie Grove Cemetery.

On the site of the old Boot Hill Cemetery now stands the **Boot Hill Museum,** a re-creation of Dodge City in the 1870s. Lining historic Front Street, where lawmen Wyatt Earp and Bat Masterson once walked, are an 1865 Fort Dodge jail, the Santa Fe Depot, and a nineteenth-century blacksmith shop. Call (620) 277–8188 or visit the Web site at www.boothill.org.

During the summertime, daily entertainment includes melodramas, old-fashioned medicine shows, stagecoach rides, reenactments of gunfights, and a real crowd favorite, the Long Branch Saloon Variety Show, where Miss Kitty's can-can girls kick up their heels. Get a reservation for this show. Afterward, stop in for a buffalo burger and ice cream at **Beatty & Kelly's Restaurant and Old Fashioned Ice Cream Parlor,** also part of the museum complex.

Hours at the museum are 8:00 A.M. to 8:00 P.M. daily June through August. From September through May, hours are 9:00 A.M. to 5:00 P.M. Monday through Saturday and 1:00 to 5:00 P.M. Sunday. Admission is $7.00 for adults, $6.50 for seniors and children ages seven to seventeen. The Boot Hill Museum also has a research library, open by appointment, where history buffs can see scores of old photos, maps, and other documents of the period.

Fort Dodge: A Home for Soldiers

*T*he Fort Dodge site was once used as a campground for wagon trains. The fort was established in 1865 to protect the wagon trains as well as mail carriers. Fort Dodge was abandoned in 1882. Eight years later it was deeded to the state of Kansas so that the adobe and sod buildings could be used as a soldiers' home. Most were veterans of the Civil War and Mexican and Indian wars. Today the fort's quiet, tree-lined walks and dignified buildings are still home to Kansas soldiers. A small museum and self-guided tour of the grounds relate the history of the fort. It's 6 miles east of Dodge City on Highway 400. Leave a message at (316) 227–2121 if you'd like more information.

You can relive the legend in Dodge. The *Dodge City Trolley* visits places where history was made along the Santa Fe Trail. Tours are daily, and schedules are in the information center. Adult fares are $5.00, children's $3.00.

Two museums share a building at 603 Fifth Avenue, across the street and west of Boot Hill. *The Kansas Teachers' Hall of Fame* is not only a memorial to the state's teachers but also a museum containing early classroom items. No admission charge. Also at this location is the famous *Gunfighter's Wax Museum.* Life-size gunfighters buried with their boots on create a scene you won't soon forget. Admission is $2.00 for adults, $1.25 for children ages six to thirteen. Both museums are open daily May 1 through October 31; call (620) 225–7311 for hours.

Santa Fe Trail Tracks, situated west of the city, are part of the original wagon trail used by early travelers westward bound between 1821 and the 1880s. It is 9 miles west of Dodge City on Highway 50 and is listed on the National Register of Historic Sites. Here 140 acres are set aside to preserve the finest remnants in existence of the Santa Fe Trail. The deep swales left by the wagons can still be seen quite clearly, especially in spring, when the prairie grass is short. Officials ask that you stay on the walkways in order to help preserve the ruts.

For morning coffee or lunch in Dodge City, stop at *Mic-Leo's* at 509 North Second Avenue (620–225–4833). Two sisters joined forces (and their

Top Annual Events in Southwest Kansas

April
Mennonite Quilt Auction & Relief Sale,
Hutchinson;
(620) 543–6633

May
Wildflower Tour,
Medicine Lodge;
(620) 886–3417;
second Saturday

June
Beef Empire Days,
Garden City;
(620) 278–6807;
first two weeks

July
Dodge City Days,
Dodge City;
(620) 227–3119; last week

Pretty Prairie Rodeo,
Pretty Prairie;
(620) 459–4653

August
Heritage Day, Yoder;
(620) 662–8472

September
Kansas State Fair,
Hutchinson; (620) 669–3600

Peace Treaty Pageant,
Medicine Lodge;
(620) 886–9815

Is It the Prairie or the Plains?

*W*hat is the difference between the plains and the prairie? One hundred degrees longitude, a line that runs north-south near Dodge City, is the approximate dividing line between the two. To the east of the line are the tall grasses—the prairies—and to the west are the short grasses—the plains. The former are better for crops, and the latter, for grazing.

names) to start this downtown restaurant, 1 block east of Boot Hill. Everything's homemade, including bread, pastries, and pie; the menu includes two dozen different sandwiches and a daily special. Hours are 8:00 A.M. to 4:00 P.M. Monday through Friday and 8:00 A.M. to 3:00 P.M. Saturday and Sunday.

For a hearty steak, head to *Casey's Cowtown* at 503 East Trail (620–227–5225). Inside, the place has an Old West feel, circa 1890s. After dinner, spend some time looking at the restaurant's collection of antique stained glass and western art. On summer weekends and during Dodge City Days (late July or early August), enjoy an outdoor barbecue and dancing. Hours are 11:00 A.M. to 10:00 P.M.

If sundown finds you in Dodge, the *Boot Hill Bed and Breakfast* at 603 West Spruce Street might have a bed for you. This elegant Victorian home across the street from Boot Hill has new owners, Craig and Claire Poe. The B&B's popularity is due in part to the breakfast served its guests; the previous owner, a former Ritz Carlton pastry chef, left some of his recipes, and the Poes have added some of their own. In addition, the landscaped yard has a gazebo (a favorite for weddings). The 6,000-square-foot mansion has six rooms available, all with private baths. One is a honeymoon suite, which comes with a romantic package. Rooms are from $79 to $139. Check out the Web site at www.bbonline.com/ks/boothill, or e-mail at boothillbb@dodgecity.net. Call (620) 225–7600.

Twenty-five miles southwest of Dodge City on Highway 56 is the little town of *Montezuma.* Every small town has its surprises, and Montezuma's is the *Stauth Memorial Museum* at 111 North Aztec. The visitors who come each month outnumber the 900 souls who live in this town. Claude and Donalda Stauth were world travelers for thirty-eight years, and "Donnie" was a professional photographer. Many of her slides have been made into laser videos featuring children, animals, or famous places. The focal point of the 10,000-square-foot museum is the permanent exhibit, "Around the World," which showcases some of the 10,000 slides and many "off-the-back" artifacts collected in their travels. These are items that people owned and used, such as the Croatian skirt completely covered with detailed embroidery and edged with handmade lace. There are musical instruments of all kinds, for example, a thumb piano from Cameroon. Statues of ivory and ebony are from Papua New Guinea and Indonesia.

Trivia

Built to Smithsonian specifications, the museum has hosted thirty-six national and international traveling exhibits. This is a not-to-be-missed place. Hours are Tuesday through Saturday 9:00 A.M. to noon and 1:00 to 4:30 P.M., Sunday 1:30 to 4:30 P.M. Call (620) 846–2527, or e-mail stauthm @ucom.net. Admission is free, but donations are welcome.

The Cimarron Route was a shorter road to Santa Fe than the Santa Fe Trail, but water was dangerously hard to find. Travelers sank a wagon bed into the quicksand to let the water seep through and fill the wagon. A wagon bed still marks the old route today at Wagon Bed Spring.

Travelers have hung their hats at the **Cimarron Hotel** (620–855–2244) at 203 North Main Street in **Cimarron,** 16 miles west of Dodge City, since 1886. The redbrick hotel has been renovated and decorated in Old West style with original tin ceilings. A rusting sign reads THIEVES, THUGS, FAKIRS, AND BUNKOSTEERERS GET OUT OF TOWN BY 10 P.M. And you'd best listen up, Pilgrim.

Owner Kathleen Holt purchased the building in 1977. Renovation of the third-floor rooms provided ten bed-and-breakfast rooms. The bathrooms are down the hall; to preserve the history and charm of the place, there are no telephones or television sets. Rooms are $35. A full breakfast is available on request; dinners for groups can also be arranged.

At the other end of Main Street, stop in at **Clark Pharmacy** on 101 South Main. The building dates from the 1930s or 1940s and still has the original tin ceiling. It also has an old-fashioned soda fountain of the same era. Call (620) 855–2242 to check hours.

The Caches

A marker 2.1 miles west of Dodge City on Highway 50 is all that is left of a well-known landmark and rest stop on the Santa Fe Trail. The marker indicates the location of the Caches, pits that supposedly were dug out of the ground. According to legend, a trading party set out from Missouri in late 1822, but their pack train was caught in a blizzard near this site. They lost most of their pack animals and were stranded for three months. In early spring of 1823, they dug pits to cache their goods and left for Taos, New Mexico, to purchase mules. On their return trip, they were attacked by a war party of Pawnees. They survived and dug up their goods and returned to Taos. The pits were left open and were a landmark on the trail for many years.

While in Cimarron, call ahead (620–855–7718 or 800–261–6251) to arrange a visit to the **Kansas Wheat House** at 102 South Main Street and try some of Shirley and Dave Voran's "Wheat Nubs," and other wheat snacks and confections. They also offer bread mixes ranging from jalepeño-cheddar to chocolate-raspberry and gift baskets of Kansas items. You can see several of the products at their Web site, www.kansasgrown.com/kswheat/.

Another option for accommodations is the **Cimarron Crossing Bed and Breakfast,** 307 West Avenue A (Highway 50) on the edge of Cimarron. This charming 1907 home was built by Joan and Gerald Vogel's great-aunt and great-uncle, who followed the Santa Fe Trail as far as this corner of Kansas before deciding they'd gone west far enough. The house is furnished in period antiques and reproductions (you'll have to look really closely to see that the kitchen stove isn't a wood burner), with modern amenities including central heat and air-conditioning and a hot tub in the herb garden. Rooms (four, all with private baths) include a hearty country breakfast with locally grown and homemade treats such as jelly made from Kansas peaches. Rates are $50 to $80. For reservations, call (620) 855–3030 or (888) 829–3232, or visit the Web site at www. cimarroncross ing.com. Or you can e-mail at Innkeeper@cimarroncrossing.com.

Stocking Your Wagon

I have traveled across Kansas many times, and I have learned that "gettin' outta Dodge" takes some forethought. If you look at a map of the state, you will realize that in western Kansas, it can be a long way from one town to the next. So check to see that your gas tank is full and your spare tire is inflated. Measure the distance between your starting point and destination. Just "eyeballing it" will leave you in the middle of nowhere at sundown. If you are traveling with children (and even if you are not), it's a good idea to use a public rest room whenever one appears.

Weather is a serious factor in Kansas. There are thunderstorms with "post-hole diggers"—that's what they call lightning around here—and thunder that will scare you to death. Blizzards seem to come from nowhere; there are floods, and, of course, tornadoes. Pay attention to weather watches and warnings. For example, a "tornado watch" means the conditions are right for a tornado; a "tornado warning" means one has been spotted in the area. It's a good idea to have a map, walking shoes, water, a first-aid kit, snacks, sunglasses, and, in winter, blankets and some heavy clothing. And you will want binoculars and a camera!

East of Cimarron on Highway 50, a historical marker points out wagon-wheel ruts (called swales) remaining from the Santa Fe Trail.

Garden City lies in beef country. You'll see feed-lots and packing plants, but some unexpected pleasures, too. The *Lee Richardson Zoo* at Finnup Park at Fourth and Maple Streets was founded in 1920. You can walk or drive through the zoo in your car, a "wild experience" the easy way. The park also boasts the largest free, out-door swimming pool in the world, occupying half a city block and holding 2½ million gallons of water. There are picnic areas, tennis courts, horseshoe pits, and a formal garden. The park is open daily year-round from 8:00 A.M. to dusk. Call (620) 276–1250.

Trivia
Garden City is the proud owner of the world's largest hairball. It is at the Finney County Museum. (I am not making this up.) It was found in a cow's stomach at the packing plant.

Long before cattle were king in this part of the state, bison roamed the prairie. You can see the state's oldest publicly owned herd of the massive creatures at the 3,670-acre *Finney Game Refuge,* south of the Arkansas River bridge on Highway 83 near Garden City. Male bison can reach 6½ feet high, 9 to 12 feet in length, and weigh more than a ton. The herd usually numbers about 150. This stretch of prairie is also home to lesser prairie chicken, quail, ground squirrels, jackrabbits, and deer. For the safety of the public, no self-guided tours are allowed, but a guided tour can be arranged by calling Friends of Finney Game Refuge at (620) 276–9400 or (620) 276–3264, or the Finney County Convention and Tourism Bureau at (888) 445–4663, ext. 9400. There is no charge, but donations are welcome.

Garden City's *Mercer Gallery* offers a simple place to enjoy a range of quality art exhibitions. Two rooms are filled with paintings, sketches, engravings, sculpture, and hand-thrown ceramics, done by students and some well-known Kansas artists. Located in the *Pauline Joyce Fine Arts Building* on the Garden City Community College campus, the new gallery was a dream turned into reality by Garden City resident Maxine Mercer Porter in memory of her late husband, Clyde Mercer.

The gallery is open from 2:00 to 5:00 P.M. Sunday and from noon to 4:00 P.M. Monday through Friday during the college year. For more informa-tion, call (620) 276–7611.

Fred and Kathryn Askerem just opened a bed-and-breakfast in their twenty-two-room brick Victorian mansion, circa 1909, at 501 North Fifth Street in Garden City. *Sunnyland Bed and Breakfast* is indeed a mansion, with a ballroom that will seat seventy-five people, seven

Prairie or Forest?

*I*n the early part of the twentieth century, the U.S. government designated a significant amount of the state's prairie as the Kansas National Forest. Beginning with 30,000 acres of seedling trees in 1905, the project had expanded to 800,000 acres by 1915, and looked very promising. But weather runs in cycles, and when a dry cycle set in, most of the trees soon died and the land reverted to prairie.

bedrooms all with private baths, and a chef who will do wedding receptions and other events. Prices are $75 to $95 a night with a full breakfast. You can visit their Web site at www.sunnylandbandb.com, or call (620) 276–0500 or (866) 453–0500.

Kathryn and her partner, Tonya Bond, own *Klass Act* at 203 East Laurel, a rubber art, stamp, and scrapbook shop with everything you need to record your adventures in scrapbook form. Hours are Tuesday through Friday from 10:00 A.M. to 5:30 P.M. and Saturday to 4:00 P.M. Call (620) 272–9904.

West of Garden City in *Lakin* is the *Windy Heights Bed and Breakfast* at 607 Country Heights Road. This B&B is a modern home on a nine-hole public golf course. With some advance notice, you can have dinner waiting for you when you're through playing. A continental or full breakfast is served in the kitchen or dining room, or outside on the terrace overlooking the golf course. Or have breakfast in bed, if that's your mood. Hosts Chuck and Dianne Jaeger have three rooms with private baths. Rooms are $50 to $60. Call (620) 355–7699 or e-mail djaeger@pld.com.

Lakin is a rural community made up of farmers and ranchers. But for a small town it has some interesting places. The most unusual is Dennis and Janice Urie's *Frontier Flowers.* They harvest weeds and grasses in the area and preserve them with a technique that keeps the plants from becoming brittle. They are happy to give tours of their operation with advance notice. Call (316) 355–6177.

Frontier Flowers' arrangements are sold at a trio of shops in town. *Blooming Field's,* 220 West Santa Fe Boulevard (Highway 50) (620–355–6867), is a florist, as you might guess by its name, specializing in live plants, fresh flowers, and silk arrangements. Hours are 9:00 A.M. to 5:30 P.M. Monday through Friday, 9:30 A.M. to 1:00 P.M. Saturday. *Perfect Arrangement,* 106 East Santa Fe Boulevard (620–355–7740), is also a florist and carries a good selection of linens. You can eat lunch here (sandwiches of all kinds or the daily special, homemade cookies and pies) weekdays from 11:30 A.M. to 1:00 P.M. Store hours are 9:30 A.M. to 5:30 P.M. Monday through Friday, 9:30 A.M. to 3:00 P.M. Saturday. *Patchwork Garden,* 404 East Santa Fe Boulevard (620–355–1441), offers fabrics and notions as well as sewing classes, or you can just buy a finished quilt. Also sold here are crafts made from old Kansas barn wood. Hours are 10:00 A.M. to 4:00 P.M. Tuesday through Saturday. *Cinnamon Bear,* also on East Highway 50 (620–355–7833), has candles, fragrances, afghans, and, of course, bears. Hours are 9:30 A.M. to 5:30 P.M. every day but Sunday.

Bob and Adriene Price have a quiet little place in **Deerfield** about 7 miles east of Lakin, which is 48 miles from the Colorado border on Highway 50. Their little log cabin sits on a private fishing pond. It is the perfect spot to just get away and enjoy some quiet time. There is no phone, no television (and in fact, no kitchen or bathroom; there is an outhouse and water outside), but lots of birds, fish, geese, and ducks. Bob will take you hunting during the season, and ice-skating is always a possibility in the winter. Call (620) 426–6291 for more about this secret retreat for $30 a night.

Next head south on Highway 25 to **Ulysses**— actually, *new* Ulysses. Old Ulysses gave itself away in 1909, when all the buildings in town were loaded on skids and moved 3 miles to the present site so that the lots could be deeded back to bondholders. The town's hotel was cut into three sections for transport. One section is now part of the **Historic Adobe Museum,** 300 East Oklahoma (620–356–3009). Call for hours. George W. Earp (first cousin to Wyatt Earp of Dodge City) became (old) Ulysses's first peace officer in 1885.

Fort's Cedar View (620–356–2570) is a bed-and-breakfast that sits on twenty acres of landscaped grounds 0.75 mile northwest of the junction of Highways 25 and 160, Ulysses. It is a quiet getaway with an indoor pool and fireside room. This modern brick-and-cedar home has four rooms, one with private bath.

> **Trivia**
>
> *An old Jewish cemetery is 4 miles north of Garden City on Kansas Avenue and 4 miles west on Highway 83, at the southeast corner of Chmelka and Lowe Roads. Four grave sites are still visible. Several Jewish colonies were formed in this part of the state in the early 1880s, and the land was permanently deeded for a cemetery in 1892.*

Owner Lynda Fort invites guests to think of the place as their own. Breakfast can be whatever guests want, from homemade cinnamon rolls to a full meal. Often the entire house is rented for business meetings. Rates are from $50 to $65 per day. Call (620) 356–2570, e-mail at fort@pld.com, or visit www.fortscedarview.com.

The next city on Highway 56 is **Hugoton,** probably the cleanest, most all-American little town you will ever see. If you'd like to stay here, try the **Shady Lane Bed and Breakfast,** at 110 North Main. Neal Gillespie hosts guests at his World War II–vintage home, which has been completely renovated and lies down a shady tree-lined lane on the northern end of Hugoton.

All four rooms have a king-size bed, large TV set, private phone line, and private bath. There's even a spa off the outdoor deck. Rates are $49 to $84. Call (620) 544–7747.

Elkhart is southwest of Hugoton, in the southwestern corner of the state. The **Morton County Historical Society Museum** on Highway 56 in Elkhart (620–697–2833) brings the covered-wagon experience alive in your imagination as you walk through. You can imagine Coronado's quest on the prairie, the Native American's life following herds of buffalo, and the freight wagons hurrying to reach the only available water on the Cimarron Cut-Off at Middle Springs. As the covered wagons came, sod houses were built in the treeless plains. The red caboose in front of the museum symbolizes the end of the Santa Fe Trail.

Stop by **Jim-n-I's** (620–697–9886) on Highway 56 (next to the El Rancho Motel). This restaurant owned by Jim and Janelle Shultz has a delightfully varied menu. Rotisserie chicken, burgers, and a noon buffet are available weekdays; Friday and Saturday nights, folks come for the prime rib and smoked chicken and ribs. Hours are from 6:00 A.M. to 9:00 P.M. seven days a week.

In early summer, two dozen of America's top collegiate baseball players descend on the town to form the **Elkhart Dusters,** one of the teams in the NCAA-sanctioned summer Jayhawk League. Local families host the

The Pride of Morton County

*M*orton County is the smallest county in the world to have not one, but two Olympic Medal winners: Glenn Cunningham ran on the 1932 and 1936 indoor track teams and won a silver medal in 1936 in the 1500 meters; in 1938 he set an indoor mile world record with a time of 4:04.4 and was selected as the out-standing track performer in the one-hundred-year history of Madison Square Garden. Thane Baker won the silver medal in the 200 meters in 1952 at Helsinki. In 1956, in Melbourne, he won a gold medal as captain of the 400-meter relay team; a silver in the 100 meters, and a bronze in the 200 meters.

Duster players, and the town turns out in big numbers to watch the games and line up for autographs. The season kicks off with **Duster Daze,** a celebration held the first weekend of June that includes a parade and picnic to welcome the players.

Ten miles north of Elkhart on Highway 27 is the **Cimarron National Grasslands,** open year-round during daylight hours. The U.S. Forest Service maintains the ecosystem here; a self-guided tour allows visitors to familiarize themselves with the natural history of the region. You'll begin to get an idea of what it was like when the first pioneers crossed that wide-open grassland. The 108,000 acres have been reclaimed as a complete ecosystem of native wildlife and plants. This is the largest area of public land in the state and is a great experience for campers, hikers, and hunters. There are elk and antelope along the 19-mile companion trail that parallels the preserved trail ruts. Call (620) 697–4621 for information.

Go north on Highway 27 to **Johnson City** to find David and Steve Parman's most unusual shop. They create kaleidoscopes for collectors at **Parman Brothers Limited** (620–492–6882), 106 South Main, at the intersection of Highways 27 and 160. A tube-shaped optical toy, the kaleidoscope produces changing symmetrical patterns as loose bits of handblown glass are moved about under a set of mirrors.

Parman kaleidoscopes, made of imbuia (a Brazilian wood), oak, and walnut with optical-quality lenses, sell for low prices, as kaleidoscopes go. The Parmans offer thirty models in a range of sizes for $35 to $150, and kaleidoscope collectors snap them up. The miniscopes, which weigh less than eight ounces, have the same optical quality as the larger ones and

"Tanking" on the Arkansas River

*T*he sport of tanking on the Arkansas River (pop quiz: How is that pronounced?) originated here. What is tanking? Well, it started as an annual race. People dragged big round aluminum horse tanks down to the river, where they were painted and decorated with streamers and balloons, then raced from Syracuse to the town of Kendall, 10 miles east. When there's enough water (Colorado and Mother Nature control the water in the Arkansas River), you can float to Lewis Landing, 5 miles downriver.

are made of beechwood, walnut, and imported wenge, a black wood. Hours are from 8:00 A.M. to 5:00 P.M. Monday through Friday.

Syracuse was once one of the most favored towns on the High Plains, a green oasis on the prairie. People in distant towns drove here to enjoy the cool beauty of its graceful poplars, weeping willows, and other trees.

At 208 North Main Street is *Cynthia's Pizzeria,* the most popular place in town. Owner Cynthia Clark makes a sauerkraut and vegetable pizza that is so good, you will want to carry one away with you. It is very good cold. The place is packed with senior citizens, high-school students, and local farmers searching out a breakfast pizza. Everyone eats here. Call (620) 384–5928. Hours are from 11:00 A.M. to 8:30 P.M. Monday through Thursday, and to 9:30 P.M. Friday and Saturday.

The *Horace Greeley Museum* (620–376–4996) is located in the old Greeley County courthouse in the small town of *Tribune.* Built in 1890 of post rock (local limestone), the structure is listed on the National Register of Historic Places. There's no proof that either the museum or the county is named for the *New York Tribune* newspaperman who penned the famous words "Go West, young man." But there is a connection; the founder of Tribune, C. K. Gerard, worked with Greeley in New York before editing his own newspaper here.

The jail that was once part of the courthouse is still there, as well as a restored courtroom. A late-1800s kitchen and schoolroom and an early-1920s filling station have been added. Among the displays on the museum's three floors is a collection of Old West branding irons. Hours are Monday through Friday from 9:00 A.M. to 4:00 P.M. and by appointment.

Following the Civil War, there was a soldier's colony in Tribune. Anxious to settle the West, the government offered soldiers 160 acres of land if they settled and "proved up" the property—building a house, farming or raising cattle, and staying a set number of years. The settlers could also file a tree claim, receiving an additional 160 acres for planting trees. Many of these Civil War veterans lived out their days here and are buried in a GAR (Grand Army of the Republic) cemetery in northwest Greeley.

Lake Scott State Park (620–872–2061) is 12 miles north of *Scott City* on Highway 83. Steep canyons and bluffs seem oddly out of place in Kansas, but then, so does Lake Scott, a cool, wet haven, and one of the few large lakes in southwest Kansas. Lake Scott is in the spring-fed Ladder Creek Valley. It is a lush oasis in a land where water is scarce. The valley is carved into the white stone of the Ogallala bluffs and watered by the Ogallala aquifer. Lake Scott's water is a natural beauty surrounded with cottonwood, elm, and walnut trees. It is much the same as the Native Americans and later the pioneers saw it. The Ogallala aquifer has provided an important and reliable water source for thousands of years. The Plains Apache people lived part of each year in the valley in the 1600s, enjoying shelter, wild fruits and berries, and easy water. Bison and antelope on nearby plains provided supplies of meat and hides.

Within Lake Scott State Park is the **Steele Home Museum.** Built in the shadow of the bluffs, the native sandstone home of the Steele family still feels the steady breeze of western Kansas after more than a century. Except for a covered porch and a few rain gutters for protection, the home looks just as it did so long ago. Inside the restored house is some of the original furniture that traveled to Kansas by covered wagon, along with other period pieces.

Herbert Steele came with his parents, brothers, and sisters in a covered wagon to the land and filed claim to it. Eliza Landon, a Tennessee schoolmarm, lived with her family on a timber claim nearby. When Herb and Liza united their frontier families in 1892, they purchased a section of ranch land with natural springs trickling from the bluffs. The couple hand-quarried blocks of sandstone from the land and built a two-story house near the cool bed of Ladder Creek.

Liza's kitchen and workroom were in a dugout surrounded by sod to protect her from the summer's heat and winter's chill. The back door was at ground level and provided a view of the cherry, apple, and peach

The Squaw's Den Battleground

*I*n 1878, Chief Dull Knife and Little Wolf of the Northern Cheyenne escaped from their reservation near Fort Reno, Oklahoma, with 235 followers, including women and children. Their escape took them through eastern Kansas, and on September 27, the men, women, and children of the Cheyenne Nation made a stand against the U.S. Army on the bluffs of Beaver Creek, just south of what is Lake Scott State Park today. This encounter with the cavalry was the last Indian battle in the state. The site became known as Squaw's Den Battleground because of the cave in which the Cheyenne women and children hid during and after the battle. Colonel William H. Lewis was wounded during the fighting and died en route to Fort Wallace, making him the last casualty of the Indian wars in Kansas. Ask at the state park office for directions to the historical marker.

orchards. Two living rooms and two bedrooms, also at ground level, faced the bluff. The walls of porous sandstone and mortar are more than a foot thick, insulating the house and trapping warmth from the kitchen below in winter. The rock floor of the springhouse built around the bubbling spring just north of the house provided refrigeration for the milk and cream from the dairy cows and for eggs from the chickens, kept in the quarried-stone chicken house on the bluff.

Rugs handwoven by Liza grace the floors; her iron kettle still hangs over the coals on the range where buffalo chips fueled the fire. Near the window in the sitting room stands a bookcase made by the Steeles' only son, Roy, who died when he was twenty. Two daughters died in infancy.

The Steeles' reputation for hospitality was well known, and their door was always open, the spring providing a cool drink to visitors. They sold nearly 800 acres of their land to the state to create a park, and the house was preserved in their honor. The spring still bubbles cool water for travelers. The home can be viewed by appointment.

El Cuartelejo Pueblo Ruins, also at the park, is an important archaeological site occupied by the Taos and Picurie Indians from 1650 to 1720. It is the northernmost Indian pueblo in the Americas. It was also the first white settlement in Kansas. Rick Stevens, park manager, can tell you all about it. Vehicle permits to enter the state park are $4.00. Camping is extra. There is no charge for viewing the museum or pueblo ruins, but donations are welcome.

Highway 83 from Lake Scott to Oakley cuts through the Chalk Hills, which contain the fossils of not only fish and sharks—which you might expect if you know the geology of the region (once an inland sea)—but also flying reptiles and swimming birds. The Smoky Hill River eroded its way down through the chalk, exposing prehistory at a glance.

Patrycia Ann Herndon's Studio/Gallery is in an 1888 landmark bank building in ***Dighton,*** east of Scott City along Highway 96. She records her surroundings in western Kansas in watercolor, pastel, or pencil. Her realistic interpretations can be seen in her studio/gallery. Patrycia is artist-in-residence at 146 East Long Street from 10:00 A.M. to 5:00 P.M. Monday through Friday, unless she's at an art show. You might want to call ahead at (620) 397–2273.

The ***Lane County Historical Museum*** at 333 North Main Street has something a little different in the Bachelor Exhibit. The museum features a dugout; inside, a mechanical man—whose creator does special effects for movies—sings the "Lane County Bachelor," a late 1800s song, at the press of a button. Close by the museum in the park is a full-size sod house, furnished the way these dwellings were when settlers lived here. Virginia Johnston is the museum curator and can be reached at (620) 397–5652. The museum is open Tuesday through Saturday 1:00 to 5:00 P.M. year-round, and Sunday from 2:00 to 5:00 P.M. Memorial Day to Labor Day. Admission is free.

If you happen to be on Highway 4 north and east of Dighton you will find the town of **Uttica** and the **Wertz Street Emporium** at 222 East Wirtz. Mark Bauer's restaurant is open only on Saturday night, and it fills up fast, so get there early. The steaks are great; serving begins at 7:00 P.M. "Supper" is served until 10:00 P.M. but the Emporium stays open and serves drinks until 2:00 A.M. In wintertime the Emporium is open for meals on Friday and Sunday nights, too, but when winter begins is entirely up to the Bauers—usually whenever it is too cold to do farm work or go to the lake. It is only 17 miles south of Castle Rock. For information, call (785) 391–2342.

Ness City is the next stop on Highway 96. It's the home of the **Prairie Mercantile,** featuring Kansas products. The Mercantile is at 102 West Main Street, inside the native stone Ness County Bank building, which is on the National Register of Historic Landmarks. All money earned in this shop is used to restore the building. (Everyone in the shop is a volunteer.) Hours are from 1:00 to 5:00 P.M. Monday through Friday. Call (785) 798–3337.

A short trip south from Dodge City on Highway 283 and west on Highway 54 is the town of **Meade,** the perfect place to "get away"—at least, the Dalton Gang thought so. The **Dalton Gang Hideout**, at 502 South Pearlette, is only one of many spots the outlaws used, but this one has been preserved, restored, and furnished as it was in the nineteenth century, complete with secret passages and a tunnel leading from the house down the hill to the barn.

The tunnel is cool and quiet in the middle of a Kansas summer; at the south end of the passageway in the loft of the barn is the **Dalton Museum.** It's filled with a fascinating collection of pioneer items, including the W. S. Dingess Antique Gun Collection. It is open Monday through Saturday 9:00 A.M. to 5:00 P.M., Sunday 1:00 to 5:00 P.M. The museum closes an hour later in summer. Admission is $2.00. Call (620) 873–2731 or (800) 354–2743.

The **Meade County Historical Museum,** 200 East Carthage (620–873–2359), contains replicas of a one-room schoolhouse, an early church, a

Pancake Boulevard

In Liberal, Highway 54 is called Pancake Boulevard in honor of the international pancake race held here every Shrove Tuesday. Women from the town run a quarter-mile course flipping a pancake. The winner's time is compared with the winning time from a similar race held in Olney, England, on the same day. The race makes TV news nationwide and abroad—a welcome and entertaining change from the usual fare.

general store, a blacksmith shop, a sod house, a doctor's office, and a barber shop. Truth be told, the favorite exhibit is a unique two-headed calf. Outside, a windmill and early farm equipment join the 1976 Bicentennial time capsule; but the place is a time capsule in itself. It is open 9:00 A.M. to 6:00 P.M. Monday through Saturday, 1:00 to 5:00 P.M. Sunday. Admission is free, donations are welcome.

You can spend the night in a peaceful country farmhouse northeast of Meade on Highway 54 near the town of *Fowler.* Dean and Mary Reese will welcome you to *Creek Side Farm* at 26131 A Road. They offer deer and pheasant hunting in season. The farm, built in the 1930s along the banks of Crooked Creek, now raises its main crop in a lush greenhouse filled with bedding plants. Two guest bedrooms with double and queen-size beds with private baths and ceiling fans await you, and a full country breakfast will be served on the enclosed porch that overlooks the farm, or in the dining room, if the weather's not right. Rooms are $45 to $65. Call (620) 646–5586 for reservations.

Most weekends Dean and Mary send guests to enjoy a meal at *Someplace Else Steak House,* 211 South Main, in a nineteenth-century hotel building. It's open Thursday, Friday, and Saturday evenings from 6:00 to 10:00 P.M. from October through July. Call (620) 646–5577. The *Neon '57* at 500 North Main is an old fifties-style diner and gift shop, open 9:00 A.M. to 4:00 P.M. Monday through Friday, 10:00 A.M. to 2:00 P.M. Saturday. Call (620) 646–5775.

Just 10 miles west of *Kismet* you will see the *"Mighty Samson of the Cimarron,"* the largest railroad bridge of its kind. It's officially known as the Rock Island Bridge and is 1,200 feet long, rising 100 feet above the Cimarron River.

The Bluebird Inn is in *Liberal* at 221 West Sixth. Rita Kenney's gracious home is just 2 blocks from downtown. There are three charming guest rooms, all with private baths and a suite with its own Jacuzzi tub for two. Guests will wake to the delightful aroma of gourmet coffee brewing. A full breakfast is served in the formal dining room or sunny garden room. Guests are served evening hors d'oeuvres next to the fireplace or in the garden room. Rooms are $60 to $85. Call (620) 624–0720 for reservations, or e-mail at urrpk@ptsi.net. You can visit the Web site at www.bluebirdinnbandb.com.

From Highway 54 take East Cedar Street to 567 East Cedar where the *Coronado Historical Museum* contains exhibits concerning the Spanish explorer who came here in 1541. Overseeing the artifacts and exhibits with typical explorer's aplomb is a bronze statue of this famous adventurer. The museum is open Tuesday through Saturday from 9:00 A.M. to 5:00 P.M. (7:00 P.M. in summer), and Sunday from 1:00 to 5:00 P.M. (6:00 P.M. in summer). Call (620) 624–7624.

The *Mid-America Air Museum* (620–624–5263), located on the former Liberal Army Air Field (now the municipal airport on Highways 54 and 83), has more than ninety airplanes on exhibit. The airfield was the training ground for more than 5,000 B–24 Liberator commanders during World War II, and the idea for the museum was born during a reunion in 1986. The 86,000-square-foot building is devoted to aircraft exhibits and displays. The facility also features a 6,000-square-foot Aviators Memorial Chapel, a library, and a gift shop, as well as a 200-seat theater.

Aircraft are on display, including a 1929 Pietenpol, the oldest vintage aircraft in the collection. This high-wing monoplane was powered by a Ford Model A engine. The restoration area, a popular part of the exhibit, is open to visitors. Another favorite is the TBM Avenger like the one flown by former President George Bush during World War II and named for his fiancée, Barbara Pierce. Bush was the Navy's youngest aviator when he received his wings in 1943; he went on to earn the Distinguished Flying Cross and three air medals.

The museum is open Monday through Saturday from 10:00 A.M. to 5:00 P.M., Sunday from 1:00 to 5:00 P.M. There is an admission fee.

What would a trip to Kansas be without a visit to Oz? At *Dorothy's House and the Land of Oz,* you can walk the Yellow Brick Road and see Dorothy and Toto, Dorothy's house (with the Wicked Witch's feet showing beneath it), Scarecrow, Tin Man, Cowardly Lion, winged monkeys, and talking trees. The address is, of course, 567 Yellow Brick Road. Summer hours are 9:00 A.M. to 5:00 P.M. Monday through Saturday, 1:00 to 5:00 P.M. Sunday. From Labor Day to Memorial Day, hours are Tuesday through Saturday 9:00 A.M. to 5:00 P.M. and Sunday 1:00 to 5:00 P.M. Admission is $5.00 for adults, $4.00 for seniors, and $3.50 for children ages six through eighteen. Call (620) 624–7624 for more information.

The Baker Arts Center at 624 North Pershing is known as the "cultural oasis on the prairie" for good reason. It is an art-education facility in a 5,000-square-foot, three-floor building. There are four galleries, a workshop area, and a Discovery Center for children. Visiting the galleries is free; fees are charged for workshops. Gallery hours are Tuesday through Friday from 1:00 to 5:00 P.M., Saturday and Sunday from 2:00 to 4:00 P.M. Call (620) 624–2810, e-mail bakerarts@swko.net, or fax (620) 624–7726.

Cheyenne Bottoms

The **Barbed Wire Museum** in the heart of Post Rock Country displays over 500 varieties of barbed wire. It is located in Grass Park at 201 West First Street, a new complex with three museums in **La Crosse,** on Highway 183. The second museum, the **Rush County Historical Museum,** is housed in an old Santa Fe Railroad Depot and focuses on local history. The third, the **Post Rock Museum,** is in a restored stone house. It was built around 1883 and serves to tell the story of the stone used for fenceposts—there were precious few trees in southwest Kansas—and the tools used to quarry it. All three museums are generally open April through September, but hours vary, so call ahead (785–222–9900 or 785–222–2719).

Highway 183 is a north–south road that rolls with river valleys and is lined with hills. It cuts right through the middle of **Liebenthal.** You can often see many out-of-state license plates in front of the old Liebenthal State Bank building at 401 Main Street. They come for **Pat's Beef Jerky** (785–222– 3341). People stop at Pat's every time they pass through to stock up on jerky, bologna, or summer sausage. Hours are Monday through Friday from 7:30 A.M. to 6:00 P.M. and Saturday from 9:00 A.M. to 5:00 P.M. You can order through their Web site at www.patsbeefjerky.com.

A strange business to be in an old bank building? Well, the structure was empty for years. It was closed during the Depression. But the building remained because on one corner of it is a small marker saying that right there is an exact point on maps, a benchmark for the U.S. Coast and Geodetic Survey. Anyone who moves that circular piece of brass is in trouble with the Feds.

Trivia

In Great Bend you can see the Kansas Quilt Walk, a site that has seven historic quilt patterns built into the sidewalks around the courthouse square. Rocky Road to Kansas, Kansas Dugout, Windmill, and the other patterns are described in a self-guided walking-tour brochure available from the local visitors bureau.

Trivia

Just east of Great Bend, along the Arkansas River from Raymond to Sterling, is a 20-mile canoe route that takes from eight to twelve hours to run. If you prefer a shorter trip, Section 2, from Sterling to Hutchinson, is 15 miles long and takes five to six hours.

Pat got into the business by accident. He was messing around with jerky, trying to invent new marinades and seasonings, and he started giving it away. His friends loved the stuff, and before he knew it, he was in business. Now Pat's turns out 22,000 pounds of jerky a year, as well as bologna and sausage. Hours are from 8:00 A.M. to 6:00 P.M. Monday through Friday and from 9:00 A.M. to 5:00 P.M. Saturday.

Great Bend, at Highways 56 and 281, derives its name from the sweeping curve made here by the Arkansas River as it loops through southwest Kansas. The town was settled in 1871, two years after the abandonment of old Fort Zarah, and the railroad reached it in 1872 on its way west. The Southern Hotel was the first building in Great Bend, and the town soon became the railhead on the Chisholm Trail. For a time, its boisterous saloons and dance halls made it a hot spot among cowboys and railroad freighters.

Lizzie's Cottage at 1315 Stone (2 blocks east of downtown) is a Victorian house that has been restored by owners Phyll and Ed Klima. Fine dining is the specialty here, but there is a two-bedroom suite upstairs (and three more rooms in an Arts and Crafts–style home nearby) where overnight stays can be arranged. The cottage also has an art gallery that includes works by Kansas artists. Rooms are $60 to $125.

The restaurant offers several different dinner menus, which include some very tempting desserts that come with the meal. The first person to make a reservation gets to choose the menu for that day or evening. Four or more courses are served by waitstaff in period costume. Lunch and dinner are served Thursday, Friday, and Saturday, by reservation, or by special arrangement for groups of ten or more. Call (620) 792–6000.

Dale and Doris J. Nitzel bought a comfortable, sprawling, old two-story farmhouse on ten acres here. It had been expanded by the previous owners, and, although it appears small when you drive up from the north, it rambles on and on to the south.

"We wondered what we were going to do with all that space when the rest of the family moved out," Doris said. They decided to try a bed-and-breakfast. The result, ***Peaceful Acres Bed and Breakfast,*** is located 5 miles from Great Bend. This sprawling farmhouse has two kitchens, one on the east side and one on the west. A low rock wall surrounds the house, and a working windmill waters the garden.

The bedrooms are on the main floor, and guests share a bathroom. Kitchen privileges are available for extended vacations, and kids can enjoy the guineas and chickens.

Everything Doris serves is homegrown. The eggs are fresh, the sausage is home cured, and she even grinds wheat for her homemade breads. Thirty-five dollars a night for two people includes a full country breakfast. One bedroom is air-conditioned, and there are plenty of trees and an attic fan to keep the rest of the house cool on summer nights. Peaceful Acres is easy to find: Call (620) 793–7527, and Doris will give you directions when reservations are made.

The *Medicine Bear Trading Company* at 1704 Highway 96 is the place to find Native American collectibles, gifts, and jewelry. There are Hopi kachinas, storytellers, rugs and baskets, flutes and drums. It also stocks medicinal herbs and spices as well as herbal gift baskets. There is a consultant of natural herbs on staff, too, to help you make your choices. Hours are 10:00 A.M. to 5:30 P.M. Monday through Saturday. You can e-mail medicinebear4@hotmail.com or call (620) 792–3256.

The *Kitchen Connection, Inc.* at 1411 Main Street is a kitchen/gourmet shop that carries everything you might ever need in your kitchen—cookware, china, and gadgets. There is also a great selection of gourmet coffees, teas, and foods. They will make specialty baskets for any occasion. The perfect gift for those folks you are about to visit. But this is the best part: You can have a piece of homemade pie or a biscotti in the coffee corner and lunch is served from 11:30 A.M. to 1:30 P.M., when you can choose among soups, quiche, and sandwiches. Hours are 10:00 A.M. to 6:00 P.M. Monday through Friday, and to 5:30 P.M. on Saturday and 8:00 P.M. on Thursdays. Call (620) 793–9339.

The *Barton County Historical Museum and Village* (620–793–5125) lets you walk into the past. A five-acre outdoor village includes a pioneer home, church, schoolhouse, post office, and railroad depot from the late 1800s and early 1900s, and a wood-vane windmill. Inside, see Native American artifacts, farm implements, and exhibits spanning history from the Paleozoic period, the Santa Fe Trail, and World War II. During the war, Great Bend was a training base for the B–29 Superfortress bomber, with its top-secret Norden bombsight (its crosshairs were made of spider webs). The village is located south of Great Bend on Highway 281 just south of the Arkansas River bridge. The museum is open from 1:00 to 4:00 P.M. Tuesday through Sunday, mid-April through mid-November. There is no admission charge, but donations are welcome.

Just west of Great Bend, near Tenth Street and Patton Road, at 5944 West Tenth Street, is the **Kansas Oil and Gas Hall of Fame and Museum.** Exhibits on geology, drilling and refining oil, and a Hall of Fame of industry leaders are housed in the main building. Tours are by appointment; call (620) 792–2750.

The **Shafer Art Gallery** at Great Bend's Barton County Community College displays the bronze western sculptures of internationally known Kansas artist Gus Shafer and other artworks. Call (620) 792–9242 for hours and other information.

Seven miles northeast of Great Bend on Highway 156 or 2 miles east of Highway 281 is an immense, 19,000-acre wildlife area, the **Cheyenne Bottoms Wildlife Management Area.** Cheyenne Bottoms is the largest inland marsh in the United States. Hundreds of thousands of migrating waterfowl can be seen here each March and October. It also provides a safe roost for bald eagles in winter. As many as 300 species, or three-fourths of all the birds sighted in the state, visit the Bottoms, and it has been designated as critical habitat for the endangered whooping crane. Hunting of nonprotected birds is permitted in season. Call (785) 233–4400 for more information.

In nearby **Ellinwood** on Highway 56, you can spend the night in **Grandma's House** at 113 West "C" Street. Built in 1878, this was the first brick house in town. The brick turned out to be soft, though, and the original owners had to have the house covered in cement in 1890. More rooms have been added, but the original metal ceilings, walnut stairway, and light fixtures, as well as the unique design of the exterior, have been preserved.

Barbara Jordan and her late husband, Keith, provided a home for more than 150 foster children over the years, so children and pets are always welcome. Everyone is welcome to use the pool table and fireplace in the family room. You can relax at Grandma's House because the antiques are sturdy and accustomed to living with children and animals—there are two small dogs and a couple of cats in residence, too. This is a warm and friendly home. The price is $35 (or a family of four can have the large room, with a queen-size bed and extra-long bunk beds, television, and wildlife decor, for $50). Call (620) 564–3278 for reservations.

There are several antiques shops in this friendly town, so walk along the brick streets and

> ### Trivia
>
> *American white pelicans are among the thousands of migrating birds that stop at Quivira or nearby Cheyenne Bottoms in the spring and fall. The endangered whooping crane has been seen here, too.*

Trivia

In 1946 Earl Kelly of Stafford bought a rooster he called "Just Bill" for $100. "Just Bill" became famous when he won a contest the next year to become the crowing rooster for Warner-Pathé Newsreels. He beat out several thousand other roosters because he could crow on cue—with the urging of Kelly, waving his arms.

explore them. *Try **James Elliott Antiques*** at 1 North Main (620–564–2400), ***Our Mother's Treasures*** at 14 North Main (620–564–2218), ***Starr Antiques*** at 104 East Santa Fe (620–564–2400), and ***The Showcase*** at 23 North Main (620–564–3224).

The town of **Susank** is north of Great Bend. (How do you pronounce it? Just remember "If Sue sank, who would save her? Ellinwood [the town you just left].") It's an old, old joke around here. Susank is one of those towns that suddenly appeared when the Santa Fe Railroad came through in 1917. It was a boomtown with lumberyards, implement dealers, a newspaper, and barber, who supposedly was a bootlegger. The town's sudden appearance and prosperity was all because of the liquid gold called "oil." No one farmed here; people were too busy supplying the steady demand for that commodity, even during the Depression. But now, Susank has a mere fifty inhabitants, and it has something else. *The Susank Café,* at 201 Main Street, has been serving food since the 1950s, albeit under various names with various owners. But like most small-town cafes, it is the gathering place for the people who live around here. Dennis Trapp, mayor of Susank, has been mayor since, "well, when did Dad retire?" he asks his wife. His father had been the mayor for twenty-five years, then Dennis was elected and has been mayor for about, "oh, ten or fifteen years." Someone else was mayor there for a while after his dad retired, but it has mostly been a family thing. And the cafe is where political decisions are made since there really is no City Hall to speak of, and the food is good, besides. Owner Mike Hickel opens the place at 11:00 A.M. for lunch and serves until 9:00 P.M. Monday through Thursday and stays open until 10:00 P.M. on Friday and Saturday nights. The building itself is interesting. It is the old school building. Well, the front of it is the old school building, the back is actually the railroad foreman's old house from when the railroad was big here. (During its heyday, over 1,000 people got their mail at this post office.) The two buildings were sort of bridged together. Well, you have to see it. Call (620) 653–2660.

The Old Township Hall in **Alden,** west of Highway 14/96 southeast of Great Bend, was built in 1905, and the Santa Fe Depot was constructed in 1884. This place has history going for it. The ***Prairie Flower Craft Shop***, 205 Pioneer Street (620–534–3551), features wicker creations of every description, quilting supplies, and works of art by local craftspeople. Sara Fair Sleeper is the owner. Hours are from 10:00 A.M. to 4:30 P.M.

Monday through Saturday. Sometimes the shop is closed at the noon hour while Sara goes to lunch.

Three miles south and west of Alden you'll find the Arkansas River again. It is a beautiful waterway here, lined with stately cottonwoods and drooping willows. Drop a line, hike on the nature trails, or canoe on this historic stream, and look sharp—wildlife abounds. Beaver join green and great blue herons along the slow-moving river. Bald eagles survey the icy waters in winter as the river slides slowly past long sandbars.

Perhaps you don't think of conquistadores when you think of Kansas, but you should in **Lyons,** on Highway 56. At 105 West Lyon, the **Coronado–Quivira Museum** (620–257–3941) contains artifacts from Coronado's trip to Kansas. In 1541, more than seventy-five years before the Pilgrims arrived at Plymouth Rock, Francisco Coronado and his expedition arrived in Kansas with just one thing in mind—gold. His party brought a force of 300 Spaniards and 2,500 horses, along with slaughter animals, cannon, and the other necessities of sixteenth-century travel.

His journey took him to the land of the Quivirans, but no gold was found. Coronado's legacy to the Indians was the horses they began using instead of travois pulled by dogs. There were no finer riders than these Plains Indians. The museum is open Monday through Saturday from 9:00 A.M. to 5:00 P.M., Sunday from 1:00 to 5:00 P.M. Admission is $2.00 for adults, $1.00 for children ages six to twelve.

On Highway 50 between Hutchinson and Kinsley is the little town of **Stafford,** the gateway to the Quivira National Wildlife Refuge. Three bed-and-breakfasts here form the hub of a retreat center. **Henderson House Bed and Breakfast,** at 518 West Stafford, is a 1905 two-story with a dozen stained- or beveled-glass windows, original brass light fixtures, and an ornate staircase. The house is on the National Register of Historic Places. It has three rooms, all with private baths. Rooms are $60.

The second of the trio, **Weide House,** is at 302 North Green. It dates from 1904 and offers four two-room suites. The third accommodation is the 1905 **Spickard House,** just down the street at 201 North Green. It has three rooms, all with private baths. Meals for guests at all three bed-and-breakfasts are prepared in the commercial kitchen here and served in two dining rooms that seat up to forty people.

Room rates at all three accommodations are $50, double occupancy, and include breakfast. Meeting or event space is available in a 1913 church at 113 Green, also part of the retreat center. Call innkeeper

Arlene Lickiss at (620) 234–6048 for reservations or information. Visit their Web site at www.hendersonbandb.com.

The **Quivira National Wildlife Refuge** is located 13 miles northeast of Stafford. Public hunting of waterfowl, pheasant, and quail is permitted in season on 8,000 of the refuge's 22,135 acres. The Quivira Refuge is an intact ecosystem. Because of the salinity of the water, the marshes have not been depleted as many freshwater marshes have. It is a gold mine for nature photographers because it provides a habitat for migrating birds on the Central Flyway, and almost one-half of all the shorebirds east of the Rockies stop at Quivira in the spring. The main roads in the refuge allow excellent viewing opportunities from a car, but birders and wildflower enthusiasts prefer the two hiking trails and the service roads. The northern part of the refuge is dominated by the Big Salt Marsh, where thousands of ducks, geese, and sandhill cranes can be seen as they migrate in spring and fall. Prairie dogs, coyote, white-tailed deer, northern bobwhite, and wild turkeys also call Quivira home. The visitors center is open Monday through Friday from 7:30 A.M. to 4:00 P.M. The refuge is open sunrise to sunset. There is no entrance fee. For more information, call (620) 486–2393.

In 1939 the *Saturday Evening Post* turned up the fact that **Kinsley** was exactly halfway between San Francisco and New York City—1,561 miles from either city on Highway 50. Not about to let an accident of geography go unnoticed, the town adopted the nickname "Midway USA." Now local boosters are giving the old moniker a new twist by making Kinsley the home of the new **National Carnival Heritage Center.** During the 1900s, six family-owned carnival companies operated out of Kinsley. What had long been part of the town's heritage is now housed in the **Carnival Museum,** located in a renovated, downtown department store building. Former carnival workers have donated to the project, including

Where's the Stockade?

*O*ne of the most frequent questions asked of National Park Service personnel at Fort Larned concerns the lack of a stockade surrounding the fort.

There never was a stockade here. It wasn't necessary. The Plains Indians didn't attack the fort. They were guerrilla fighters, ambushing small groups of soldiers traveling to and from the fort. Because the prairie in the 1860s was nearly treeless, building a stockade would have required shipping logs from Colorado or Missouri.

some of the canvas backdrops used by burlesque queen Sally Rand, who once appeared in carnival shows. One carousel is already operating there. Artist Bruce White, a nationally recognized master carver of carousel horses, has been commissioned to create a second carousel. Using the framework and mechanical workings of a two-story German-made carousel dating from 1900 that once delighted children in Denmark's Tivoli Park (alas, the animals were all sold to collectors years ago), White is hand-carving replacement horses. Each will be a replica of different historical carved horses of American and European carousel makers.

To complete the carousel, White will include an animal of his own design, a Pegasus, done in his own style. You can see the work in progress. Call the chamber of commerce at (877) 464–3929 for more information.

Little Things, at 720 East Fifth, is the largest miniature shop between Kansas City and Denver. Jane and Thayne Mellick have every kind of miniature you can imagine: dolls, musical instruments, flowers, dollhouses, and everything that goes into them. Most items are handmade and range in price from $50 to $2,700. Jane says she carries less expensive pieces for people just beginning their collections.

Hours are usually from 9:00 A.M. to 5:00 P.M. Monday through Friday and weekends by appointment, but the Mellicks suggest you call (620) 659–2240 to make sure they're in. E-mail carouselminis@midway.net, or visit their Web site at www.midamin.com.

Larned is located at the junction of Highways 56 and 156, midway along the historic Santa Fe Trail. By the 1850s the stream of soldiers, wagon trains, mail coaches, and miners headed for the goldfields of California, and later Colorado, and the mail stations built on their hunting grounds were too much for the Native Americans to tolerate. Established as a military post in 1859 to protect travelers on the trail, Fort Larned served as a base for operations against the Plains Indians (who saw the wagon trains as trespassers).

Fort Larned National Historic Site has been magnificently restored to its original condition. All but one of the sandstone buildings were constructed after the Civil War ended, when more time could be spent on the "Indian Problem." The fort was constructed in the shape of a quadrangle.

Larned Schoolhouse

Six miles west of Larned on Highway 154, a 100-foot-tall wooden flagstaff still towers over the fort, miles from any interstate highway. The fort attracts more than 40,000 visitors a year, despite the same isolation it endured so long ago.

Neatly arranged around the still-intact original parade ground, nine sandstone buildings dating from 1866 to 1868 and a blockhouse stand guard along the Pawnee River, just as they did more than a century ago. Forty interior rooms are restored and furnished in period style, including crowded troops' quarters, where broad bunk beds in the barracks slept four men, two up and two down. A gloomy blacksmith shop and a nineteenth-century post hospital are startlingly real. The isolation of the fort, the relentless wind, the hot sunshine, and the endless flat plains are also striking. The park shows the stark reality of life on the prairie for those who were daring enough to brave the Santa Fe Trail.

One barracks has become a visitors center, with audiovisual programs, and a museum. The museum has grim photographs, archaic tools, and old uniforms; one case details the role of the "Buffalo Soldiers"—the black men of the Tenth Calvary stationed at Fort Larned.

Park rangers and volunteers give tours and do living-history programs. Admission is $2.00, with a maximum of $4.00 per family. It is open from 8:30 A.M. to 5:00 P.M. daily except Thanksgiving, Christmas, and New Year's

Day. Call (620) 285–6922, or check the Web site at www.nps.gov/fols.

The **Santa Fe Trail Center,** 2 miles west of Larned on Highway 156, exhibits the lifestyles of the early Kansas settlers. This fine regional museum has archival and research facilities. A replica sod house and dugout—a practical solution to Kansas's extremes of heat and cold—are on the grounds. The museum focuses on the history of commerce and trade along the Santa Fe Trail and civilian life near Fort Riley. The exhibits trace transportation from the covered wagon to the railroad. It is open daily Labor Day through Memorial Day from 9:00 A.M. to 5:00 P.M. The rest of the year the hours are the same, but the museum is closed Monday. Admission is $3.00 for adults, $2.00 for young people ages twelve to eighteen, and $1.00 for children ages six to eleven. For tour information, call (620) 285–2054.

The **Central States Scout Museum** at 815 Broadway has one of the best collections of worldwide Boy and Girl Scout memorabilia in the country. Admission is $1.00 for youth, $2.00 for adults. Scout troops and other groups can stay overnight at a Boy Scout camp 1 mile out of town that has a dormitory; the charge is $4.00 per person plus a $10.00 utility charge. The museum is open from 9:00 A.M. to 9:00 P.M. most days year-round, but call ahead to be sure (620–285–8938).

Outside Larned is a unique spot that is really off the beaten path. Vicki Dipman has built a barnlike, two-story structure and filled it with antique English and American furniture, lamps, and art glass. Daughter and son-in-law Sandi and Jeff Bates have joined this growing business, which also includes kitchen remodeling, interior design, and custom-made lamp shades and rugs. **Memories Restored** is worth searching out: Go 1.25 miles west of the historic site on Highway 156, then 3.25 miles north. Hours are from 10:00 A.M. to 5:00 P.M. Tuesday through Saturday. Call (620) 285–3478, e-mail memories@larned.net, or visit www.memoriesrestored.com.

The Fiddlers Three is a pair (there *used* to be three) of talented Larned artists with a studio at 606 Topeka Street. What began as "just fiddling around" making Santas for friends blossomed into a popular business. Nancy and John Adams use no patterns, and no figure is exactly like another. Their special Santas can be made with your own remnants of Grandmother's wedding gown or fur coat, or bits of antique toys, or even Grandpa's old pocket watch. They can also personalize a Santa to reflect the interests of the individual for whom it's intended—Santa dressed in University of Kansas colors, wearing a tartan and playing bagpipes, or playing golf. Prices start at $200. Their work is on display in a shop window next door (they're looking for bigger quarters). Hours at the studio are seasonal; call ahead (620–285–2053) or e-mail santa@kaws.com.

Rose Manor at 707 State Street belongs to Yvonne Rose Wittig and is both a bed-and-breakfast and a restaurant. This 8,100-square-foot home is a small mansion. The renovation of this 1904 Georgian home exposed a lovely old spindle staircase. Fine dining is available. Meals are served in a lavishly decorated dining room complete with a crystal chandelier. Afternoon teas are available, and tours are free. During the holiday season, Wittig decorates more than thirty Christmas trees throughout the home. Call for a calendar of events. The 1,150-square-foot honeymoon suite has a gold-leaf fireplace, maple floors, and antique furniture. The bath has heated towel racks and marble floors with a sunken, whirlpool tub. Two other rooms with private baths also are available. Rates range from $95 to $195, including a four-course breakfast. Call (620) 285–6292 for information or reservations.

Heartland Farm in Rush County is eighty acres of homestead, organic gardens, and cropland owned and operated by the Dominican Sisters. It is a ministry of healing and simple living and is open to people as a retreat. Stay in a rustic one-room cottage and try your hand at organic gardening or explore holistic health, conservation, and alternative energy sources, including solar power.

Meals created with natural whole foods are not strictly vegetarian but emphasize a naturally healthy diet. Therapeutic massage is available for $35 per hour. Suggested offering is $15 a day for lodging and $10 for a full day of meals. For information, write to Heartland Farm, Route 1, Box 37, Pawnee Rock 67567, call (620) 923–4585, or e-mail hfarm@gbta.net. No one is excluded from sharing the experience of Heartland Farm because of financial stress. Bartering of contributed services and extended time payment may be prearranged.

Amish Country

*H*utchinson lies on the north bank of the Arkansas River. Built in a level valley, the town boasts long, straight streets. The discovery of salt led to almost a dozen salt plants by 1888. In fact, the Morton Salt Stabilized Highway was built accidentally between the Morton plant and Main Street as salt spilled from trucks onto the soft road. It soon became a satisfactory road for heavy trucks.

A shallow inland sea once covered the land here 300 million years ago, slowly receding, drying, and concentrating its salt near Hutchinson; the area has the world's largest salt deposit—100 miles by 40 miles, 325 feet thick, mined from underground passages. It yields 44.1 million tons of salt each year; that'll salt a lot of homegrown tomatoes!

If you're a golfer, then Hutchinson has something special for you. The **Prairie Dunes Golf Club,** 4812 East Thirtieth Avenue, is one of the top fifteen courses in the country. It was designed by Perry and Press Maxwell. The course is designed like a Scottish links course and offers "a touch of Scotland" in Kansas and also what is reputed to be the world's most difficult hole—number 8, a long par 4 that is 422 yards of rolling hills.

Prairie Dunes is a private club but has reciprocal privileges: If you belong to another private USGA facility, you are welcome here, but you must call ahead for a tee time. There is a fine restaurant here with a very large selection of unusual dishes. Call (620) 662–0581, or visit the Web site at www.prairiedunes.com.

The **Kansas Cosmosphere and Space Center,** at 1100 North Plum, is affiliated with the Smithsonian Institution in Washington, D.C. The Cosmosphere's Hall of Space Museum houses the largest collection of space artifacts outside the National Air and Space Museum. It also can boast of the largest collection of space suits in the world and the most complete collection of Russian space artifacts outside Moscow.

The Hall of Space traces the Space Race from Sputnik to the space shuttle. On display are rare 1930s German V–1 and V–2 rockets, artifacts from the Gemini and Mercury programs, the actual Apollo 13 command module *Odyssey,* a 30-ton SR 71 Blackbird spy plane more than 107 feet long (it could fly over Kansas east to west in ten minutes), a Northrop

Those "Amber Waves of Grain" Explained

*B*esides wheat, the important crops of central and western Kansas are alfalfa, sorghum, barley, and broomcorn. Sorghum is a tall, grasslike plant that looks somewhat like corn. The grain, leaves, and stalks are used as cattle feed. The juice of one kind of sorghum is used for making molasses. Broomcorn is related to sorghum. Brooms and brushes are made from the stiff branches of the plant. Broomcorn is grown in the irrigated areas of southwestern Kansas.

T–38 (the aircraft used to train shuttle astronauts), and a full-scale replica of the space shuttle *Endeavor*. The *Liberty Bell 7*, the Mercury spacecraft that sank after splashing down in 1961, was recovered in 1999 and restored at the Cosmosphere. After a national tour, the capsule is now on permanent display here.

Also at the Cosmosphere are the Carey IMAX Theatre, with a 44-foot tilted dome screen, and the Justice Planetarium, where a star projector produced simulated views of the night sky and laser light shows. The Cosmosphere is open Monday through Saturday from 9:00 A.M. to 9:00 P.M., Sunday noon to 9:00 P.M. The Hall of Space Museum has an admission charge. IMAX and planetarium shows are additional; reservations are recommended. Call (620) 662–2305 or (800) 397–0330. Visit the Web site at www.cosmo.org.

Ready to come back to Earth? The **Hutchinson Art Center** at 405 North Washington displays the work of some local artists and many touring exhibits that change every month. The gallery is open Tuesday through Friday from 9:00 A.M. to 5:00 P.M., Saturday and Sunday from 2:00 to 4:00 P.M. Call (620) 663–1081.

If you're looking for a B&B in Hutchinson, Lola and Ray Ediger's **Wrought Iron Inn** at 1500 North Main Street is an elegant three-story Victorian built in 1909. The name comes from the wrought-iron fence surrounding the property, complete with austere lions guarding the front steps. There's a swing on the wraparound porch and a good breakfast to lure you out of bed in the morning. The five rooms all have private baths. Call (620) 664–5975 for reservations.

There is a most interesting shop downtown at 22 Main Street. **Ten Thousand Villages** offers handicrafts from Third World countries around the globe. There is a large selection of what they refer to as "fairly traded handicrafts" for you to peruse. Hours are Monday through Saturday from 9:30 A.M. to 5:00 P.M. Call (620) 669–8932.

The downtown area has a good-size antiques district featuring high-quality antiques and collectibles. Walk down South Main Street. Twenty South Main Street is **Yesterday's Treasures** (620–662–4439), 24 South Main is **Heartstrings Craft & Antiques Mall** (620–669–9997). The home of **Armstrong Antiques** (620–664–5811) is 121 South Main, 123 South Main is **Memory Lane Antiques** (620–662–1883), and 129 South Main houses the **Old Town Antiques Mall** (620–663–2014) and **Down Home Antiques** (620–665–6670). Browsing **Stratton Antiques** at 201 South

Main (620–727–4574), *P. Lee's Antiques & Memories* at 213 South Main (620–665–5033), *Necessities of the Past, Present, and Future* at 622 South Main (620–664–9406), and *Brokers Antiques* at 820 South Main (620–665–7040) will give you a good walk; then get off of South Main Street and wander down West Avenue B to *Bishop's Interiors* at 22 West Avenue B (620–921–0409) or along East Sherman to 11 East Sherman to the *Dancing Grouse* (620–669–5115). Wow, that was your workout for the day. Worn out yet? Sylvan Park is nearby for a quiet resting spot. You have earned a good meal, too, with all those walking points. Wherever your feet give out along South Main Street, you will find some good eating places. *Tiffany House* at 20 South Main (620–662–4439), *Anchor Inn Mexican Restaurant* at 128 South Main (620–669–0311), where you can enjoy an authentic Mexican buffet on Friday and Saturday, or *Brenda's Café* at 304 South Main (620–663–1579) will be waiting to cool you down or warm you up, depending on the season.

While you're in Hutchinson, visit the *Dillon Nature Center* at 3002 East Thirtieth Avenue. The Discovery Center includes an observation beehive and large aquariums teeming with native fish. Surrounding the center are terraced beds of perennials and some 1,500 annual flowers, planted each spring by dedicated volunteers. There is an abundance of wildlife in the tallgrass prairie area, woodlands, and marsh. You can picnic or canoe, and hikers are welcome on the trail system, which is a National Recreational Trail. Red fox, raccoons, coyotes, deer, and more than 180 species of birds have been seen here. Hours at the Discovery Center vary with the season, so call ahead. The park is open from 8:00 A.M. to sunset weekdays, 10:00 A.M. to sunset Saturday, and 1:00 P.M. to dusk Sunday. There is no

Pretty Prairie's Big Rodeo

*T*he state's largest night rodeo is held in Pretty Prairie in July. It is a world-class rodeo, and it offers visitors a picture of small-town America at its best. The twang of country music fills the air, and everywhere are people clad in blue jeans, boots, and sequined blouses. Even the parking lot is interesting. You'll see every model of pickup truck ever made. The rodeo offers $50,000 in prize money, so it attracts the top 250 cowboys on the circuit. Some eschew the pickups, however, and arrive in private planes. So put on your biggest belt buckle and get close enough to touch the clowns and animal stock. Pretty Prairie is off Highways 17 and 54. There are special rodeo signs for you to follow. For more information, call (316) 459–4653 or (800) 638–2702.

admission charge. For more information, call (620) 663–7411.

Five miles west of Hutchinson is the ***Mennonite Dutch Kitchen Restaurant*** (620–662–2554), 6803 West Highway 61. If you're partial to pies or bonkers over bread, this is the place. They bake them fresh each day, and also sweet, spicy cinnamon rolls. Hours are 6:00 A.M. to 8:00 P.M. Monday through Saturday.

Also west of Hutchinson on Highway 96 at **Nickerson** is the most unusual animal farm/bed-and-breakfast combo you'll ever find in the state. Joe and Sondra Hedrick are hosts at the ***Hedrick Exotic Animal Farm*** and the ***Hedrick Bed and Breakfast***, at 7910 North Roy L. Smith Road. A family hobby of raising exotic animals soon became a petting zoo. Now you can watch a small herd of zebras, see a huge white camel move with dignity among the other dozen or more camels, try to count a band of fast-moving kangaroos and wallabies, Sicilian donkeys, giraffes, several llamas, a number of ostriches, and probably a partridge in a pear tree, if you look long enough. A stay at the bed-and-breakfast includes a hands-on tour, as well as petting and feeding the giraffes and zebras. Kenya, one of the farm's half-dozen giraffes, witnessed a marriage proposal here and was invited to a Colorado couple's wedding. (She was unable to attend.) The bed-and-breakfast has seven rooms behind the building's facade, which gives the appearance of a frontier bank, general store, hotel, and saloon, with animal-influenced decor and private baths. Color television and home-cooked, farm-style breakfasts are part of the package. Rooms are $59 to $120 Friday and Saturday. Call (620) 422–3245 or (888) 489–8039 for reservations.

Northeast of Hutchinson, you enter lovely, alien lands: the Flint Hills. Here the deep, silty deposits eroded away, leaving the bony outcroppings of flint or chert that girdle the landscape. Lonely prairies remain virtually unchanged here from presettlement days; the stony land didn't lend itself easily to agriculture. These rolling prairie uplands flow in auburn hues.

You can see forever from the tops of some of these hills, perhaps 100 miles in any direction on a clear day; you begin to understand how alone the first settlers must have felt.

Yoder, a small town southeast of Hutchinson on Highway 96, lets you step into the gentle world of the Amish community. A general store, a bakery, and a gift shop here in the quiet Kansas countryside make you feel as if you've tumbled backward into the last century. You'll find a blacksmith, a harness maker, and a buggy shop among the businesses in Yoder.

Most do not have telephones and there are not too many addresses on the buildings, but once you are in town, just wander around and find what you find. Watch for the *Kansas Station* at Highway 96 and Yoder Road, where George and Lori Montgomery invite you to take a ride around town in an Amish buggy on select Saturdays. There's a buggy inside that you can inspect, too, or you can shop among the goodies—chocolates, wheat straw creations, and gifts—or sit down and enjoy a snack from the deli counter. Phone (620) 465–9800 or (800) 269–6055, or e-mail llm@south wind.net. Open Monday through Saturday 10:00 A.M. to 8:00 P.M.

Yoder Meats is also with the Kansas Station. Joyce and John Yoder sell hormone-free, fresh-from-the-farm chicken and corn-fed beef. Stock up on sausage, as well as Amish cheeses and beef jerky. Buffalo, elk, and other exotic meats are available, along with lamb, pork, and the best, the very best, hickory-smoked ham and bacon around. Call (800) 952–6328 to order.

The Dutch Mill Bakery is the home of cinnamon rolls like you wish your Grandma made, along with cakes, cookies, pies, and breads—all without preservatives. The *Bontrager Harness Shop* at 5913 East Greenfield Road and the *Bontrager Blacksmith Shop* are fascinating to see in this age of computerized automobiles. *Yoder Wood Products* at 10409 South Yoder Road will also give you a look at quality handcrafted furniture, from china cabinets to gazebos. The showroom takes you back to an era when craftsmen used time as well as tools to fashion heirloom furniture. *Country Traditions* at 9815 South Main Street has a fine collection of Amish quilts, Howard Miller grandfather and wall clocks that will stay in your family for generations, collectibles, and gifts. There is a large Thomas Kinkade gallery filled with the "painter of light" prints and gifts. The shop is open Monday through Saturday 10:00 A.M. to 8:00 P.M.

There has been a hardware and lumber store on the corner of Main Street and Lawrence Avenue in Yoder since the late 1890s. *Yoder Hardware and Lumber,* 9816 South Main Street, is truly an old-time hardware store with horseshoes, hand tools, crocks, butter churns, hand meat grinders, and sausage stuffers. Rod and Peggy Fry sell nails in bulk, weighing each purchase on an old metal scale. The shop carries a full line of Radio Flyer metal wagons, tricycles, bicycles, and toys, as well as their line of miniatures and collectibles. One of the specialties of the store is an oil-lamp

Gypsum Hills Scenic Drive

*T*o enjoy a beautiful 29-mile drive to nowhere, travel west of Medicine Lodge on Highway 160 for a little more than 3 miles. There a scenic-drive sign will point you south. About a mile down the road, you will round a curve and begin to see the beauty of the Gypsum Hills. About 2.5 miles south, just before you reach the crest of the hills, it is worth a long look to the east down one of the most beautiful valleys. Six miles south of Highway 160, you will turn west onto a dirt road. Just after the turn look to the north, and you will see the back side of Twin Peaks. Look to the northwest and you will see Flowerpot Mound. About 11.5 miles down the dirt road, turn left, or north, at a Y-shaped intersection, and 5 miles later, you will be back at Highway 160. A turn to the right, or east, will take you back to Medicine Lodge. Within 4 miles you will be at a scenic overlook, which will give you an opportunity to see the valley and hills to the south.

A mile to the east (mile marker 217), a cross sits atop a hill, and for the next mile Twin Peaks will clearly be in view to the south. (Another paved pull-off is on the south side near mile marker 219.) Continue on to cross Cedar Creek and return to Medicine Lodge. Call (620) 886–9815 for information, or get a map at the Stockade Museum.

selection, with oil lamps and lanterns in many sizes, price ranges, and descriptions, as well as parts to fix up your old lamps and lanterns. Take a look at their Web site, www.yoderkansas.com/yoder_hardware.htm.

John and Sharon Covert own the **Yoder Market & Deli.** They carry a full line of groceries and bulk foods; this is a good place to stock up on fresh spices. There is a daily lunch special with homemade pies and cakes. You can buy straw hats (black & natural) for adults and children. Amish black felt hats are also available. They carry the *Yoder Cook Book,* containing more than 450 recipes, and will ship any product to anyone in the country. Phone (620) 465–3645 or e-mail yodermarket@yoderkansas.com.

Will wonders never cease? The town, for all its shortage of telephones, automobiles, and modern gewgaws does indeed have a Web site at www.yoderkansas.com.

Carriage Crossing Restaurant at 10002 South Yoder Road (620–465–3612) has really good cooking and is open for breakfast, lunch, and supper. There are specials every day and fresh homemade pies for dessert. Order from a huge menu, or try family-style all-you-want-to-eat dinners. There's even a gift shop inside. Restaurant hours are from 6:00 A.M. to 9:00 P.M. Monday through Saturday. Horse and carriage rides are often offered here on nice Saturday mornings in summer. Most Amish businesses are located on Yoder Road or Red Rock Road, Yoder's main street. Folks at the Carriage Crossing will be glad to give you directions to any place you can't find.

Near the banks of the Chikaskia River you'll find the town of *Argonia.* The *Salter House National Historic Site,* at 220 West Garfield, was the home of Susanna Madora Salter, who was elected the first woman mayor of Argonia (and of the world) in 1887. (Not bad for a presuffragist.) The 1884 house was built from brick fired in a kiln near the site. An adjacent museum in the old Mayfield church holds antiques and artifacts of the area's culture.

Gyp Hills

edicine Lodge lies on a hillside overlooking the Medicine River and its wooded valley. The landscape here is unusual for Kansas. Red bluffs, mesas, and buttes extend from this part of the state into Oklahoma and the Texas Panhandle, and turning south here is like entering another world.

Stormy temperance leader Carry Nation, known for her ax-swinging crusade against demon liquor, lived in Medicine Lodge during her most colorful years. Even though Kansas was, by law, a dry state, Medicine Lodge in the late 1880s had seven saloons. Nation closed the first in

The First Medicine Lodge

he Kiowa tribe made their home in this beautiful area, where vast herds of buffalo, elk, deer, and antelope grazed in the valleys and bear, turkey, and other game birds inhabited the woods. There were swift-running streams, sweet native grasses, and abundant natural shelter in the bluffs and canyons. The Kiowa believed that the Medicine River was endowed with healing properties. Every year they came to a spot where the river joined a creek. They pitched their tepees, bathed in the river, and drank its mineral waters. They also discovered the healing properties of many of the herbs and plants that grew on the banks of the streams. The Kiowa built a great medicine lodge out of slender tree trunks set on end in a circle, their tops bent toward the center and covered with rushes and earth. They heated large stones, placed healing herbs on them, and poured water on the stones to make clouds of aromatic steam.

Carry Nation's Home

1899 by singing in front of it, the second by praying in front of the door. Before the end of the year, all the saloons in town closed.

Nation traveled to other Kansas towns, using stones and a cane to wreak havoc on saloons there. In 1901 she descended on Wichita, and it was there that she first used her famous hatchet to attack a saloon. In the months following, she was arrested and jailed many times and paid her fines by selling souvenir hatchets.

Carry Nation's Home, now a National Historic Landmark, is a small house at 211 West Fowler in Medicine Lodge. It is furnished with many of her personal belongings and is open daily from 10:30 A.M. to 5:00 P.M. Call (316) 886–3553 for information.

Every three years, in the fall, Medicine Lodge is the scene of the *Peace Treaty Pageant,* a huge spectacle dating from 1927, when citizens looked for a way to commemorate the Medicine Lodge Peace Treaty, signed at the confluence of Elm Creek and the Medicine River in 1867. The treaty allowed settlers to move onto the lands of the Apache, Comanche, Cheyenne, Kiowa, and Arapaho in Kansas, and

Trivia

Sharon, 10 miles east of Medicine Lodge on Highway 160, is the hometown of country singer Martina McBride.

moved the Indians to Oklahoma. It takes more than 500 American Indian and military reenactors to re-create the scenes surrounding the treaty. An intertribal powwow and a rodeo take place the same weekend. Call (316) 886–9815 for information.

Stop at the Medicine Lodge High School on El Dorado Avenue to see the *Equatorial Sun Dial.* This monster of a clock is made of Colorado granite and weighs one ton. It was engineered for this exact location to help students understand the movements of our solar system.

Gypsum Hills Trail Rides takes horseback and horse-drawn-wagon riders out on the trails through the area's spectacular scenery. The red gypsum bluffs overlook canyons richly carpeted with wildflowers. Downy phlox, ragwort, and native cedars tint the canyons. This is one of the country's most colorful sights: stark red bluffs and buttes flecked with white gypsum and capped with deep green cedar trees.

The trail day ends around a campfire, where steaks sizzle to savory perfection, seasoned with the kind of hunger you work up only outdoors. Riders sing cowboy songs, and in the distance you can hear coyotes howl. The trail rides begin at the Gant–Larson Ranch about 9 miles west of Medicine Lodge on Highway 160. This is strictly a BYOH affair—you must have your own horse to ride; if you don't have a horse, you can ride in one of the horse-drawn wagons. Either way, if you want to see the incredible color of the "Gyp Hills," there is no better way to do it. The combination of cedar trees and the unusual formations of the hills is what the Wild West movies were made of.

Bob and Charlene Larson own the ranch and provide campsites and food; everything else is up to you. Riders bring their own equipment. This is no dude ranch; it is a real working outfit, smack in the middle of some of the most beautiful scenery in the state. Saddle clubs, as well as smaller groups, are welcome. Call the Larsons to make arrangements at (620) 886–5390.

Kasey Kuhn (620–886–5293) organizes trail rides on the Larson ranch during the first three weekends in May. Make your plans well in advance; there is a 250-rider limit, and they fill up early. Riders come in on Friday night, and the ride begins at 11:00 A.M. Saturday morning. Sunday morning breakfast and dinner at noon are also provided for $65 (adults) or $50 (children ages six through twelve). Kasey is a wealth of information about the area and the history of Medicine Lodge.

The **Sagebrush Gallery of Western Art** (620–886–5163), at 115 East Kansas Street, is also owned by the Kuhn family. Here Earl Kuhn exhibits western paintings and sculptures Monday through Saturday from 8:30 A.M. to 5:30 P.M.

Folks around **Zenda** enjoy the seafood buffet the third Saturday of every month at **The Lumber Yard,** 311 North Main Street. Yes, it is actually in a lumber yard in this old town, but there's a full menu of steaks, ribs, and chicken, and people travel out of their way to get there. There are the occasional nights when something special is featured. Open Thursday from 5:00 to 9:00 P.M. and Friday and Saturday nights until 11:00 P.M. Phone (620) 243–6000.

Anthony is southeast of Medicine Lodge at the junction of Highways 2, 44, and 179. If you're here in July, you're in luck because Kansas's oldest race meet is held here at **Anthony Downs** with two weekends of pari-mutuel horse and greyhound races.

Begun in 1904, the meet has grown large enough to attract 5,000 people. An equally enthusiastic crowd comes for the **Sunflower Balloon Fest** on Mother's Day weekend each May. Weather permitting, you can watch a mass launching of twenty-five hot-air balloons Saturday morning and evening and Sunday morning. Call the chamber of commerce for more information at (620) 842–5456.

It seems every town has its favorite eating place, and here in Anthony it's the **Smokehouse Cafe** at 110 West Main. The menu has such diverse dishes as stuffed pizza, Tex-Mex foods, and soup in a bread bowl. The noon buffet features a salad bar and pizzas (great buffet idea!). Hours are Monday through Thursday from 9:00 A.M. to 9:00 P.M., Friday and Saturday from 9:00 A.M. to 10:00 P.M. Call (620) 842–3282.

South of Medicine Lodge on Highway 281 in the town of **Hardtner** is Bob and Sue Sterling's restaurant, **Yur Place.** The food here is typically Kansas with a lunch special every day: Tuesday is Mexican, Wednesday, chicken-fried steak, and Thursday, fried chicken. Yur Place opens for breakfast at 5:00 A.M. (yes, sir, you read that right) and stays open until 2:00 P.M. On Sunday, there is a lunch buffet from 11:00 A.M. to 2:00 P.M. Call (620) 296–4477.

North of Medicine Lodge on Highway 281, in the town of **Pratt,** a covered wagon stands ready to take you back on an imaginary trip to the

1880s at the **Pratt County Historical Museum**, 208 South Ninnescah (Ninnescah and Second Streets, 1 block off either Highway 54 or Highway 281). The covered wagon on display tempts children to climb aboard and feel the sodbuster plow settlers carried west.

Several galleries and an Old Time Main Street show visitors the ingenuity settlers used to survive. Gallery One traces history up to the late 1800s. Gallery Two re-creates a sodbuster's home, right down to the rug beater and cream separator, and a one-room school with McGuffey Readers, slate boards, and desks with inkwells. Gallery Three houses old-time farm implements, while Gallery Four salutes agriculture, the railroad, and the oil industry. Completing the museum's collections is an early Main Street with a drugstore, a tonsorial shop, a photography studio, a bank, a livery stable, a telephone office, and a hotel. A harness maker's horse is hitched to a buggy and stands ready for an imaginary ride. Upstairs is a wedding chapel, still used on occasion.

For genealogy and history buffs, there is a research library with land patents, marriage licenses, census and cemetery records, and newspapers, open by appointment.

The museum is open every afternoon from 2:00 to 4:00 P.M. Admission is free, but donations are accepted. Call (620) 672–7874 for information or special tours.

Pratt Guest House at 105 North Iuka Street is listed on the National Register of Historic Places. Experience the luxury accommodations of another time. Climb the elegant oak staircase and admire the leaded glass and quartersawn oak cabinetry. The hearty morning meal is satis-

---

"Cannonball" Green and Carry Nation

*T*he town of Greensburg was named for D. R. "Cannonball" Green, a stagecoach driver along the route followed by Highway 54 (still Cannonball Highway to locals). His nickname was earned from the speed at which he drove. Cannonball was a colorful guy. Carry Nation rode with him often during her temperance crusade. Once, when she was a passenger, Cannonball lit a huge cigar. Nation reached through the window, snatched it from his mouth, and threw it into the dirt. The story goes that Cannonball stopped the coach, lifted her down, and drove off without a word, leaving her miles from town. Temperance is one thing, but "a good cigar is a smoke."

fying and delicious. Hosts Richard and Diane Ring will pamper you. Rooms range from $50 to $90, and all the rooms and suites have private baths. Call (620) 672–1200 for reservations, or check the Web site at www.prattguesthouse.com.

Charley's Pizza Taco comes highly recommended by the Pratt locals. Try the great folded taco pizza. Charley's is at 105 West First Street and it's open from 10:00 A.M. to 2:00 P.M. and from 4:00 P.M. to 8:00 P.M. (except Wednesday nights) Monday through Saturday. Call (620) 672–3649.

If you're hungry, you might want to head over to ***Coldwater.*** Known around here as "the eating-out town," Coldwater has about ten sit-down restaurants. Eating out is the social pastime of the town, so if you sit down in any one of them, you probably won't be alone long.

One-fourth of a mile southwest of Coldwater on Highway 183 is ***Lake Coldwater,*** a 250-acre lake in a 930-acre park. Coldwater is the only lake in southwestern Kansas that allows water sports. There are facilities for boating, fishing, and camping. A nine-hole golf course is just east of the lake.

The towns of Coldwater, ***Protection,*** and ***Wilmore*** have outdoor artwork created by artist ***Stan Herd,*** a Protection native. You may have seen aerial photos of Herd's incredible "field art": The artist's immense canvas is the earth itself, and his paints are the various soils and vegetation he plants. Somehow he keeps all this beauty straight in his mind from the back of a tractor. He also creates permanent rock mosaics on the ground. Contact the local chambers of commerce for locations, or the artist at (620) 622–4501, or e-mail him at stan@stanherd.com. He also has a Web site, www.stanherd.com.

Hardesty House, at 712 Main in ***Ashland,*** on Highway 160/183 west of Coldwater, is a small, turn-of-the-last-century hotel. The owner is Les Moore, and his daughter Heather manages the restaurant. Specialties include steak, smoked meats, and seafood. Lunch is served from 11:00 A.M. to 2:00 P.M. Monday through Friday and dinner from 5:00 to 8:00 P.M. Tuesday through Thursday and until 10:00 P.M. on Friday and Saturday. Sunday buffet is from 11:30 A.M. to 1:30 P.M. and is by reservation only. It is a private restaurant because the county is dry except for social clubs. But if you're from out of town, you can sign in as a guest at the restaurant and enjoy the facilities.

Six rooms and two apartments are available, all with private baths and all decorated with antiques. Call (620) 635–4040.

The ***Rolling Hills Bed 'n Breakfast*** is in Ashland at 204 East Fourth Avenue (Highway 160). There are three rooms with shared baths, a spa, and an outdoor pool. Rates are $50 to $55, including a full breakfast cooked by hosts Jess and Essie Waits. This is a "down-home," comfortable, country place. Call (620) 635–2859 for reservations.

Travel 15 miles north toward ***Clark State Fishing Lake***, through Church's Canyon and Horseshoe Bend, where rugged terrain provided hiding places for rustlers when those cattle drives came through. There are photo opportunities aplenty here.

The ***World's Largest Hand-Dug Well*** is at 315 South Sycamore, ***Greensburg.*** The "Big Well" was dug here in 1887 and furnished water for the city and railroad until 1932. It measures 32 feet across and 109 feet deep, a marvel of pioneer engineering.

Crews of about a dozen men were hired to dig the well and to quarry and haul stone from the Medicine River, 12 miles away, for the casing of the well. Dirt from the well was hauled away by the same wagons, which had slatted beds. By opening the slats in low spots, roads to the site were "leveled"—these guys were ingenious. You can walk the 105 steps to the bottom; but remember, you'll have to come back up the same way. Summer hours are from 8:00 A.M. to 8:00 P.M. daily. Winter hours are from 9:00 A.M. to 5:00 P.M. Looking at the well from the top is free, but the climb down and up is $1.50 for adults, $1.25 for children ages five to thirteen. Call (316) 723–2261 or (800) 207–7369 for information.

Next to the well, you can see a 1,000-pound pallasite meteorite found east of town years ago. It must have created quite an impact when it struck earth, experts think, about the time of Christ.

West of Greensburg on Highway 54 near the town of ***Mullinville,*** you will see colorful metal artwork on Highway 154 at the west edge of town. Just 3.5 miles south and 1.75 miles west of Mullinville is the site of the historical ***Round Barn.*** It is just an amazing thing to see. It is not just big, it is huge, and it is not actually, technically, round, it is polygonal—having sixteen sides—but of course, you noticed that right away. It was built in 1912 and took a trainload of shingles to roof. Inside are twenty-eight horse stalls and a circular alleyway big enough to allow a grain wagon to be pulled through. A sixteen-sided granary in the center of the first floor is 16 feet across. The dome covers two haymows. It cost $8,000 to build back then. It is being restored by the Kiowa County Historical Society, who received it as a gift in 1993.

PLACES TO STAY IN SOUTHWEST KANSAS

DODGE CITY
Econo Lodge,
1610 West Wyatt Earp
Boulevard,
(620) 225–0231 or
(800) 553–2666

Gunsmoke Campground,
11070 108 Road,
(620) 227–8247 or
(800) 789–8247

GARDEN CITY
Budget Host,
123 Honey Bee Court,
(620) 275–0677

KOA,
4100 East Highway 50,
(620) 276–8741

GREAT BEND
Best Western Angus Inn,
2920 Tenth Street,
(620) 792–3541

Travelers Budget Inn,
4200 Tenth Street,
(620) 793–5448

GREENSBURG
Best Western
J-Hawk Motel,
515 West Kansas Avenue,
(620) 723–2121 or
(800) 528–1234

Kansan Inn,
800 East Highway 54,
(620) 723–2141 or
(800) 523–2141

HUTCHINSON
Anchor Inn,
128 South Main,
(620) 669–0311

Astro Motel,
15 East Fourth,
(620) 663–1151 or
(800) 633–1168

LARNED
The Burgerteria,
417 West Fourteenth Street,
(620) 285–3135

LIBERAL
Best Western LaFonda
Motel,
229 West Pancake
Boulevard,
(620) 624–5601 or
(800) 550–3111

Holiday Inn Express,
1550 North Lincoln,
(620) 624–9700 or
(800) HOLIDAY
(800–465–4989)

Kansan Motel,
310 Pancake Boulevard,
(620) 624–7215

Western Ho Motel,
764 East Pancake
Boulevard,
(620) 624–1921

PRATT
Days Inn,
1901 East First,
(620) 672–9465

SCOTT CITY
Airliner Motel,
609 East Fifth Street,
(620) 872–2125

Chaparral Inn Motel,
102 Main,
(620) 872–2181

96 Motel,
503 East Fifth Street,
(620) 872–5560

ULYSSES
The Peddler's Inn,
1 Mile West–Highway 160,
(620) 356–4021

YODER
The Hitchin' Post RV,
(620) 663–8884,
e-mail: kegli@prodigy.net

PLACES TO EAT IN SOUTHWEST KANSAS

DODGE CITY
Cowtown Club,
503 East Trail,
(620) 227–5225

Silver Spur Supper Club,
1510 West Spruce Street,
(620) 225–9362

GARDEN CITY
Adams Rib,
1135 College Drive,
(620) 275–7427

Kokomo Café,
2414 East Kansas Avenue,
(620) 276–6009

HUTCHINSON
Amarillo Grill,
1401 East Eleventh Street,
(620) 669–6868

Flores Mexican Grill,
1500 East Eleventh Street,
(620) 664–5555

KINSLEY
Mary D's Restaurant,
800 East Highway 50,
(620) 659–3299

LARNED
Country Inn,
135 East Fourteenth Street,
(620) 285–3216

LIBERAL
Gateway Restaurant,
720 East Pancake Drive,
(620) 624–2020

MEDICINE LODGE
Indian Grill,
307 West Fowler,
(620) 886–3791

Raykies Grill & Dairy,
110 West Fowler,
(620) 886–5938

PRATT
Uptown Café & Club D'Est,
202 South Main Street,
(620) 672–3481

SCOTT CITY
Scott City Sports Center,
1213 Main Street,
(620) 872–2338

Selected Chambers of Commerce and Visitors Bureaus

Medicine Lodge Convention and Visitors Bureau,
108 West First, P.O. Box 274, Medicine Lodge 67104;
(620) 886–3417;
www.medicinelodge.com

Dodge City Convention and Visitors Bureau,
400 West Wyatt Earp Boulevard, P.O. Box 1474,
Dodge City 67801; (620) 225–8186 or
(800) OLD–WEST; fax (620) 225–8144;
www.dodgecity.org

Garden City/Finney County Convention and
Visitors Bureau,
1511 East Fulton Terrace, Garden City 67846;
(620) 276–3264 or (800) 879–9803

Hays Convention and Visitors Bureau,
1301 Pine Street; (785) 628–8202 or (800) 569–4505;
www.haysusa.net

Great Bend Convention and Visitors Bureau,
3111 West Tenth Street; (620) 792–2750

Liberal Tourist Information Center,
1 Yellow Brick Road; (620) 626–0170;
e-mail: tourism@swko.net

Larned Chamber of Commerce,
502 Broadway, P.O. Box 240, Larned 67550;
(620) 285–6916 or (800) 747–6919;
www.larned.com

North Central Kansas

Part of the Central Lowlands, the landscape here is made up of rolling hills and valleys. The Flint Hills, south of the Kaw River, are in the area known as the Osage Plains. Limestone, chert, shale, and other rock underlie this area; wind and water have carved it into escarpments—long cliffs or bluffs—formed by rocky ledges that eroded more slowly than looser soils and sediments. Between the escarpments are gently undulating plains.

Although most of Kansas has been cultivated, the Flint Hills remain largely in native grass because much of the ground is too rocky for cultivation. Used by ranchers for pasturing cattle, it is one of the last preserves of the tallgrass prairie of bluestem, Indian grass, and switchgrass. Except around rivers, trees are rare in the Flint Hills, partly because ranchers burn off the hills every spring to eliminate weeds and small trees.

In the mid-1800s, the Oregon Trail provided a route to the Northwest; when gold was discovered in California in 1848, traffic became heavy. Part of the trail followed the Kaw River to Topeka, then continued north into Nebraska. Alcove Springs, between Blue Rapids and Marysville, was a well-known stopping place. Watering holes were at a premium, and stones in the area contain initials and dates carved by those early travelers. Highway 36 follows the old Pony Express Route and Oregon Trail.

Lieutenant Zebulon Pike (of Pike's Peak fame) traced the Osage River west and found Pawnee, Osage, and Kansa Indians growing corn, beans, and pumpkins on land called "incapable of cultivation and uninhabitable by people depending on agriculture for their sustenance." Because it had been seen as worthless, the eastern Indians (Delaware, Shawnee, Wyandot, and Kickapoo) were moved to the "Great American Desert," which has since become the breadbasket of the country.

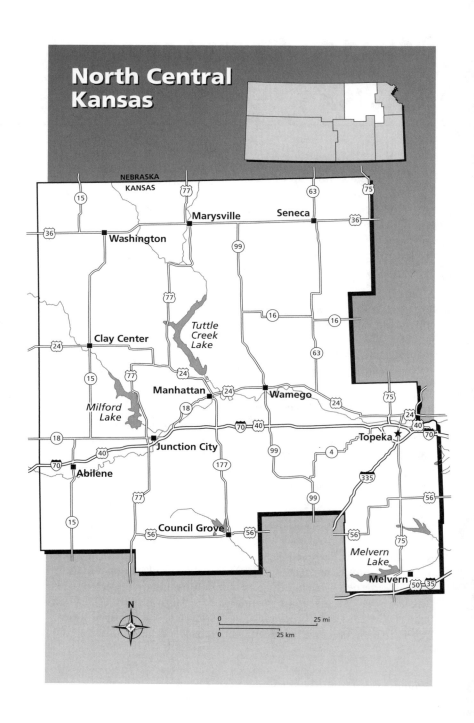

North Central Kansas

Tallgrass Prairie

AUTHOR'S TOP TEN IN
NORTH CENTRAL KANSAS

Eisenhower Center

John Steuart Curry murals at the Capitol

Konza Prairie

The Woodward

Seelye Mansion

Junction City's Kansas Vietnam Veterans Memorial

Kirby House

Combat Air Museum

Hays House Restaurant

Paxico

Topeka is the capital of Kansas, so let's start there and take the East Topeka exit (182) off Interstate 70. The city is bisected by the Kansas River and extends across the bowl of the fertile valley; the Oregon Trail crossed the river here.

Topeka has that nice blend of big city/small town; people here are both city-sophisticated and down-home friendly. Handsome green and gold *Topeka Trolleys* carry you around the downtown area Monday through Friday over the noon hour. Catch them at Eighth and Kansas or around the Capitol. Summers bring trolley tours through the historic district, full of interesting bits of history. These relaxing, scenic rides are by reservation only (785–354–9571).

The high point on this tour is **Potwin Place,** a quiet, untouched neighborhood established as a separate village in the 1880s. Here brick roadways—designed for buggies, but negotiable by cars—curve among homes set back on cool, shaded lawns. Turreted Queen Annes and handsome Italianate villas give this Victorian neighborhood its charm, but at Christmas it becomes a fairyland of shimmering lights. It's not hard to find; just take Sixth Avenue to Woodlawn and Greenwood Streets.

Nine blocks from the Potwin Place neighborhood stands the city's most famous landmark, the Greek Revival **Ward–Meade Home** at Meade Park, 124 Northwest Fillmore Street, built in 1870. This beautiful estate also has a reconstructed frontier log cabin, an authentic one-room schoolhouse, a depot dating from the turn of the nineteenth century, a general store, and a drugstore that serves up ice-cream treats from its vintage soda fountain. The grounds contain a splendid botanical garden with more than 500 varieties of trees and shrubs, 9,000 annual flowers, and 5,000 tulips.

Enhance your time traveling: Have a Victorian dinner on fine china and silver in the elegant dining room, a family-style meal at the cabin (hearth-cooked ham, Dutch-oven biscuits), or a picnic-basket dinner in the garden. Call (785) 368–3888 for museum information or for meal reservations.

The garden is open daily from 8:00 A.M. to dusk; the home, Tuesday through Friday from 10:00 A.M. to 4:00 P.M. with tours at 11:00 A.M. and

The constitution that was adopted when Kansas became a state in 1861 is still the law. It is one of the oldest state constitutions in use.

1:30 P.M., Saturday and Sunday (April–October) from 1:00 to 4:00 P.M. with tours at 1:00 or 2:30 P.M. Admission is $3.00 for adults, $1.25 for children ages five to twelve.

The copper-domed **State Capitol Building** at Tenth and Harrison Streets was constructed of native limestone and designed in the French Renaissance style. It is home to the famous **John Steuart Curry murals,** including one of abolitionist John Brown, and murals by other native Kansans, as well as statues of Dwight D. Eisenhower, Amelia Earhart, and other noted Kansans, each weighing a ton. There's also a hand-operated passenger elevator dating from 1923. It is open year-round Monday through Friday from 8:00 A.M. to 5:00 P.M. For tours, call (785) 296–3966.

Across the street from the capitol is the **First Presbyterian Church,** 817 Southwest Harrison Street, noted for its original Tiffany stained-glass windows. Call (785) 233–9601 to schedule a tour of the century-old church.

One of the country's newer national parks is **Brown v. Board of Education National Historic Site.** The visitors center is located on the second floor of the Main Post Office at 424 South Kansas Avenue in downtown Topeka and offers exhibits and a film on the landmark school segregation case that went all the way to the U.S. Supreme Court. Nearby Monroe Elementary School, where plaintiff Oliver Brown's child attended, will open to the public as a museum upon completion of renovations. Although the

Capitol Controversy

*C*onstruction of Kansas's elaborate state capitol was a thirty-seven-year project—begun in 1866 and finally finished in 1903 at a cost of $3.2 million. The central portion was completed last, so for a time, the east and west wings were connected only by a covered wooden walkway dubbed "Cave of the Winds."

Mired in controversy from the beginning, much of the criticism centered on the art inside, according to the Kansas State Historical Society. Ceres, the mythological goddess of

agriculture, was chosen to adorn the dome, then rejected. Twelve-foot-high murals of Grecian women were removed in 1902 after being deemed too risque.

Even the highly prized murals by Kansas native John Steuart Curry were criticized by the public in the 1930s. The mural project came to an end when the executive committee refused to remove eight pieces of marble that the artist felt interrupted the story his murals told, and the artist refused to sign his work.

case also represented plaintiffs from Virginia, South Carolina, Delaware, and Washington, D.C., it retained the Brown name. For more information, call (785) 354–4273, or visit the National Park Service's Web site at www.nps.gov/brvb.

Cedar Crest, One Cedar Crest Road, Topeka (Interstate 70 and Fairlawn Road), is the governor's residence. The 6,000-square-foot French-style chateau dates from 1928 and is listed on the National Register of Historic Places. A $4 million renovation of the property was completed in 2000. Free tours are offered on Mondays at 1:00 and 4:00 P.M. Call (785) 296–3636.

Topeka residents are proud of **Gage Park,** and rightly so. The 160-acre city park at Sixth and Gage Avenue is home to the **Topeka Zoological Park** (785–272–5821), exhibiting about 400 animals, and the **Reinisch Rose Garden** (785–272–6150), where 6,500 plants in 400 varieties bloom from May through October. There is no charge to visit the rose gardens. Admission to the zoo is $4.50 for adults, $3.50 for seniors, and $3.00 for children ages three through twelve. Zoo hours are 9:00 A.M. to 6:00 P.M. April 1 through October 31, 9:00 A.M. to 5:00 P.M. November 1 through March 31. Ticket office closes one hour before the zoo. Also in Gage Park, enjoy a mile-long ride on a mini-train and a spin on **The Carousel in the Park,** a historic carousel built in 1908, with traditional music from a 1909 Wurlitzer organ. Take a mile-long scenic ride through the park on the mini-train and see all the attractions. Hours are seasonal (call ahead), and admission is charged.

In addition to being the headquarters for the Kansas State Historical Society and an excellent source of genealogy material, **The Kansas History Center,** 6425 Southwest Sixth Avenue, operates the Kansas Museum of History. Among its features: a full-sized Cheyenne tepee, a Wichita tribe grass lodge, a log house, an 1880 Atchison, Topeka, and Santa Fe Railroad locomotive, and exhibits on the Bleeding Kansas and Civil War periods. Admission is free. It's open from 9:00 A.M. to 4:30 P.M. Monday through Saturday, 12:30 to 4:30 P.M. Sunday except some holidays. Phone (785) 272–8681.

TOP ANNUAL EVENTS IN NORTH CENTRAL KANSAS

April

Tulip Festival, Wamego; (785) 456–7849; third Saturday

Victorian Tea and Historic Homes Tour, Waterville; (785) 363–2170 or 363–2041

June

Wah-Shun-Gah Days, Council Grove; (800) 732–9211; intertribal powwow and festival, third weekend

September

Apple Days, Fort Riley; (785) 239–2022 or (800) 528–2489

Topeka Railroad Days; (785) 232–5533; e-mail: rrdays@kspress.com

October

Polka Fest, Paxico; (785) 636–5544; second Saturday in October

December

Home Heritage Tour, Abilene; (785) 263–7336; first weekend

The Junior League of Topeka's major fund-raiser occurs annually in the fall and is called the "Next-to-New Sale." It includes housewares, arts and crafts, books, antiques, jewelry, electronics, furniture, lawn and garden supplies, hardware, sporting goods, plants, toys, shoes, linens, and clothing for the entire family, at reasonable prices. Over the years it has generated over $1.3 million for the Junior League of Topeka's sponsored programs. For more information, e-mail the organization at email@jltopeka.org.

If you don't have the time to travel to England, the next-best thing is right here in Topeka. **The Woodward,** a bed-and-breakfast at 1272 Southwest Fillmore Street, resembles the elegant residences of English nobility. The two-and-one-half-story library was inspired by the great hall of King Henry VIII's Hampton Court Palace in Surrey, England. The home was completed in 1925 and is on the National Register of Historic Places. It contains a premier collection of antique cobalt blue glassware and the original dining room table, which is also listed on the National Register of Historic Places. Owner Elizabeth Taylor's love of this home is obvious in the attention lavished on the decor. A breakfast of oven-puffed pancakes stuffed with fresh fruit and drizzled with orange-maple syrup and an evening dessert are served to overnight guests. Prices range from $105 to $175, depending on the size of the bed. Guests have the use of the indoor sauna and outdoor hot tub. Call (785) 354–7111 or (888) 321–9407. See photos of the rooms at the Web site: www.thewoodward.com.

Another bed-and-breakfast in a unique setting is the **Brickyard Barn Inn** at 4020 Northwest Twenty-fifth on the northern edge of Topeka. A 1927 redbrick dairy barn with attached silo houses three guest rooms furnished with English antiques, all with private baths. Owners Scott and Truanna Nickel also have a catering business, so the barn includes

Fleeting Fame

*C*harles Curtis (1860–1936) was born in North Topeka. In 1907 he was the first native-born Kansan to represent the state in the U.S. Senate. He was elected vice president on the Republican ticket with Herbert Hoover in 1928, becoming the thirty-first person to hold that office. Curtis's home, at 1101 Southwest Topeka Boulevard, is open for tours. Call (785) 357–1371. Another Topeka resident, Alfred Mossman Landon, served two terms as governor of Kansas. In 1936 he was the Republican nominee for president of the United States. He lost to President Franklin Delano Roosevelt.

a dining room that seats seventy. Breakfast might include such spe-cialties as blueberry-stuffed French toast or Swiss quiche pie. Scott's omelets are great, too. Depending on the season, guests can curl up in front of a crackling fireplace, or cool off in the in-ground pool on the four acres of grounds. Rates are $75 to $95 per night, including a full breakfast. Call the Nickels at (785) 235–0057, fax them at (785) 234–0924, or e-mail umoo2me@cjnetworks.com. Their Web site is www.brickyardbarninn.com.

The Elderberry Bed and Breakfast is at 1035 Southwest Fillmore Street. Innkeepers Jerry and Carol Grant invite you to enjoy their restored 1887 Queen Anne home with its beveled-glass windows, oak woodwork, and pocket doors. It's listed on the National Register of His-toric Places. There are two rooms, both with private baths. The rooms are $55 to $60, with a full breakfast, served in the dining room or in your own room. An evening snack is offered, too. Call (785) 235–6309, e-mail elderberry@kbba.com, or visit the Web site www.nhouse-design. com/elderberry.

If you want to get so far off the beaten track that finding the place is part of the fun, and worth the effort, search out ***Porubsky's Grocery and Deli.*** This is a tiny "mom and son" store, the way Lydia and her son Charlie Porubsky want it to be, and as it has been for fifty years. In the deli sec-tion, an old-fashioned bar stretches down one side; booths line the other.

The food is known all over the capital; autographed photos of gover-nors and senators line the walls. A sign over the bar says GOOD CHILI AIN'T JIST FOR BREAKFAST, ANYMORE, and between the first Monday in October and March 29 (Monday through Thursday only) you can taste the best chili on the planet; well, at least according to the politicos at the capital. Porubsky's serves thick deli sandwiches with Charlie's own homemade tongue-roasting, melt-in-your-mouth pickles. Regulars love to wait for visitors to chomp into them the first time: "We have ignition. . . ." Charlie says the pickles have a little horseradish, a little mustard, a few hot peppers . . . but he's not about to give away the secret. The crazy part is that the whole sandwich is just $2.35.

Porubsky's is in "Little Russia," a Polish–German neighborhood. Now, pay attention and it's easy to find: Cross the Kansas Avenue Bridge into North Topeka, turn right onto Morse (the second street), and north at the top of the Sardou Bridge onto Porubsky Drive. The address is 508 Northeast Sardou, but don't let that confuse you. Porubsky's is open from 11:00 A.M. to 2:00 P.M. every day but Sunday. Call (785) 234–5788 for more information.

Profiles in Courage

South of the Kansas River in the neighborhood known as Oakland, in a sleepy-looking residential area, hides a little restaurant that has been snoozing here for more than forty years. People who are looking for real Mexican food search it out by the hundreds. It was one of the first authentic Mexican restaurants in this town. *La Siesta* is at 201 Northeast Woodruff. Owners Connie and Frank Herrara bought the restaurant from Connie's sister Lola Gonzales. They continue to serve basic Mexican food to the tacos-and-enchiladas crowd, but they also serve such items as chiles rellenos (an old family recipe), tamales, sanchos, and sopapillas.

When many customers began looking for low-cholesterol dishes, Lola created chicken enchiladas. New items such as potato Mexicana (a not-so-low-cholesterol baked potato stuffed with meat, chili con queso, guacamole, and sour cream) joined the well-loved chili con queso, made with a sauce so popular that the Herreras began bottling it to sell in grocery stores across Kansas.

The secret to the food here is the real cheddar cheese and the seasoning. Only the freshest ingredients are used. Nothing is microwaved, and everything is made to order—so you might have to wait a bit, but it is worth the wait, and you get to enjoy the Mexican music and appreciate the art on black velvet. Or you can pop back into the kitchen. Connie loves to have the customers come back and visit her there.

La Siesta is open from 10:30 A.M. to 2:30 P.M. Monday through Friday and from 5:00 to 9:00 P.M. Friday and Saturday. The restaurant seats only fifty-five people, so reservations are suggested; call (785) 354–1325.

The *Combat Air Museum* at Forbes Field Airport on "J" Street (Hangars 602–604), 5 miles south of Topeka on Topeka Boulevard, is a must-see for military or aviation history buffs. About two dozen military aircraft from both world wars, Korea, Vietnam, and Desert Storm are on display. Visitors can also watch ongoing restoration of additional aircraft in an on-site workshop. Along with such gems as a Grumman F11F-1 Tiger (the plane flown by the Blue Angels) and a replica of a World War I Curtiss "Jenny" trainer, you'll find military vehicles, missiles, re-creations of

Trivia

The Kansas Memorial Building in Topeka contains a historic sword. It was picked up on the Kansas plains near Council Grove centuries after it was dropped by one of Francisco Coronado's men, who passed through here in 1541.

a German POW barracks, a field kitchen and chapel, as well as a gallery of military aviation art. Forbes was built for training Air Force pilots. The museum is open Monday through Saturday from 9:00 A.M. to 4:30 P.M., with last admission at 3:30 P.M., and Sunday from 10:00 A.M. to 4:30 P.M., with last admission at 3:30 P.M. Admission is $5.00 for adults, $4.00 for seniors, and $3.00 for military and students ages six through seventeen. Call (785) 862–3303. Or you may visit the Web site at www.combatairmuseum.org.

Also at Forbes Field, in building 301, is the **Kansas National Guard Museum.** Tours are by appointment and include artifacts from the Kansas Militia and National Guard from 1854 to the present. Several vehicles and aircraft are also displayed. Admission is free. Call (785) 862–1020 for information.

Topeka is an arts and antiques center; the **Topeka Art Guild Gallery** (785–273–7646), at 4131 Gage Center Drive, features handmade jewelry, sculpture, paintings, hand-pulled prints, and pottery, all by Kansas artists. It is open from 11:00 A.M. to 5:00 P.M. Tuesday through Saturday.

Stop in at **Topeka Antique Mall** (785–273–2969) at 5247 Southwest Twenty-eighth Court. It is open seven days a week, from 10:00 A.M. to 5:00 P.M. You can stop in and pick up a brochure listing other shops.

General James Henry Lane, Father of Free Kansas

*I*n 1861, when Kansas joined the Union as a free state, James Henry Lane was elected as one of its first U.S. senators. Arriving in Washington just as the Civil War began, he organized a Frontier Guard to protect the White House. Lane established a firm relationship with President Abraham Lincoln, who named him a brigadier general and sent him home to fight. In the Senate and on the back roads of his home state, he called for total emancipation and the enlistment of black troops. "I would like to see every traitor who has to die, die at the hands of his own slave," he said. In 1862 he began recruiting two regiments of black soldiers. One of those, the First Kansas Colored Infantry, became the first black unit to see combat alongside white troops.

*For more information about Lane, visit **Lane's BBQ,** 1306 South Kansas Avenue (785–232–3610), a few blocks from the state capitol, where Harold Lane, one of the general's descendants, will share his story with you.*

In **Auburn,** a southwestern suburb of Topeka, you'll find **Lippincot's Fyshe House Homestay** at 8720 West Eighty-fifth Street. Enjoy the intriguing collection of fish paraphernalia collected by innkeepers Jan and Toni Lippincot. Call (785) 256–2772; fax (785) 256–2436.

This rustic ranch house on twenty acres of forest is about thirty minutes from downtown Topeka. Lippincot's is decorated around a central motif of fish, which the resident greeter cat, Muffin, must find intriguing. The Lippincots will pamper you with featherbeds and handcrafted quilts. You can indulge in a bubble bath or hot tub, and home-cooked gourmet meals served country style will make your stay memorable. The great room, library, and front porch are all yours to enjoy. The dolphin garden and rose garden will bring peace to your soul. Cozy down in a four-poster bed to enjoy a snack basket and bottled water in your room. A full or continental breakfast awaits you each morning. Rooms are $60 to $80.

About 30 miles southwest of Topeka on Highway 31 are the town of **Harveyville** and **Jepson Studios,** where Barry and Jill Jepson make handthrown pottery. Barry has his studio and shop just outside town. Take Interstate 70 to the Auburn exit, then go 10 miles to Auburn. There's a sign directing you to Harveyville, but please call the Jepsons for directions to their studio (785–589–2324); they often travel to shows.

The Kansas Turnpike system is today what the Santa Fe Trail was in its time, a much-beaten path. So we will leave Topeka on Highway 75, avoiding the southbound Kansas Turnpike, and head for Tecumseh and **Pomona Lake**, created by the Marais des Cygnes River.

Chuck and Shirley Linn had a summer place near **Tecumseh,** east of Topeka, an 1850s, tin-roofed, limestone house with walls so thick and air circulation so good that no air-conditioning was needed in the hot summer months. A few years ago they decided to renovate the place and move to the forty-acre spread permanently.

Now colored Angora goats roam the pasture and twenty English angora rabbits live in the seventy-five-year-old barn cooled by an attic fan and ceiling fans. **Shirley Linn's Studio** is in the granary, where she spins, weaves, and creates garments of the soft natural angora. Shirley invites other area artisans to join her at the farm each fall for a show and sale. Call for dates. The granary/studio (785–379–0421) is located at 7541 Southeast Sixty-first Street. From Topeka, head east on Forty-fifth Street to Stubbs Road. Follow it south to Sixty-first Street. It's at the southwest corner of Sixty-first Street and Stubbs Road. E-mail Shirley

| **Trivia** |

Looking for a canoe route? The Section 3 Kaw River access ramp is near Interstate 70 at Topeka. This stretch ends 34 miles later at Burcham Park in Lawrence. It's about a twelve- to fourteen-hour trip.

at slinn2@mindspring.com, or visit the Web site at www.rockbottomfarm.com.

Old Stone House Bed and Breakfast Along the Oregon Trail, in Tecumseh at 6033 Southeast Highway 40, has a name as long as the trail, but whether you are a history buff or just relish the peacefulness of the country, you will enjoy this 1850 native limestone farmhouse. If you are interested, hosts Alan and Sabra Shirrell will tell you tales of Indians, slavery, and Kansas's struggle to become a free state. They cater to vegetarians, so you can expect a fine meal if that is your inclination. Rooms are $55 to $85. Call (785) 379–5568 for reservations, or e-mail oldstone1@mindspring.com.

South of Topeka on Highway 75 and east on Highway 56 is the town of ***Overbrook,*** which makes a good day trip from the capital city. ***Fieldstone Bed and Breakfast Inn, Orchards, Vineyard and Country Store*** at 7049 East 149th is 2 miles east of Highway 56 and Maple and 1 mile north. The Mennonites who built the original barn in 1909 meant it to last a while; the sandstone walls are 2 feet thick. It has since been transformed into a French Provincial house. The loft became second-story bedrooms, and the hay doors, great windows. Now Nancy and Ken Krause have added a third-story suite with a king-size bed, private bath, and Jacuzzi. The loft boasts a living room, pool table, bar, and minikitchen with a microwave and refrigerator. The other two bedrooms share a bath.

Nancy serves a real country breakfast, with eggs fresh from the barn and bacon from their own hogs, along with homemade muffins, juice, and coffee. The loft is $110 (plus tax) and the other rooms are $75 (plus tax) for two people. Call (785) 665–7643 for reservations, or e-mail kkrause@sftnet.org, or check the Web site at www.fieldstonee.com.

Fieldstone is situated on 180 acres of working farm with $8^1/_2$ acres of vineyards, 1,000 apple trees, and (are you ready for this?) $2^1/_2$ acres of asparagus. There are seven ponds, five of which are stocked with catfish, bass, and crappie.

Asparagus season is from April 15 to May 30. Blackberries and cherries are available about June 15. Or perhaps apples or apple cider sounds good. The processing building and sale barn are open for tasting from late August to December 1. But the grape season, August 15 to September 15, is most interesting because you can rent crushing and pressing equipment and make your own wine. At the vineyard you'll see French hybrid wine grapes such as vidal blanc, seyval blanc, and vignole, as well as native Concord grapes. The country store offers farm products, honey, apples, pears, and ciders. Call for a fruit availability report at (785) 665–7643. Hours April 15 through December 1 are 8:00 A.M. to 6:00 P.M. Monday through Saturday, noon to 6:00 P.M. Sunday.

While in Overbrook shop at *From the Heart Country Gift Shop* at 401 Walnut in a cute Victorian house. Owner Cindy Keefover carries Boyd's Bears for collectors, along with baskets, birdhouses, and other country gifts. It is always Christmas in the little shop on the second floor. The shop is open Tuesday through Friday from 10:00 A.M. to 4:30 P.M., Saturday from 10:00 A.M. to 4:00 P.M. Call (785) 665–7512.

Have lunch at *Shirley's* at Highway 56 and Maple Street, where Shirley Simmons serves home-style cooking, including a daily special. Hours are Tuesday through Saturday from 6:30 A.M. to 9:00 P.M. and Sunday from 7:00 A.M. to 3:00 P.M. On Sunday, a fine smorgasbord is served from 11:30 A.M. to 3:00 P.M. Call (785) 665–7101.

The *Overbrook Quilt Connection* at 500 Maple Street showcases a display of large quilts and more than 1,000 bolts of fabric. Carolyn Meerian and Roxanne Fawl have quilting classes on Saturdays. Open Tuesday through Saturday from 10:00 A.M. to 5:00 P.M. Call (785) 665–7841 for a class schedule or to be added to the mailing list, or e-mail oqc@sftnet.org.

Tucked between Highways 50 and 56, *Americus* (just seven minutes northwest of Emporia), founded in 1857, is the home of *Marlow Woodcuts* (620–443–5589) at 706 Locust. It's a family business; Wanda Douglas, her son Brad, daughters Pamela and Rita, and Rita's husband, Steve, make more than 8,000 original woodcuts each year. They have had visitors from more than fifty-five countries since 1985.

The woodcuts, made of black walnut and ranging in size from a tiny inlaid pin to a 20-by-40-inch farm scene, are priced from $2.00 to $495.00. Shop hours are from 8:30 A.M. to 4:00 P.M. weekdays, Saturday from 10:00 A.M. to 4:00 P.M. (1:00 to 4:00 P.M. after Christmas until May 1).

Americus is also home to *Mel's Country Brass*, at 558 Mulberry, where Melba Rhudy will engrave metal or glass or "anything that stands still long enough." She has made some unique gifts for the people-who-have-everything types. Want to engrave a photo of the old homestead on Grandpa's old saw? Or maybe something more romantic, such as champagne glasses for a wedding? Coffee mugs with funny sayings, vases, gun stocks, knives—just about anything you can think of, she can engrave. She can draw from a photograph or freehand. The brass engravings are her favorite because they make such special gift items. "I'm just country through and through," she says, and she obviously loves her work. Hours are by appointment. Call (620) 443–5828, or e-mail melscountry@americusks.net.

If you have never experienced the Kansas Turnpike, now's your chance, but take it only as far as the scenic route, Highway 56, where you will turn west to *Council Grove.*

On the edge of the Flint Hills in the fertile Neosho River Valley, Council Grove was the last outfitting post between the Missouri River and Santa Fe and a natural stopover on the Santa Fe Trail. Because of its abundant grass and timber, Native Americans had used it for centuries. The U.S. government negotiated with the Osage for a passage across their lands in 1825; this became the Santa Fe Trail. The city was named after that

Marlow Woodcuts

council with the Osage. The stump of Council Oak remains where the treaty was signed, east of the present-day Neosho River bridge. In 1846 a new treaty with the Kansa, or Kaw, Indians gave them a 20-square-mile reservation where the city now stands (some treaty).

There are eighteen historic sites in "the Grove," as locals call it, and you can pick up a tour guide at the visitors bureau at 212 West Main Street, or call (800) 732–9211.

In a grove of trees along the Neosho River is the stately *Kaw Mission,* built in 1850 as a Methodist mission school for Native American children of the Kansa tribe. Now a museum and state historic site, the two-story limestone building at 500 North Mission houses Native American artifacts and items related to Council Grove history. It's open Tuesday through Saturday from 10:00 A.M. to 5:00 P.M., Sunday from 1:00 to 5:00 P.M. Admission is free. A tour of Council Grove's historic sites and the new Neosho Riverwalk also begins here.

At the east entrance to the Riverwalk, you'll see the *Guardian of the Grove,* a 10-foot-tall statue of a Native American warrior, honoring the Kaw tribe. It is by local artist Mark Sampsel.

Another historically significant figure is represented at the corner of Union and Main Streets. *Madonna of the Trail,* a 10-foot-tall statue of pink algonite stone, depicts a pioneer woman with two children and pays tribute to the courage of women who moved westward. It is one of eleven erected along the Santa Fe and Oregon Trails by the Daughters of the American Revolution in 1928.

You can't miss the *Farmers and Drovers Bank* at 201 West Main Street. The ornate two-story redbrick building with the limestone trim, stained-glass windows, Romanesque arches, and Byzantine dome dates from 1892 and is listed on the National Register of Historic Places. The bank continues to operate at this site.

The Last Chance Store, West Main and Chautauqua Streets, was built in 1857; it was the last supply stop on the Santa Fe Trail. It is not open for tours. One block east of the bridge on Main Street is the trunk of a 300-year-old bur oak known as the Post Office Oak. Letters for passing wagon trains and pack trains on the Santa Fe Trail were left from 1825 to 1847 at the base of this ancient oak tree. A stone building dating from 1864 stands next to the tree and houses a museum, open Sunday afternoons in the summer and by appointment.

A block west of the Last Chance Store is an American Four Square house built in 1913 and now the ***Flint Hills Bed and Breakfast Inn,*** 613 West Main Street. Owner Merry Barker invites guests to enjoy her home, which is filled with antiques and has a personality all its own. The sitting room is open to guests and has a television, refrigerator, and coffeemaker. The two large porches offer a place to sit and take in the beauty of the surrounding hills. You can enjoy a full country breakfast in the dining room and then stroll the 2 blocks to downtown. Rooms are $50 with a queen-size bed or $70 for a two-room suite with a queen-size bed and private bath. Call (620) 767–6655 or e-mail flinthills@kbba. com for reservations. Visit the Web at www.flinthillsbedandbreakfast.com.

Hays House Restaurant (620–767–5911), at 112 West Main Street, is the oldest continuously operated restaurant west of the Mississippi River, in business since Seth Hays built it in 1857. It is considered one of the finest in the state.

A lot of history could be whispered by these walls: Hays was the great-grandson of Daniel Boone; Kit Carson was his cousin. But old family recipes are the only history being spoken here—Beulah's ham, marinated brisket of beef, and crispy fried chicken. The current owners are Rick and Alisa Paul; Rick's also the chef. The restaurant opens at 6:15 A.M. Tuesday through Sunday for coffee, with breakfast service beginning at 7:00 A.M. It closes at 3:00 P.M. on Sunday, at 9:30 P.M. the rest of the week. But those are just the summer hours. Hays House changes its closing hours with the seasons, and that includes the K State football season, so it's a good idea to call ahead if it's even remotely near closing time. It closes in the summer at 9:30 P.M., 8:30 P.M. in the fall, that is, until the football season is over, then 8:00 P.M. in the dead of winter. Are you taking notes? Call ahead.

The ***Hays Tavern*** is on the second floor and is open Tuesday through Saturday from 5:00 P.M. until the restaurant closes.

The Cottage House Hotel at 25 North Neosho began as a three-room cottage and blacksmith shop in 1867. In 1871 a two-story brick house engulfed the cottage, and it became a boardinghouse. In 1879 a 5,000-square-foot, two-story Queen Anne addition was added, and the boardinghouse became

> ## Trivia
>
> *The William Young Archeological Site is an occupational site of an Archaic culture (which dates from 6000 B.C. to 81 B.C.). The group, who inhabited the area about 3000 B.C., is known as the Munker Creek Culture. They lived on the floodplain of Council Grove Lake about a mile north of Council Grove on Highway 177/57. Most of the site is underwater, but there are artifacts at the project office by the dam.*

A Taste of Ostrich

If you want to try ostrich, **Baker's Apple Market** *in Council Grove carries ostrich steak, ground patties, and jerky. Call (316) 767–5219.* **Rockin' V Steakhouse** *in Herrington has ostrich steaks on the menu. Hours are Wednesday through Saturday from 4:00 P.M. to midnight and Sunday from 11:00 A.M. to 2:00 P.M. and 4:00 to 10:00 P.M. Call (785) 258–3200.*

a hotel. Continental breakfast is served in your room or in the coffee room. Prices range from $65 to $175 for rooms and suites; all have private baths. There are two honeymoon cottages with bed, whirlpool bath, and a kitchenette/sitting room. Many rooms have more than one bed, and several are adjoining, family-style. Call (316) 767–6828 or (800) 727–7903 (reservations only). You can e-mail at cotthouse@cgtelco. net, or visit the Web at www.travelguides.com/ home/cottagehouse.

A monument 2 miles south of Council Grove marks the vicinity where Father Juan Padilla, a Franciscan priest who accompanied Coronado, returned in 1542 to convert the Indians. He was killed that same year and became the first Christian martyr in the United States.

Double D Ostrich Farm (620–767–6638) at 1412 West Highway 56 near Council Grove belongs to C. H. "Chuck" and Charles Downes, a father and son partnership. Tours to see their lovely birds can be arranged by the visitors and convention bureau. Call (800) 732–9211. Ostrich graze on grass just like cattle and weigh about 230 pounds when they are fully grown. Ostrich meat is "the other red meat," and is favored because it is low in fat and cholesterol.

Junction City, at the confluence of the Republican and Smoky Hill Rivers, is in the heart of the gently rolling Flint Hills. It was developed as a trading point for soldiers from the Fort Riley Reservation.

Stop at Heritage Park, at Sixth and Washington Streets, near Junction City's downtown. Over the northeast entrance to the park is the **Civil War Memorial Arch.** It was erected in 1898 by veterans of the Grand Army of the Republic. Inside the park, the **Kansas Vietnam Veterans Memorial** is similar to the memorial in Washington, D.C., honoring veterans of the same war. Thirteen feet high and 46 feet long, the ebony-colored granite stone lists the names of the 797 Kansans killed or still missing in action during the Vietnam War. When the remains of any of them are recovered, a star is added by the name. Life-size statues of soldiers of the Vietnam era stand beside a large replica of a Purple Heart Medal.

The **Buffalo Soldier Memorial Statue** can be seen at Eighteenth and Buffalo Soldier Drive. A 9-foot-tall bronzed statue of a soldier and his horse honors the African-American men, or Buffalo Soldiers, who made up the Ninth and Tenth Cavalry Regiments. The soldiers, many of them Civil War veterans, served on the frontier in Kansas and other western states through the 1880s, building forts and protecting stage, mail, and rail routes from outlaws and marauding bands of Indians. For more information, call (800) 528–2489.

The Bartell House at Sixth and Washington Streets was once a hotel and is now the home of *Ericka's Guest House,* a restaurant. The 1880 redbrick hotel was host to Wild Bill Hickok, John Wayne, Gloria Vanderbilt, and Sally Rand. It is listed on the National Register of Historic Places. The restaurant used to be famous for its buffalo tongue dinner. Now Ericka's serves more traditional fare. The restaurant is open 11:00 A.M. to 9:00 P.M. Monday through Saturday. Call (785) 762–6414 for more information.

Fort Riley is located just north of Interstate 70 and Junction City. Home of "America's Army," the post was originally built for defense of the Santa Fe and Oregon Trails. The fort is one of the largest inland military reservations in the country.

Fort Riley has excellent historical sites and museums. And why not, since some of the most famous names in army history were here: Buffalo Bill Cody, George Custer, and George S. Patton.

The *U.S. Cavalry Museum* at the corner of Custer and Henry Streets was built in 1854 as a post hospital, later becoming post and Cavalry School headquarters. The museum contains artifacts emphasizing the role of the U.S. Cavalry in the expansion of the West and the integral part the fort has played in U.S. history, producing leaders in every war. During peacetime, the fort fields Olympic equestrian teams. The museum features

Trivia
The Osage chiefs opened the Santa Fe Trail in 1825 when they sold the right-of-way through their land for $800.

murals and dioramas, as well as a picture and sculpture gallery. It also carries an excellent selection of cavalry and military history books and limited-edition fine-art prints. It is open year-round Monday through Saturday from 9:00 A.M. to 4:30 P.M., Sunday from 12:30 to 4:30 P.M. For information, call (785) 239–6727.

Adjacent to the U.S. Cavalry Museum is the *First Infantry Division Museum,* where you can trace the exploits of the "Big Red One," as the division is known, from World War I through Desert Storm. The division's First Brigade still trains at Fort Riley. Museum hours are 10:00 A.M. to 4:00 P.M. Monday through Saturday, noon to 4:00 P.M. Sunday. Closed Thanksgiving Day, Christmas Day, and New Year's Day.

Also at Fort Riley, in the Camp Whitside portion of the post (once a pioneer settlement called Pawnee City), is the *First Territorial Capitol of Kansas.* This two-story native limestone building served briefly as the territory's capital in 1855. The first territorial legislature met here in July of that year; the slavery issue was hotly discussed, with division over the issue leading to the "Bleeding Kansas" era and Civil War. The museum is open Thursday through Saturday from 10:00 A.M. to 5:00 P.M., Sunday from 1:00 to 5:00 P.M. Tours can be arranged by calling (785) 239–6727. The adjoining *Kaw River Nature Trail* is open from dawn to dusk every day.

The Custer House at 24 Sheridan Avenue was constructed in 1855 of native limestone. It is the only surviving set of quarters from the fort's earliest history. It depicts military life on the western frontier during the Indian wars period. (General Custer was at the fort in 1866.) Open Memorial Day through Labor Day. Hours are 10:00 A.M. to 4:00 P.M. Monday through Saturday, 1:00 to 4:00 P.M. Sunday. The rest of the year, tours can be arranged by calling (785) 239–6727.

Trivia
The Episcopal Church (785–238–2897) at 314 North Adams, Junction City, is the oldest Episcopal church in continuous use in the state, dating from 1859. Services are on Sunday at 8:00 and 10:00 A.M.

Across the street is the statue of *The Old Trooper,* known here as "Old Bill." The soldier and his mount have become the symbol of the proud heritage of the horse cavalry. It was designed and constructed by two soldiers in 1960, and marks the grave site of "Chief," the last cavalry horse registered on the government payroll.

The first nine holes of the *Custer Hill Golf Course* on Fort Riley are a Robert Trent Jones design. It is a pleasantly demanding course, with tree-lined fairways and two ponds strategically located with bunkers and fairly small greens. The course is open to the public, but members of the military have priority. Call (785) 762–5688 for tee times.

Calico Inn Restaurant (785–485–2622), 105 South Broadway in *Riley* (north of Junction City on Highway 24), is owned by Trixie Fasse, who has filled the little restaurant with antiques. The food is 100-percent homemade-from-scratch and includes not only the usual fried chicken, gravy, and homemade pies but also a weekend barbecued rib special that draws people from Fort Riley and Manhattan. The restaurant holds only about thirty-five people "when it's packed," according to Trixie, and that is often. The inn is open from 11:00 A.M. to 8:00 P.M. Tuesday through Saturday and from 11:00 A.M. to 2:00 P.M. Sunday.

You can take Interstate 70 from Junction City to Chapman and search out the **Windmill Inn,** 1787 Rain Road, 9 miles south of exit 286, for an intimate weekend in the country. Surrounded by acres of farmland, this carefully restored farmhouse and a 45-foot-tall windmill re-create the charm of a bygone era. The inn features beautiful oak woodwork, brilliant stained glass and beveled glass in the common areas, and a wraparound front porch that lures you to come out and relax in a swing or rocking chair and watch the courtship dances of the greater prairie chicken—a rare sight worth bringing a camera to capture. Hosts Tim and Deb Sanders are fine cooks, too. In the morning you'll awaken to the aroma of home cooking, and a full country breakfast will be served in the large, sunlit dining room. You can sip coffee and eat a homemade muffin on the front porch and enjoy the tranquil gardens.

In fact, with some advance notice, you are invited to enjoy dinner with the Sanderses, too. Guests who make early reservations can influence the chef's choice for the evening meal. Since the inn caters receptions and meetings, the menu contains everything from beef to seafood: thick pork chops with maple pan gravy, grilled lamb chops with herbs, Chicken a la Windmill simmered with herbs and pearl onions, and what they call the Ultimate Meat Loaf (not like Mom used to make).

The home has four guest rooms, all with private baths. Room rates are from $80 to $110. Call (785) 263–8755, or e-mail windmillinn@access-one.com. The Web site is www.access-one.com/windmill.

A scenic route to Salina is the road along wooded Smoky Hill River on Old Highway 40.

This route will also take you through **Chapman,** home of Joe Engle, one of three Kansas astronauts, and the site of one of the area's beautiful post-rock churches, **St. Michael's Catholic Church** on East Sixth Street. Other post-rock buildings and homes are all along Old 40, many with towers and balconies.

Old 40 continues across Mill Creek to **Abilene.** It is an excellent road paralleling the interstate (without the traffic), with fields of hay and milo nestled in rocky hills. Short stacked-stone walls line the fields along the roadway, creating the feel of the New England countryside rather than Kansas—except for the occasional oil well.

Abilene bears one of the most famous names of the Old West. It was the first cattle boomtown and the end of the famous Chisholm Cattle Trail, the western terminus of the railroad in the days of the cattle drives. In the five years from 1867 to 1872, nearly three million head of cattle were moved to Abilene and shipped to eastern markets on the Kansas Pacific Railroad.

Founded in 1857 as a stagecoach stop, the crude little village was inundated with cattle traders. It grew almost overnight from a population of 300 to 3,000, with the largest stockyards west of Kansas City, several hotels, a dozen saloons, gambling houses, and bawdy houses. Texas Street was the Broadway of the Plains.

Marshal Tom Smith became a hero here. Sadly, after bringing law and order to the town, he became the first U.S. marshal killed in the line of duty. He was succeeded by Marshal Wild Bill (James Butler) Hickok, the best-known gunman in the Old West. The six-gun was the law in this tough town, known as the roughest in the West.

Abilene's most famous citizen wasn't a lawman, but the thirty-fourth president of the United States. Dwight D. Eisenhower lived in Abilene from 1898 (when he was eight years old) until leaving for West Point in 1911. "The proudest thing I can claim is that I am from Abilene," Eisenhower said. Abilene is proud of him as well.

The *Eisenhower Presidential Center,* at 200 Southeast Fourth Street, honors his contributions to his country while serving as commander of the Allied Forces in World War II and during two terms in the White House. Included in the complex are five structures. The visitors center houses an auditorium, where a short film on Eisenhower's life is shown. The *Eisenhower family home,* located on its original site, contains furni-

Kids Like Ike, Too

*A*t the Eisenhower Presidential Center, you'll see an 11-foot-tall bronze statue of Abilene's most famous son as an adult. But local schoolchildren wanted to honor their hometown hero as a boy.

So the Abilene Kids Council, a fifteen-member board of elementary and middle school children who act as an advisory group to the local city council, led local kids in raising almost $21,000 for a likeness of Eisenhower as a boy.

The "Little Ike" statue was erected in 1999. It stands in a downtown park at East First Street and Buckeye Avenue, near Abilene's Civic Center.

While Eisenhower's birthday, October 14, is not an official state holiday, the Kansas legislature did declare it a state commemorative day. Children in schools all over Kansas study about and honor Eisenhower— the boy and the man—on that day each year.

ture and other items belonging to the family. The *Eisenhower Museum* is built of Kansas limestone and was dedicated on Veterans Day 1954 during Eisenhower's first term in office. Exhibits include military and World War II memorabilia; a timeline of his presidency including the cold war, Civil Rights, and the space race; gifts given to Ike by other world leaders; and a tribute to Mamie Eisenhower's role as First Lady. The *Presidential Library* contains some three million documents related to Eisenhower's public life. Dwight D. Eisenhower, his wife, Mamie, and their firstborn son, Doud Dwight Eisenhower, who died during childhood, are buried at the *Place of Meditation,* which includes a chapel designed by Eisenhower.

In this region tall grass stretches as far as you can see, and winds play across the nearly treeless landscape, creating swirling patterns of wheat and grass. Native Americans learned to survive in this unsheltered country, and ranchers still follow their ancient custom of burning off pastures to encourage new growth. Flames often cast an orange glow in the skies here. In the spring, rain transforms the blackened landscape into vibrant shades of green.

The Eisenhower Presidential Center is open from 9:00 A.M. to 4:45 P.M. every day except Thanksgiving Day, Christmas Day, and New Year's Day. For information, call (877) 746–4453.

Abilene is also known for the *Greyhound Hall of Fame Library.* It is across the street from the Eisenhower Center, at 407 South Buckeye Avenue. Honoring this magnificent racing dog that has lineage dating from 5000 B.C., the exhibit traces the greyhound's history in a short movie. Two resident greyhounds demonstrate the breed's lovable nature by enjoying hundreds of pats and hugs every day. The hours are from 9:00 A.M. to 5:00 P.M. seven days a week. Call (785) 263–3000.

There is now an organization called Greyhound Pets of America, which places dogs past their racing prime (from four to five years old) and young dogs who haven't been successful at the track in homes across the country. The local chapter, called T.L.C. Greyhound Adoption, can be reached at (785) 655–2208. There are chapters in every state.

The First Great Cattle Town

*A*bilene was the first of the great cattle towns on the Chisholm Trail. In 1867 about 35,000 head of cattle were brought to town. The number soon rose to 600,000 head of Texas cattle, which were shipped by rail to eastern markets. Like other cattle towns, Abilene was rowdy and lawless until 1870, when Tom Smith was hired as city marshal and peace was restored.

Also in town is a wonderful antique railroad—the *Abilene and Smoky Valley Railroad*—that leaves from the depot at the Greyhound Hall of Fame for a one-and-a-half-hour round-trip through the Smoky River Valley to Enterprise. Ride in a restored coach or diner car, pulled by a diesel-electric locomotive dating from 1945. The railroad has restored and is using a 1919 steam locomotive. Dinner excursions are also available. Fares are $8.50 for adults, $5.50 for children, and $30.00 per person for dinner trains. Trains run Tuesday through Sunday, Memorial Day through Labor Day, and weekends in May, September, and October. Call (888) 426–6687 for schedule information, or visit on the Web at www.asvrr.org.

The *Heritage Center,* east of the Eisenhower Center at 412 South Campbell, houses two Abilene museums. The *Museum of Independent Telephony* honors Clayson Brown, a local man who started an independent telephone company here, then purchased others across the state and country, until today we know the company as Sprint. The museum has an extensive collection of antique telephones.

The *Dickinson County Historical Museum* is famous nationwide for its circa 1900 *C. W. Parker Carousel,* a National Historic Landmark. It's restored and operating; you can ride it for $1.00. It's outdoors, along with an 1867 log cabin, a barn dating from 1915, a 1920s corner store, a blacksmith shop, and other pieces of local history.

Both museums can be reached at the same number, (785) 263–2681. A single $2.50 ticket is good for admission to both. Hours are Monday through Saturday 9:00 A.M. to 8:00 P.M., Sunday 1:00 to 5:00 P.M. Memorial Day through Labor Day; and Monday through Friday 10:00 A.M. to 4:00 P.M., Saturday 10:00 A.M. to 5:00 P.M., and Sunday 1:00 to 5:00 P.M. the rest of the year.

Tour the *Seelye Mansion,* a twenty-five-room Georgian mansion at 1105 North Buckeye Avenue, dating from 1905. Along with eleven bedrooms, the home includes its own bowling alley, a ballroom, and a Tiffany-designed fireplace. The original Edison light fixtures and most of the family's furniture are there, too. The period gardens have also been restored. Dr. A. B. Seelye, for whom the home was built, owned a successful patent medicine company, and many artifacts from the business are displayed in the *Patent Medicine Museum* here. Tours are at 10:00 A.M. and 2:00 P.M. Monday through Saturday and at 1:00 P.M. Sunday. During the month of December, the home is decorated for the holidays. (Closed Christmas Day.) Admission is $10.00 for adults, $5.00 for children ages six to twelve. Group rates are available. Call (785) 263–1084 for information.

Also open, by appointment, is the *LeBold Vahsholtz Mansion* at 106 North Vine. The twenty-three-room Italianate mansion was built in 1880 by banker and Abilene mayor C. H. Lebold, and served as an orphanage and home for single female telephone operators before being restored. It is listed on the National Register of Historic Places. Call (785) 263–4356 to arrange a tour.

Many other privately owned mansions are open for tours the first week-end in December, when Abilene hosts an annual *Christmas homes tour.* Call (800) 569–5925 for information. The rest of the year you'll have to be content with driving or walking streets such as Buckeye, Cedar, and Third, and viewing the exteriors.

At 300 North Mulberry Street is an old limestone church that looks like a medieval castle. Wild Bill Hickok and Dwight Eisenhower both wor-shipped here. Terry Tietjens left the enormous stained-glass windows intact and transformed the building's interior to the *Tietjens Center for the Performing Arts.* Theater performances featuring professional actors from all over the United States are staged here. It seats almost 200 people and is handicapped accessible. Each season, the theater offers seven plays, with multiple performances of each, plus a children's the-ater production. Tickets for a single performance start at about $17; season tickets are also available. Call (785) 263–4574 for information on what's currently playing.

See and shop for fine Native American arts and crafts at the *American Indian Art Center* at 206 South Buckeye. You'll find dolls, pottery, paintings, jewelry, and carvings by one hundred artists from thirty dif-ferent tribes in the region. Call (785) 263–0090 for hours.

Farmers' Drovers Art Gallery at 309 Buckeye (785–263–0240) is a showcase for Kansas artists. Housed in a historic building, the gallery sells original works of art at reasonable prices. Hours are Monday through Saturday from 10:00 A.M. to 5:00 P.M.

Bow Studio and Gallery (785–263–7166), 921 South Buckeye, is on the western edge of the Flint Hills just off Interstate 70. Inga and Bob Bow established the studio to display unique designs in clay tiles and plates handmade from local clays. The soft clay is rolled into large slabs, and Kansas wheat and wildflowers are impressed into it; the tiles are then cut, glazed, and fired. Terra-cotta sculptures, fountains, and lava-bos are also available. Hours are 10:00 A.M. to 7:00 P.M. every day.

If you're a doll collector, stop by the public library at 209 Northwest Fourth Street to see the *Abilene Library Doll Collection.* The collection includes dolls owned by Mamie Eisenhower, Works Progress Administration (WPA) dolls, and foreign dolls. They can be viewed at no charge during regular hours. Call (785) 263–3082 for information. Another collection can be viewed at the **Antique Doll Museum** at 1709 Buckeye Avenue by appointment. Call (785) 263–2800.

Also of interest in Abilene is the **Vintage Fashion Museum** (785–263–7997) at 212 North Broadway. It features clothing dating from 1860 to the 1970s. Hours are 10:00 A.M. to 4:00 P.M. Monday through Saturday, 1:00 to 4:00 P.M. Sunday. Admission is $3.00. Children under age twelve are free.

Sports buffs will enjoy the **Kansas Sports Hall of Fame** at 213 North Broadway. There are displays on Kansas high-school sports, as well as college and pro team memorabilia. Interactive displays let you watch video, research your favorite athletes and teams, and test your sports knowledge. The Hall of Fame includes NFL great Barry Sanders, a Kansas native. Hours are Monday through Saturday from 9:00 A.M. to 4:30 P.M., Sunday from 1:00 to 4:00 P.M. Admission is $3.00 for adults. Children ages twelve and younger are free with an adult. Call (785) 263–7403 for information.

The Kirby House (785–263–7336), now a restaurant, is located at 205 Northeast Third Street (1 block east of Buckeye Avenue). It was built in 1885 and has been restored to its original Italianate appearance, complete with tower and a new front porch.

A picket fence surrounds the stately home. The foyer has a parquet floor and walnut staircase. The front parlor has lead-glass and bay windows and a maple fireplace. Guests are seated in nine dining rooms on all levels of the mansion—even the tower, where there is a secluded table for two. It's a long climb, so there is a $25 extra charge for the waitress, but it's so romantic, it's worth it.

Now, let's talk about food. The specialty of the house is a spicy country-fried steak (with cream gravy), so big it hangs over the edges of the plate, barely leaving room for the baked potato and vegetables. There is also perfect prime rib, as well as chicken and seafood. Kirby House is open daily for lunch from 11:00 A.M. to 2:00 P.M. and for dinner from 5:00 to 8:00 P.M.; closed Sunday evenings. Visit www.kirby-house.com.

Another Abilene restaurant with an interesting history is the **Brookville Hotel,** at 105 East Lafayette, just off I–70. Four generations of the Martin family ran the hotel-turned-restaurant in neighboring Brookville, but a lack of a city sewer system there led them to relocate the business. Rather than attempt moving the 1870 structure, the Martins chose to replicate it, from the tin ceilings and vintage wallpaper to the old oak tellers' cages from the Brookville bank that became an additional dining room for the restaurant during its years there.

The menu didn't change; there's still just one item on it—fried chicken. Platters of it are served with mashed potatoes, gravy, biscuits, corn, coleslaw, and dessert. Adults pay $10.95; children ages three to eleven are $5.95. Hours are 5:00 to 8:00 P.M. Tuesday through Friday, 11:00 A.M. to 2:00 P.M. and 4:30 to 8:00 P.M. on Saturday, and 11:00 A.M. to 2:30 P.M. and 5:00 to 7:30 P.M. on Sunday. Reservations are a very good idea on weekends; call (785) 263–2244 for reservations.

Victorian Reflections Bed-and-Breakfast Inn (785–263–7774) at 820 Northwest Third Street is in one of Abilene's fine old historic homes. Third Street is lined with lovely old homes with an early 1900s feel. This nine-bedroom "painted lady" offers five guest rooms, all with private baths, and is filled with antiques; each room reflects comfortable elegance. Owners Don and Diana McBride serve a gourmet breakfast daily, featuring such delights as egg soufflé, homemade bread, and fresh fruit. Rooms are $70 to $95.

God's Garden is in Abilene, so if you want a private, quiet moment, find this six-acre spot at 1774 Camp Road. There is night lighting in the garden until 10:30 P.M., but a daylight stroll will show you eighty varieties of roses. The garden is open daily spring to fall, and there is no admission charge; it is supported by donations only. Phone (785) 479–5901.

Abilene's historic downtown area has quite a few specialty shops filled with antiques, gifts, toys, quilts, and more. If you are looking for a **Made in Kansas** item, this shop of the same name at 302 North Broadway is the right place to look. Barb Rehberg not only carries gifts handmade in Kansas, but you can also sit down and have some soup, a salad, and a sandwich homemade in Kansas. Her hours are 9:00 A.M. to 5:30 P.M. Monday through Friday and until 4:00 P.M. on Saturday. Call (785) 263–4944.

The *Balfours' House Bed and Breakfast*, just 1.5 miles south of Abilene on Highway 15 at 940 1900 Avenue, is a contemporary country home with a spa that holds three. Built into a shaded hill and surrounded with greenery and rock work, this is a place where you can kick off your shoes and relax. Owners Gilbert and Marie Balfour offer two suites, both with private entrances. Sliding-glass doors lead to a large, comfortable living area with two bedrooms and a natural stone fireplace (plus a television, VCR, and piano). A separate bungalow, decorated in Southwestern style, is completely private. It has a queen-size bed and two futon couches.

Both suites sleep six comfortably. A full breakfast (fruit, homemade rolls, coffee) is served in the gazebo or on the patio, which has an incredible sunrise view so unobstructed you can see the curve of the earth and more than a fair share of stars at night. The suites rent for $85 per couple. Call Marie at (785) 263–4262 for directions and reservations, or e-mail her at balfours@ikansas.com. Her fax number is (785) 263–2162. Visit on the Web at www.balfourshouse.com.

Ehrsam Place (103 South Grant) is a bed-and-breakfast in **Enterprise,** 5 miles east of Abilene. Mary and William Lambert will pamper you in this 1879 mansion on twenty acres along the river. The accommodations are luxurious, and you will receive complimentary snacks and soft drinks. You'll even find a guest robe in your room. The beds are queen- and king-size. After a good night's sleep, you'll awaken to a full breakfast in the morning. Rooms are $65 to $105. Call (785) 263–8747, or fax (785) 263–8548. Visit the Lamberts' Web site at www.ehrsamplace.com, or e-mail them at innkeeper@ehrsamplace.com.

Mr. K's Farmhouse (407 South Van Buren; 785–263–7995) is a farmhouse restaurant on top of a hill off old Highway 40. The family-style dinners include generous portions of steak, chicken, and seafood. There is a paddle hanging on the wall that was supposedly used on President Eisenhower on one of his visits home. No, it is not the Kansas way of telling the chief of staff we don't agree with his politics; it was done when he had been out of office for a while. Or so they say. See, good food and history, too! Hours are 11:00 A.M. to 2:00 P.M. every day but Monday, 5:00 to 9:00 P.M. Tuesday through Saturday.

The last stop before leaving Abilene must be the **Russell Stover Candy Factory,** near the edge of town on the south side of Interstate 70, at 1993 Caramel Boulevard. Even if you don't plan to buy any of the famous Midwestern chocolate-covered nuts and cremes, stop by for a taste. It's free and the people here know if you taste one, you will just have to buy enough to last you the rest of the year. Hours are Monday through Saturday from 9:00 A.M. to 6:00 P.M., Sunday from noon to 5:00 P.M. There is a demonstration kitchen; call ahead to see if they're making candy, if you'd like to watch (785–263–0463).

The view to the west is vast. Soft green hills touched with blue are spotted with the occasional oil well. The towns and cities of western Kansas have wide streets—wide enough for a herd of cattle to traverse—some of them the original brick; homes are set back on large lawns. Nothing is crowded or cramped here.

Pony Express Country

Wakefield, on Highway 82 East off Highway 15 North, is a quiet little community of only 800 souls, a great place to get away from it all. Enjoy some solitude at the *Kansas Landscape Arboretum,* on Highway 82 near Wakefield. If you've ever wondered what a bald cypress or golden rain tree looks like, and whether it would grow in Kansas, you'll find your answer here. There are 328 trees in 140 different varieties planted as memorials. Walk one of the mulched paths through the woods, or drive the winding road near the Milford Lake. Visit sunrise to sunset; there is no admission fee. For information, call general manager Pansy Beaudoin at (785) 461–5322.

Also along Milford Lake are a state park, a nature center, and a wildlife management area. *Milford State Park* offers trails for hiking and horseback riding, picnic shelters, campsites, and a boat ramp. The park entrance is off Highway 57. A vehicle sticker is $4.00; camping is additional. Call (785) 238–3014 for more information. The *Milford Nature Center* has exhibits and live animals, and in winter offers a popular program on eagles. You can visit the outdoor portions of the nearby fish hatchery anytime, but the nature center can arrange indoor tours in April when the fish are hatching. The nature center and hatchery are below the dam. Nature Center hours are 9:00 A.M. to 4:30 P.M. Monday through Friday, 1:00 to 5:00 P.M. Saturday and Sunday, April through mid-October, except for special programs. Admission is free. Call (785) 238–5323 for information. The wildlife management area provides habitat for pheasant, quail, whitetail deer, and other animals. Hunting is permitted in season. The rest of the year, hikers will find signposts and map boxes throughout the area. Call (785) 461–5402 for information.

A very secluded getaway near *Leonardville* is in a restored century-old farmhouse with newly added rooms. The *Lost Sheep Farm* at 15265 Walsburg Road, is the home of Jeanette Benney. She serves breakfast in the sunroom parlor. There are three rooms, one with private bath. Rates are $60 to $95, double occupancy. The lace curtains and cozy quilts in the private loft overlooking the duck pond make you feel as though you have escaped the city, never to return. Call (785) 293–4471 for directions, e-mail at benney@kansas.net, or visit the Web at welcome.to/lostsheepfarm/.

Northwest of Wakefield and Leonardville on Highway 9 are two little towns, Clifton and Vining. *Clifton* has what can only be described as some of the world's unique shopping all in one town block. Dan Deaver has constructed **Whatnot City** (The sign says JUST ANOTHER PLACE, but it's more than that!). It is a collection of old outbuildings that he has moved here from all over the county, and some that have been constructed on-site. They have false fronts, giving the block the feel of an Old West town. Whatnot City is a work in progress. As each building is finished, it is filled with antiques, used furniture, and flea-market items and opens for business. Deaver also works on the "Yellow Brick Quilt," another ongoing project. For a $15 contribution to a local scholarship fund, your name and city will be embroidered on a yellow quilt square and added to the quilt. From April to mid-December the city is open from 10:00 A.M. to 4:00 P.M. Monday through Saturday. The third weekend in August is the annual Daniel Lee Wild West Frontier Show, and a good time to visit Whatnot City. Call (785) 455–2250.

When the road changes from asphalt to gravel, look for **Brett's Club** on Parallel Street in **Vining** for the best steak around. It's open from 5:45 to 10:00 P.M. every day. Call (785) 455–3438.

Head east on Highway 36 to **Washington**'s rich river valleys. While you're there, please visit **Kansas Specialty Dog Service**, where guide and social dogs are trained for the blind, handicapped, and nursing homes. They use golden retrievers, black and yellow Labradors, German shepherds, and boxers. A puppy raiser takes an eight-to-ten-week-old puppy and houses it for twelve to eighteen months. When the pup returns to the facility, it will learn about forty commands. An additional six months is required to complete this cycle of training. A disabled individual will spend two to four weeks training with a dog that is matched to him or her. A tour of the facility is encouraged unless a class is in the process of receiving dogs. Call (785) 325–2256.

Connie Allen and Marilyn Hanshaw, owners of **Marcon Pies** at 124 West Eighth, Washington, welcome you to visit their pie production facility, where pies are baked daily and delivered to area stores and restaurants. The aroma of freshly baked pies is sure to interest you in sampling the product and purchasing one or two to take home. Marcon is 1 block south of Highway 36 at D Street, and $1/3$ block east. Tour hours are 7:00 A.M. to 5:00 P.M. Monday through Friday. Call (785) 325–2439. Call ahead for tour reservations.

South of Highway 36 is the town of **Greenleaf.** Just past Greenleaf, Kathy Dawson and Fred Cairns have **Lynes Unlimited** at 172 Upland Road (785–747–2612), a small shop where their award-winning, handcrafted wooden toys are made.

Kathy says they make playthings for children, but they also make very specialized and detailed adult toys from pine and hardwoods, sleds and sleighs, for example. Prices range from $6.00 for a toy car or truck to $1,200.00 for a 6-foot-long scale-model train. The shop is 9 miles south of Greenleaf on a paved road (the last mile is gravel) and is easy to find. Hours are by appointment.

Slightly north of Highway 36 on Highway 15 East is **Hanover.** The ***Hollenberg Pony Express Station*** is 2 miles northeast of Hanover, just a mile east of Highway 243, and is the only remaining original, unaltered Pony Express station in its original location in the United States. It was built in 1857, the most westerly station in Kansas (123 miles from St. Joseph, Missouri), and in 1859 was the western terminus of railroad and telegraph lines. From that point, travel by wagon or stagecoach was slow. The Butterfield Overland Mail Company covered the distance in twenty-two days.

In 1860 the Pony Express was inaugurated by the firm of Russell, Majors & Waddell, proving that mail could be delivered faster. Charges were set at $5.00 a letter; it makes our present-day stamps look pretty good. The visitors center includes a mural depicting the Oregon Trail and exhibits about the Hollenberg family who lived at and ran the station. It is a state historic site. There is no admission, but donations are welcome. Hours are 10:00 A.M. to 5:00 P.M. Wednesday through Saturday, and 1:00 to 5:00 P.M. Sunday. Call (785) 337–2635, or visit the Web site at www.kshs.org.

Grace Riepen and her daughter Kathy Gastmann are co-owners of *A Season's Harvest* at their home at 411 East Elm Street in Hanover. The home is surrounded by herb gardens, and the women offer wreaths and arrangements created from the flowers and herbs grown here. But they don't stop with sweet-smelling wreaths; they also offer garden tours—June is the most fragrant time—and herbal dinners.

What's an herbal dinner, you ask? It is meat, potatoes, vegetables, and dessert all flavored with herbs; it also includes herbal legend and lore. The dinners, $16 per person, are scheduled for groups. They have recently opened a tearoom in the shop, so you can stop in and have a bite to eat. Call Kathy at (785) 337–2553. She also does herbal bridal showers, weddings, and Victorian tea parties for groups by reservation, and offers a Christmas open house featuring a program about Christmas herbs. The shop visits and garden tour are by appointment only, but do go; the fragrance in your vehicle will be improved tremendously for the rest of your trip. You can e-mail at gastmann@kansas.net.

Gloria's Coffee & Quilts, on West Highway 9 in **Barnes,** is in the nineteenth-century home of Gloria Moore. Guests choose from three rooms with a queen-size bed and private bath. Rooms are $40.00 to $75.00 for a single plus $5.00 for each additional person, including a full breakfast (pecan waffles are the favored choice). Call (785) 763–4569 or (888) 511–4569.

Oregon Trail

You see them in the city parks and anywhere else you look in **Marysville.** The unusual black squirrel is the city mascot that appears on the city flag and is protected by city ordinance.

Legend has it that a boy who didn't like to see animals in cages turned a batch of them loose at a carnival in 1912. Others say the black squirrels have been seen in the area from as early as the late 1800s.

> ## Trivia
>
> *When the town of Haddam, west of Marysville, held a municipal election in 1901, women won the offices of mayor, city clerk, police judge, and the entire city council—even though women were not given the right to vote until 1920. The women decided a jail needed to be built and had a stone one built within five months. The jail, on its original site, is ½ block south of Haddam's main street.*

The Pony Express came though Marysville in the 1860s. The **Pony Express Barn-Museum** is the oldest building in Marshall County and the only original home station along the Pony Express route still at its original site. A bronze Pony Express horse and rider still appear to thunder across the prairie at the west edge of town at Pony Express Park. A perfect replica of a Rope Ferry used to pull wagons and livestock across the Big Blue River is at Historic Trails Park. The original ferry was very near this location from 1851 until 1864 when a bridge was built. Thousands of pioneers and hundreds of wagons camped for days waiting for a turn to cross. There were many graves near the crossing as settlers fell to illnesses during these long waits. A rope crossed the river above the ferry, which rode a pulley back and forth. A wheel guided another rope to shift the ferry away from swift river currents. For more information about any of these, call Marysville Travel and Tourism at (800) 752–3965.

The magnificent **Koester Block** of Marysville, on Highway 36, has been restored to its late-nineteenth-century splendor. Two stone lions guard the walkway, and a brick wall surrounds the two Koester homes, one now a museum.

The white-clapboard, 1876 **Koester House Museum** at 919 Broadway still has the original furnishings. It was donated to the city by fourth-generation heirs in 1972 and is open May to October from 10:00 A.M. to noon and 1:00 to 4:30 P.M. Tuesday through Saturday; 1:00 to 4:30 Sunday; and by appointment. Admission is $2.50 for adults, $1.00 for children ages five through twelve. Call the museum at (785) 562–2417 or, in the off-season, Joy Stewart at (785) 562–2678.

Take Highway 77 from Marysville, and follow it south and west to the town of **Waterville.** On **Banker's Row** nineteenth-century Victorian mansions stand behind rolling lawns along East Hazelwood Street. There are theater productions at the old opera house in town, which also houses City Hall.

North on Highway 178 just before you reach Seneca is the town of **Benedict,** or St. Benedict, depending on whom you ask, and formerly known as Wild Cat before the post office officially named it. Anyway, in Benedict is **St. Mary's Church,** circa 1881–94, a remarkable example of preservation and restoration that is on the National Register of Historic Places. The limestone for the late Roman-style exterior was quarried by parishioners about 3 miles north of town, who then aided masons in the construction. That kind of devotion is still apparent today as the one hundred families who make up the parish donate a great deal of both time and money to accomplish this amazing restoration. Even the pipe organ, circa 1916, was restored after sitting unused for more than twenty-five years. The paintings, ceilings, and wall decorations were carefully photographed and documented and faithfully restored. The six Bavarian-made transept windows, dominated by hues of ocher, amber, azure, and crimson leaded glass, are in paired arch sections. A saint is depicted in hand-painted glass within each section. This is truly worth the drive to see, especially on a Sunday morning.

In the town of **Seneca,** farther east on Highway 36, is **Stein House Bed and Breakfast** (314 North Seventh). Ray and Rosann love to show off their ancestral home, built in the early 1900s. Enjoy the quiet, or visit one of the nearby casinos. There are three rooms with shared baths; rates are $55 to $60 with a full breakfast. For reservations call (785) 336–3790 or e-mail steinhouse@galaxyispc.com.

Just off Highway 63 North on Highway 71 East is the town of **Bern.** A warm country welcome awaits you at **Lear Acres** (785–336–3903), a livestock and grain farm. The large, two-story farmhouse is owned by Byron and Toby Lear; it was built by Byron's father in 1918, and Byron was born there. It offers space to move about, a peaceful atmosphere,

Trivia

The town of Irving was near Frankfort, just off Highway 9 between Highways 99 and 77. But it doesn't exist anymore; it's a ghost town. The people of Irving are still alive, however, and the town site has a marker and a mailbox so that folks can leave messages for one another when they are passing through. There is even an Irving reunion and picnic every summer.

and, because it sits on a hill, a panoramic view. Breakfast is farm-raised, from the fruits and breads to the meat and eggs.

Toby fixes a country breakfast of eggs (go get your own, if you want to), bacon or sausage, muffins or rolls made with flour from their own wheat, and homemade wild plum jelly. Rates are $38 for a double room with shared bath. There is air-conditioning. Toby can direct you to some small antiques shops nearby.

Head southwest toward Tuttle Creek Lake and Highway 16. At 429 East Highway 16 in *Olsburg,* you'll find a roadside steakhouse known simply as *Bricks.* You can get a buffalo steak done to perfection Wednesday through Saturday from 11:00 A.M. to 1:00 P.M. and 5:00 to 9:00 P.M. and on Sunday from 4:00 to 8:30 P.M. Their phone number is (785) 468–3517.

From Olsburg head east on Highway 16 until it turns into a winding road that leads southeast to *Westmoreland* on Highway 99. About 1 mile south of Westmoreland on Highway 99, stop to see the life-size covered wagon pulled by a yoke of bronzed oxen—a tribute to the travelers of the Oregon Trail.

Manhattan (known hereabouts as "The Little Apple") is home to Kansas State University. As in most college towns, there is a lot going on—plenty of places to eat, an abundance of motel rooms, and some interesting bed-and-breakfast inns, too.

Anyone with an appreciation for plants must see the *Kansas State University Gardens.* A living laboratory for students enrolled in the college's horticulture program, the gardens are student designed and installed. When completed, the gardens will cover twelve acres.

Near a historic conservatory dating from 1909, where butterflies fly freely among tropical plants, a native plant garden, a butterfly garden, a cottage garden filled with old-fashioned varieties of flowers, and a day lily garden are already planted. A fountain sets off the rose garden, which will be enlarged and complemented by an iris garden. In the next few years, two ponds, a waterfall, a children's garden, a woodland garden, a sensory garden for the physically challenged, and a commons with a gazebo for weddings and other events will be added. The gardens are off

Denison; park by the old dairy barn or the conservatory. Call (785) 532–6170 for more information.

Also on the K-State campus is the **Marianna Kistler Beach Museum of Art,** near Fourteenth and Anderson Avenue. The museum specializes in twentieth-century American art, with an emphasis on Midwestern artists. Hours are Tuesday through Saturday from 10:00 A.M. to 5:00 P.M. except Thursday, when it closes at 8:30 P.M. Sunday hours are 1:00 to 5:00 P.M. Call (785) 532–7718 for information, or visit the Web at ksu.edu/bma.

For those of you who just can't pass up a new museum, the **American Museum of Baking** is tucked away in its own room at the Emerson Library at 1213 Bakers Way (785–537–4750). There are priceless samples of Egyptian bread and cake more than 3,800 years old, Roman bread, and grain from the colonies in North Africa. Wooden and pottery bread stamping tools from Roman Byzantium and many other artifacts, along with a collection of cookbooks more than 200 years old, can be seen here. The display follows the development of commercial baking in North America leading to sliced white bread, the all-American favorite. This is considered to be one of the most important collections on the history of baking in the world.

Near Manhattan is the **Konza Prairie,** a stretch of 8,616 acres of untouched native tallgrass prairie. Named for the Konza Indians who once lived in the region, it is owned by The Nature Conservancy and used for study by Kansas State University. Along with grass that can exceed 8 feet in height, the prairie is home to 600-plus species of plants. More than 200 species of resident and migratory birds have been recorded here. A bison herd of about 200 animals grazes about a quarter of the preserve, so that scientists can study the effects of grazing on the prairie. Sections of the prairie are also burned each spring, and its effects studied.

Fourteen miles of hiking trails are open to the public daily from dawn until dusk, weather and trail conditions permitting. A self-guided tour brochure is available at the entrance. Group tours are available by appointment. Other facilities at Konza Prairie, including the 1900s limestone ranch house, are for the use of researchers only. To get to Konza Prairie, take I–70 exit 307 and head northeast on McDowell Creek Road about 6 miles. For more information, call (785) 587–0441, or visit the Web site at www.ksu.edu/konza.

Manhattan has plenty of history, too. At 2309 Claflin Road are three historic attractions, the Goodnow House, the Riley County Historical Museum, and the Hartford House. For tours of these properties, the Pioneer Log Cabin in City Park, a one-room schoolhouse near Tuttle Creek Boulevard and Barnes Road, or the Wolf House Museum, an 1868 boardinghouse at 630 Fremont, call the Riley County Historical Museum at (785) 565–4750.

The *Goodnow House* dates from 1861 and belonged to Issac Tichenor Goodnow and his wife, Ellen, who came to Kansas to help in the free-state efforts. The house has some unusual features. Ellen insisted on having a window centered in her bedroom wall, so the chimney detours around it. Worried that a horse might be injured jumping a fence with pointed pickets, she had the house surrounded by a stone wall topped with curved iron rods. Many of the period furnishings are from the Goodnow family. Hours are 2:00 to 5:00 P.M. Saturday and Sunday, or by appointment. Admission is free, but donations are welcome. Information is also available at the Kansas State Historical Society's Web site at www.kshs.org.

The *Riley County Historical Society Modern Museum Building* houses changing exhibits on Riley County history and the Seaton Research Library, a wealth of archival material for history buffs and genealogists. The library is open by appointment only.

The *Hartford House* is a prefabricated house (perfect for the nearly treeless prairie) brought by steamboat in 1855, along with more than one hundred folks from Ohio determined to populate the state with abolitionists. The steamboat was headed farther west but stopped here when it ran aground due to low water. One eastern name was traded for another when the existing settlement, Boston, became Manhattan.

Four miles west of Manhattan, tucked in the side of a steep hill, are a stone house and barn built from limestone quarried in the nearby Flint Hills. The barn has beams made of tree trunks with the bark still on them. It is now an antiques shop called *The Barn at Kimble Cliff* and is filled with vintage goods from the late 1800s to the mid-twentieth century. Buttons, ceramics, glassware, furniture—you can find it all here. The address is 6782 Anderson Avenue; hours are 1:00 to 5:30 P.M. Friday, Saturday, and Sunday, or by appointment. Call (785) 539–3816 for directions.

Voted "best steak in Manhattan," the *Little Apple Brewing Company* at 1110 Westloop Place lives up to its reputation. Open seven days a week. Call (785) 539–5500 for hours, or to make a reservation if there are six or more in your party.

If you're looking for conveniently located lodging, try the 1908 Prairie-style ***Morning Star Bed and Breakfast on the Park*** at 617 Houston Street. The three-story Queen Anne, circa 1902, is in a historic district near K-State; you may be sharing the house with a visiting faculty member. Three rooms have down pillows and comforters; one has a private bath, and two are available with a private or shared bath. All rooms have queen- or king-size beds, a two-person Jacuzzi, and phone and dataports. A full breakfast featuring such specialties as eggs Benedict, walnut pancakes, Greek omelets, or apricot coffee cake is served in the dining room, or outside on the porch when weather permits. Rates are $89 to $179. Call (785) 587–9703, fax (785) 539–0442, e-mail kaszer@swbell.net, or visit the Web site at www.morningstaronthepark.com.

Other bed-and-breakfasts in Manhattan include the ***Casement Inn Christian Bed and Breakfast,*** 1905 Casement Road. One suite with private bath and a full breakfast is available at $55 to $65 per night. Call innkeeper Joan Akin at (785) 776–6037 for reservations. The ***Guest Haus Bed and Breakfast,*** 1724 Sheffield Circle, offers two rooms with shared baths. Rates are $55 to $70 per night and include a continental breakfast. E-mail the hosts, Mike and Gloria Heiberger, at guesthaus@juno.com, call (785) 776–6543, or visit the Web at www.guesthaus.com.

The ***Old Dutch Mill*** at the city park on Fourth Street in ***Wamego*** is a town landmark. Built of native limestone in 1879—an authentic Dutch mill in Kansas—it was erected in 1879 and is listed on the National Register of Historic Places. Look for the sculpted bust of Ceres, the Roman goddess of grain, above the window.

The mill, originally located 12 miles north of Wamego, was donated to the city in 1924. It was dismantled, each stone numbered, and hauled into town by horse-drawn wagons; here it was rebuilt by volunteers. This is a working mill, grinding local wheat to stone-ground flour. The flour is for sale. You won't see the wheat being ground (the apparatus is all enclosed), but you can visit the mill from 10:00 A.M. to 8:00 P.M. Thursday, Saturday, and Sunday and from 1:00 to 5:00 P.M. the rest of the week, or by appointment.

Try to plan your visit during the Tulip Festival, when thousands of Holland tulips are in bloom, or over the Fourth of July. These are two of the biggest small-town celebrations and parades in the state. Wamego's nighttime Christmas parade has spectators lining the streets awaiting the arrival of Santa in his lighted sleigh. At the ***Oregon Trail Nature Park*** east of town is a huge silo mural done by local artist Cindy Martin. The park has several walking trails and a shelter house for picnics.

Old Dutch Mill

Stop in Wamego and get a room at the *Eagle View Inn Bed and Breakfast* (785–456–9053) in the William Boyd building at 520 Lincoln Avenue. It was originally the Boyd Blacksmith Shop, built in 1885. The upstairs was a boardinghouse. Now innkeepers John and Martha Powers welcome you to their B&B. Four rooms are available with queen- and king-size beds. They range in price from $55 to $75. Breakfast is served in *The Friendly Cooker Restaurant* (785–456–9053), located on the first floor of the building. It is famous for its down-home cooking, and inn guests enjoy a breakfast of homemade buttermilk pancakes, with hosts John and Martha picking up the tab. E-mail them at eaglevi@kansas.net. The popular restaurant opens at 6:00 A.M. and doesn't close until 8:00 P.M., six days a week. Sunday hours are 7:00 A.M. to 8:00 P.M.

The *Columbian Theatre Museum and Art Center* is the locale for cultural and civic activity. It has been elegantly restored in a $1.8 million renovation project. Its murals are a wonder; they date from the 1893 Columbian Exposition in Chicago. The 250-seat theater hosts dramatic and musical performances. For show and ticket information, call (800) 899–1893.

Detour in a Canoe

The *Antique Emporium* (785–456–7111) at 509–511 Lincoln Avenue is where twenty dealers sell vintage glassware, pottery, furniture, coins, and postcards. There is even a certified appraiser on staff. Hours are Monday through Saturday from 10:00 A.M. to 6:00 P.M., Sunday from 1:00 to 5:00 P.M.

If you have never ventured off the interstate before and have any kind of phobia about it, *Paxico* is a good place to begin your therapy. Tell yourself the interstate will not go away and Colorado will not close down, and get off at the Paxico (334) exit. You can stop off in this antiques-happy little burg, leaving Interstate 70 at one exit and returning to it at the next interchange. Paxico is remarkable because it has a series of historic buildings in near-original turn-of-the-nineteenth-century condition.

It's possible to canoe on the Kansas River and its tributaries all the way from Junction City to Kansas City. One of the most scenic sections is a 15-mile stretch through the Flint Hills from Odgen to Manhattan. For information on access points, water levels, and difficulty ratings, check the Kansas Canoe Association's Web site, www.kansas.net/~tjhittle.

Paxico boasts a retail pottery outlet, art gallery, flea market, winery, and lots of antiques. There were eight antiques shops at last count. Steve "Bud" and Kathy Hund, owners of *Mill Creek Antiques*, are the drive behind the comeback of Paxico. Bud started with a two-story building and a part-time antiques business. Today the buildings are full, and people drive from Lawrence, Topeka, and Kansas City to shop for the bargains to be found here.

The Hunds sell American furniture and old lamps, but Bud's specialty is stoves. He has a regular museum of heating and cooking stoves that burn coal, wood, or gas. Big stoves and little stoves of cast iron are all here. He buys rusty and snaggle-toothed specimens at farm auctions, sands them, repairs them, and lines them up in his shop to await new homes. Call (785) 636–5520. Hours are Monday through Saturday from 9:00 A.M. to 5:00 P.M., Sunday from noon to 4:30 P.M.

Paxico Inn, a bed-and-breakfast above the general store, also belongs to Kathryn and Bud. All of the antiques in the rooms are for sale, so you can shop till you drop, quite literally! All rooms have private baths with claw-foot tubs. A common sitting area with a balcony overlooks the town's antiques district. Rooms are $75 to $85. Call (785) 636–5520 for reservations and more information.

The winery and tasting room of *Fields of Fair* are here, too. (The vineyards are in St. George.) The tasting room offers visitors a sampling of

WORTH A VISIT

Melvern Lake

Council Grove Lake

Milford Lake—
  Junction City

Marion Reservoir

Osage State Fishing
  Lake and Wildlife
  Area—Reading

their fine wines Monday through Saturday from 8:00 A.M. to 6:00 P.M. and Sunday from noon to 6:00 P.M. The wines include a dry Beaujolais-style red, a dry white, and a Prairie Dew blush wine. One of the most interesting wines, called Flint Hills Red, has a bouquet reminiscent of newly cut hay or clover— very Kansas. You can reach the winery at (785) 636–5560 or (800) 732–1984.

If you are pulling a trailer or driving a motor home, **Mill Creek Campground** (785–636–5321) is a natural. As the name suggests, the wide, rocky Mill Creek flows through the campground. Beautiful cliffs rise to one side, and you can swim, fish, canoe, or picnic. Owners Dan and Judy Meinhardt have tried to restore the Old West feeling of the campground, but it has 100-foot, level, pull-through parking sites, and can accommodate everything from a tent to an Airstream.

Get off Interstate 70 onto the Skyline Mill Creek Scenic Drive and wander over this scenic byway for breathtaking vistas of the Flint Hills. You'll encounter a variety of native stone buildings, and of course, good eating places. This road-less-traveled goes through *Alma,* where maps are available at the **Wabaunsee County Historical Museum** at Third and Missouri between the hours of 10:00 A.M. and noon and 1:00 to 4:00 P.M. Tuesday through Saturday, and 1:00 to 4:00 P.M. on Sunday. Call (785) 765–2200.

This "City of Stone" is built of locally quarried limestone, and the unique architectural features of many of the buildings draw architects from around the country. The **Alma Bakery and Sweet Shoppe** is downtown at 309 Missouri. The sweet scent of freshly baking breads, cinnamon rolls, and cookies will lure you in. Baker Jeanette Supernaw fills shelves with turnovers and puff pastries to tempt you, and assorted sweets such as fudge, brittle, and toffee will beg to go home with you. Try the popular Bierock, a meat-and-cabbage-filled meal baked in a roll. Hours are from 8:00 A.M. to 3:00 P.M. Tuesday through Friday and from 7:00 A.M. to noon on Saturday. Call (785) 765–2235. **T.D. & Co. Restaurant,** just down the block at 327 Missouri, offers down-home cooking with a special every day that includes dessert. It is open Tuesday through Friday from 8:00 A.M. to 7:30 P.M., Saturday from 8:00 A.M. to 8:00 P.M., and Sunday from 11:00 A.M. to 2:00 P.M. Call (785) 765–2527.

Travelers at the north edge of Third Street should bear left where the gravel road forks. This road runs parallel to Mill Creek and continues to *Alta*

Vista. Watch for impressive stone houses and barns along the way as well as two old stone schoolhouses. Alta Vista is about 12 miles along this road.

North out of Alta Vista, take Highway 177, which winds through some of the area's most enchanting hill country, or even better, follow the Skyline Drive signs leading out of town. Narrow lanes of blacktop or gravel parallel the highway and waist-high stone fences extend to the horizon. These fences were built by hand by the region's early settlers.

Surrounded by bluestem prairie and secluded, wooded valleys, the area is home to many varieties of wildlife and wildflowers. It is one of the best places to see the "sea of grass" as it once was. Year-round beauty marks this area. In the spring young prairie grasses form a backdrop for the explosion of wildflower colors. In late summer and autumn, bluestem grass ripens into tall, golden plumes, and giant sunflowers dot the prairie.

PLACES TO STAY IN NORTH CENTRAL KANSAS

ABILENE
Covered Wagon RV Resort,
2502 Mink Road,
(785) 598–2221 or
(800) 658–4667

Days Inn,
4709 Buckeye Avenue,
(785) 263–2800 or
(800) 701–1000

Diamond Motel,
1407 Northwest
Third Street,
(785) 263–2360

COUNCIL GROVE
Cottage House Hotel &
Motel,
25 North Neosho,
(620) 767–6828

GREENSBURG
Kansan Inn,
800 East Highway 54,
(620) 723–2141 or
(800) 532–2141

JUNCTION CITY
Econo Lodge ,
211 West Flint Hills
Boulevard,
(785) 238–8181

Selected Chambers of Commerce and Visitors Bureaus

Topeka Convention and Visitors Bureau,
1275 Southwest Topeka Boulevard, Topeka 66612-1852;
(785) 234–1030 or (800) 235–1030

Manhattan Convention and Visitors Bureau,
501 Poyntz Avenue; (785) 776–8829 or
(800) 759–0134

Council Grove Convention and Visitors Bureau,
212 West Main; (316) 767–5882 or
(800) 732–9211

Abilene Tourist Information Center,
201 Northwest Second; (785) 263–2231 or
(800) 569–5915

Junction City/Geary County Convention and
Visitors Bureau,
(785) 238–2885 or (800) 528–2489

Homestead Motel,
1736 North Washington
Street,
(785) 238–6662

Thunderbird Marina RV
on Milford Lake,
6515 West Rolling Hills
Road,
(785) 238–5864

TOPEKA
Best Western,
700 Southwest Fairlawn
Road (I–70, exit 357),
(785) 228–2223

Comfort Inn,
1518 Southwest
Wanamaker Road,
(785) 273–5365 or
(800) 228–5150

Country Club Motel,
3732 South Topeka Avenue,
(785) 266–3732

Ramada Inn,
420 East Sixth Street, off
Interstate 70,
(785) 234–5400 or
(800) 272–6232

WASHINGTON
Washington Motel,
310 West Seventh Street,
(785) 325–2281

PLACES TO EAT IN NORTH CENTRAL KANSAS

ABILENE
Victorian Restaurant
Garden,
1708 North Buckeye
Avenue, (785) 263–1997

CLAY CENTER
Bill's Place Elks Dining,
611 Fifth Street,
(785) 632–5626

COUNCIL GROVE
Hays House,
112 West Main Street,
(620) 767–5911

HANOVER
Pony Express Cafe,
Junction of Highways
36 and 148,
(785) 337–2617

JUNCTION CITY
Chubby's BBQ,
203 South Washington
Street,
(785) 762–2773

Gashaus Erika,
610 North Washington
Street,
(785) 762–6414

MANHATTAN
Granny Smith's,
706 Anderson Avenue,
(785) 537–9340

Little Apple Brewing Co.,
1110 West Loop
Shopping Center, off I–70,
(785) 539–5500

Sirloin Stockade,
325 East Poyntz Avenue,
(785) 776–0516

Texas Star Café,
608 North Twelfth Street,
(785) 539–9393

SENECA
Bob's Sirloin Room,
103 North Street,
(785) 336–2982

Valentino's Of Seneca,
604 North Eleventh Street,
(785) 336–3575

TOPEKA
Paisano's Ristorante II,
4043 Southwest Tenth
Street,
(785) 273–0100

Patty's Place,
2134 North Kansas Avenue,
(785) 235–9101

WASHINGTON
Longhorn Club,
320 "C" Street,
(785) 325–3178

Mom & Pop's Family
Restaurant,
605 "B" Street,
(785) 325–2357

Northwest Kansas

*Y*ou are about to enter the ***Smoky Hills,*** tucked between the Flint Hills and the High Plains. The landscape is grand in scale, sculpted and folded by the many creeks and rivers flowing through it. In the northwest corner, numerous dry draws run into branch lines of the two main waterways, the Beaver and Sappa Creeks, which then join the Republican River. The resulting landscape is one of high plains and rolling countryside tilting gently toward the creek bottoms.

Millions of buffalo roamed here, along with deer and antelope, as you know, from singing "Home on the Range" (the Kansas state song, by the way) in day camp. The Cheyenne and Pawnee lived here and met Coronado in 1541.

The Dakota Sandstone hills on the east, Post Rock Country in the middle, and the Blue Hills along the western edge define the area. Although this territory is larger than Vermont, New Hampshire, or New Jersey, the population is spread thin; the sky reaches all the way to the horizon, with little to clutter the view.

At one time dust storms darkened the sky. From as early as 1883, there is a record of the Sioux Indians telling a man named John Christiansen that the sodbusters had the earth "wrong side up"—the Indians only split the sod to plant corn. Years later, in the time of the Dust Bowl, thousands of tons of topsoil were blown away, and the settlers learned the lesson the Native Americans had tried to teach them.

It's a long way between cities here, with a lot of land in between. Prairies are not flat but have easy slopes, graceful rolls that resemble the heavy swell of the ocean after a storm. Roads weave through fields of wheat, corn, milo, and remnants of virgin short-grass grazing lands. Prehistoric inland seas helped sculpt the land, laying down hundreds of feet of sedimentary rocks; it is a fossil hunter's paradise.

Interstate 70 parallels the Old Smoky Hill Trail that led to the goldfields of Denver in 1859. (There is an excellent chance that you are already on Interstate 70; it is called "the Main Street of Kansas" and shoots like a

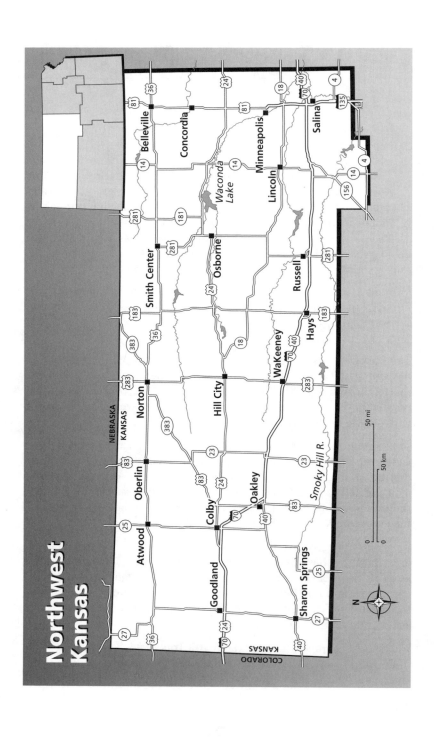

tunnel through the state at a posted 70 miles per hour.) But off this freeway lie some of the most fascinating towns in the state. The choice of motels is endless, but there are also more than fifteen bed-and-breakfasts and restored old hotels tucked in unexpected places and waiting for you.

Main Street U.S.A.

We begin in **Salina.** The town lies in a basin near the confluence of the Saline and Smoky Hill Rivers. The scenic Smoky Hills gently rise and fall all around the city.

Post Rock Tours begin in Salina and travel along Highway 18; it's an easy way to see many of the massive buildings constructed from post rock, a layer of particularly fine quarrying limestone that extends from Nebraska to WaKeeney. The stone, plentiful in this part of the country, was used extensively as fence-post and building material by the clever pioneers, who found a chronic shortage of wood in this nearly treeless land and recognized the impermanence of sod for building. Contact Duane Vonada (785–526–7369) for more information.

If you didn't stay at a bed-and-breakfast and are looking for breakfast (or lunch or dinner), folks will direct you to a place called **Russell's Restaurant and Sweet Shoppe** at 649 Westport Boulevard (corner of Crawford Street and Highway 81 in Salina). It is always open, twenty-four hours a day, seven days a week. You know the old maxim about asking a trucker where the best food is to be found? Russell's is that place. The restaurant is famous for its anytime breakfast menu (Mexican omelet, Belgian waffles) and hickory-smoked dinners (Thursday is all-you-can-eat chicken night) and the bakery is a wonderland of strawberry chiffon pies and other desserts. Call (785) 825–5733. It is simply the best food in town.

The **Central Kansas Flywheels, Inc.** (785–825–8473), at 1100 West Diamond Drive, Salina, is made up of families who are interested in preserving the heritage of the state. The group started collecting antique tractors and named itself for one of the engine parts. An unlikely looking metal building off Interstate 70 (exit 252) houses an 1880s print shop, and so many pieces of old machinery are lovingly displayed that it is well worth the donation at the door to the all-volunteer organization. Open April through October, CKFI has an annual Antique Engine and Threshing Show, held in October. Admission for adults is $3.00; children age twelve and younger are free. Closed on Monday, but any other time you just stop by and see if anyone's there, or visit the Web at www.centralkansasfly wheels.org.

If you're shopping for antiques, there are numerous shops downtown, including *Auld Lang Syne Antique Mall* (785–825–0020) in the former First National Bank building at Santa Fe and Iron Avenues. A map of the antiques and specialties shops is available from the chamber of commerce at Seventh and Ash (785–827–9301).

The *Smoky Hill Museum* at 211 West Iron Avenue features local history, a country store, and period rooms. You can purchase wheat weavings by local artist Donna Morgenstern at the museum. It is open Tuesday through Friday from noon to 5:00 P.M., Saturday from 10:00 A.M. to 5:00 P.M., and Sunday from 1:00 to 5:00 P.M. Call (785) 826–7460.

The *Salina Art Center,* at 242 South Santa Fe, has been called the best contemporary art institution in the state. Visitors can find everything from photographs to sculpture in a 1920s Spanish Revival building. This art center hosts continually changing exhibitions by talented regional artists as well as recognized masters. It offers programs for adults and children that are related to the exhibitions. The Imagination Zone is a hands-on laboratory where children can touch, weave, draw, design, and go on scavenger hunts Tuesday through Saturday from noon to 5:00 P.M., Thursday from noon to 7:00 P.M., and Sunday from 1:00 to 5:00 P.M. Call (785) 827–1431 or (800) 284–6022.

Just 1 block north of the center, the *Salina Art Center Cinema* (150 South Santa Fe) is in a renovated storefront in the downtown historic district. This is the place for offbeat, imaginative, and thought-provoking films that you might not find in a conventional theater. Call (785) 452–9868 for show times.

Popular with the locals is the *Hickory Hut* at 1707 West Crawford Street (785–825–1588). Or there's the *Cozy Inn,* 108 North Seventh, a six-stool eatery serving tiny hamburgers with fried onions, just the way it has for eighty years. Call (785) 825–9407. Or try *Scheme,* at 123 North Seventh (785–823–5125), for pizza and sandwiches.

If the children have too much stored-up energy to be in the car one more minute, get off I–135 at the Crawford exit and, just off Centennial Road at 1634 Sunflower Lane, find *Jumpin' Joe's Family Fun Center,* the place to let off some steam. There is a thirty-six-hole miniature golf course, go-carts zooming around a track, a laser-tag room, and a video-game area. There is even a soft play area with tubes and tunnels for preschoolers to take off their shoes and play in. Call (785) 827–9090. The outdoor things, of course, are seasonal, but the laser tag and video area are open year-round.

At **Rolling Hills Zoo** (625 Hedville Road), just outside Salina, there's a lot more here than buffalo. Thriving in this prairie landscape are a 7,000-pound Indian rhinoceros, some exotic snow leopards, a couple of orang-utans, and white rhinos. More than sixty-one endangered species and about 200 animals call this place home. It is open to the public and features the Education/Discovery Center, a gift shop, and a restaurant. Hours are 9:00 A.M. to 5:00 P.M. daily. Admission is $8.00 for adults, $7.00 for seniors, and $5.00 for children ages two to twelve. Tram rides are available for $2.00. Call (785) 827–9488 for more information.

Back in 1919, more than 250 acres of grapes were planted in the fields around Salina. Now Kay Bloom and Steve Jennings have converted an old riding stable into a winery. **The Smoky Hill Vineyards and Winery** at 212 West Golf Link Road produces twenty-eight wines including dry chablis, clarets rich in oak and tannins, light, semi-dry blushes, and a dessert *Icewein*. Sunshine is essential for creating good wine, and Kansas has abundant sunshine as well as rich soil. The grapes are hand

Trivia

If you have a canoe atop your van, the Smoky Hill River has a public canoe trail that begins 20 miles west of and ends 4 miles southeast of Kanopolis. It is 10.5 miles long and takes about four or five hours to complete. Call the Army Corp of Engineers office (785–546–2294) for the entry location.

tended from spring pruning through fall harvest. Add to this the best equipment and the wine-making skills of Steve and Kay, and the results are wines that rank among the best in blind tastings of American and European wines. Wines are sold from the tasting room at the winery (as well as in Wilson and Wichita); tours and tastings are free. Hours are Monday through Saturday from 10:00 A.M. to 8:00 P.M., and Sunday from noon to 6:00 P.M. Call (785) 825-2515.

The town of **Smolan** is southwest of Salina on I–135. The old high-school building now houses **The Hickory Tree Restaurant,** at Third and Walnut Streets. Some of the classrooms are used for private parties and the main restaurant is in the gym. Kathy and Lee Holzwarth "retired," he calls it, here from much more strenuous careers and now just cook for as many as 500 people. This is barbecue heaven with an extensive menu—all barbequed, smoked, seasoned, and glazed—and an all-you-can-eat philosophy for $11.00 (children only $4.95) that includes drink, dessert, and tax. This school is open only on weekends: Friday and Saturday from 5:00 to 9:00 P.M. and Sunday for lunch from 11:00 A.M. to 2:00 P.M. If you are headed west, Lee is from St. Francis, up in the northwest corner of the state, and he can tell you a lot about the history and landscape of that area, which they explore with horses and motorcycles. His parents own one of the last inhabitable sod houses in the state and love to show it off to visitors. Phone (785) 668–2164.

Trivia

*If you are looking for a scenic drive, take Highway 14 from Ellsworth to Mankato. You can get that buffalo burger you have been wanting to try at **Buffalo Roam.** Call (785) 378–3971 for hours and directions.*

Too full to travel now? The **C & W Ranch** has a room waiting for you. This is a real working ranch headquarters with home-raised, home-made food. The quiet country atmosphere and pretty antique decor make it a perfect place to relax. If you are hauling horses, they have stalls as well. The ranch welcomes hunting groups and is fine for receptions, reunions, and all kinds of retreats. Look at the Web site at www.candwranch.com or call (785) 668–2352. The ranch is at 4000 South Halstead Road just south of the I–70 and I–135 interchange at Salina.

Fourteen miles southwest of Salina on Highway 140 is **Brookville,** home of a special bed-and-breakfast. **The Castle Rock Ranch,** at

1086 Twenty-ninth Road, is a modern ranch built around the original 1917 farmhouse. There are eight rooms, all with private baths, and some with fireplaces, hot tubs, or private decks. Rooms are $75 to $150, including a full country breakfast. Evening meals are available at an additional cost. Every window has a panoramic view of the Smoky Hills. This 160-acre spread has hiking paths to the top of Castle Rock Hill. The ranch has four stalls in the stables for your horses, for an additional $20. Call (785) 225–6865 or (888) 225–6865, or e-mail crr@castlerockbnb.com.

Not far from Brookville, **Kanopolis Lake and State Park,** off Highway 141, is perfect for fishing, boating, and camping. The park also contains **Kanopolis Trails,** a 26-mile hiking and horse trail, which is also open to mountain bikes. You can get a self-guided driving tour of the area on **Legacy Trail,** which focuses on the history of the valley. It will guide you to places such as pioneer cemeteries and old homesteads along the old Butterfield Stage Coach route. For trail information, contact the Kanopolis State Park office at (785) 546–2565.

> ### Trivia
>
> *The COWBOY Society (Cock-eyed Old West Band of Yahoos) was created to preserve and encourage the cowboy stories of Kansas. You can visit their Web site at www.drovers mercantile.com.*

Two miles south and 2.5 miles west of Highways 140 and 141 near Ellsworth is **Mushroom Rocks State Park,** unique for its Dakota sandstone formations that mimic mushrooms. It's managed by the state park office at Kanapolis, (785) 546–2565. You will need a vehicle sticker for your car at both parks, available for $4.00.

Two miles north of New Cambria, **Iron Mound** passes (in Kansas) for a mountain, with an elevation of 1,497 feet. Visible from Interstate 70, it is crowned with greenhorn limestone, the easternmost outcropping of Cretaceous limestone in Kansas.

Continuing southwest on Highway 140 brings you to the town of **Ellsworth.**

Armin and Norma Meitler are the team who create **Meitler's Hand-Carved Birds** at their home at 308 Forest Drive. Armin carves more than fifty-eight varieties of birds, mostly indigenous Kansas species, and also wooden cribbage boards. Most of the birds are made of basswood, but some are carved from more exotic woods such as sumac and poison ivy. (Yes! But he insists it won't bother you.)

Norma does the painting with acrylics, and the couple has sold more than 10,000 birds in all fifty states and twenty-seven countries. They don't advertise, and they don't sell in shops or craft shows—just to people stopping by to look. The birds range in price from about $20 for the natural wooden birds to $50 for the hand-painted ones. Stop by or call for an appointment at (785) 472–4326. No large groups please; Armin is in his 90s now.

The **Ira E. Lloyd House Bed and Breakfast** is at 1575 Avenue JJ in Ellsworth. This three-story Victorian, circa 1895, is named for the state senator who lived there when he was elected in 1887. There are three rooms, one with private bath, all filled with period furniture. Host Clovia Katzenmeier gives seniors a 10 percent discount on the rooms, which are $59 to $79, including breakfast. Call (785) 472–5100, or visit the Kansas Bed and Breakfast Association Web site, www.kbba.com.

Drover's Mercantile (119 North Douglas) is run by cowboy Jim Gray. He dresses the part and sells all manner of western goods—boots, clothing, gear, and reproduction 1870s shields, lances, and tomahawks made by the Lakota Sioux of South Dakota. Jim and his partner, Linda Kohls, also carry a large selection of books on the Old West. There is a real chuckwagon that was on Jim's family ranch, and the walls of the shop are covered with siding from a family barn. Get Jim started telling stories, and you can plan on spending the rest of the day in the shop if you want to. He loves talking about Ellsworth's cow-town history. In the 1870s, Ellsworth was the end of the trail for longhorns. The herds passed down the street right in front of where the Mercantile stands now. Call (785) 472–4703 to speak to Jim. Hours are from 10:00 A.M. to 5:00 P.M. Monday through Saturday.

Next door at 121 North Douglas is another cowboy, John Barr, at **Johnny Bingo's Hats.** He sells more than hats, though. John has a large supply of antique hat boxes and old cowboy-movie posters. His hours, Monday through Friday 9:00 A.M. to 6:00 P.M. and Saturday noon to 6:00 P.M., are irregular. Stop by or call ahead (785–472–3090).

Another Ellsworth business is the **Tack Room** at 121 East First Street. Doug Evans, who specializes in saddle and boot repair, has a number of old saddles on display and has made a few of his own. Call (785) 472–3720 for hours.

The town also has two antiques malls, **Ellsworth Antique Mall** at 210 North Douglas (785–472–4659) and **Smoky Hill Antiques Mall** at 220 North Douglas (785–472–3582). Hours are Monday through Saturday 9:30 A.M. to 5:30 P.M. and Sunday 1:00 to 5:00 P.M. at both malls.

As you near Wilson Lake, past Salina on Interstate 70, you will notice the dramatic silhouette of the two 80-foot-high wind generators built by the U.S. Army Corps of Engineers. This area has the most constant wind in the state. They generate 86,000 kilowatt-hours of power annually to the Smoky Hill Electric Cooperative. The object is to substitute clean power for fossil fuel, and it's about time. A scale model of a Wilson Lake wind generator is in the Aerospace Museum at the Smithsonian Institution in Washington, D.C.

For some breathtaking views, get off Interstate 70 at exit 206 and turn north on Highway 232. You'll be on the *Post Rock Scenic Byway,* driving along *Wilson Lake.* The lake occupies 100 miles of shoreline and 9,000 acres of water. Highway 232 goes to Lucas, the "Grassroots Art Capital" of Kansas. Turn west on Highway 18. You can see Wolf Creek Valley, a part of the Smoky Hills greenhorn limestone escarpment. Notice the bluffs south of the valley and the level valley floor. In the roadside park in Luray is the first log cabin built in Russell County.

Continue on Highway 18 to Paradise to see the limestone water tower, or head south on Highway 281 at the junction of Highway 18 and 281. Highway 281 cuts though layers of limestone, revealing outcroppings of Dakota, Graners shale, and greenhorn limestone. The Saline River Valley provides some rugged landscape and dispels the notion that Kansas is flat.

Trivia
Russell is the hometown of former senator Bob Dole.

From Interstate 70, pull off at the *Wilson* exit and take something from Kansas home with you. Just about anything you want, as a matter of fact, can be found at the *Kansas Originals Market* at 233 Highway 232. It features fine folk art, crafts, and food. The huge steel building houses art and crafts from most of the artists mentioned in this book, so if you are having second thoughts about a piece you didn't buy somewhere in the state, you might be able to find something like it here: stained glass, quilts, pottery, wood carvings, and jewelry. You can also take home apple cider, kolaches, jams, and wheat snacks. The market is open from 9:00 A.M. to 6:00 P.M. Monday through Saturday and from 11:00 A.M. to 6:00 P.M. Sunday. Call (785) 658–2602 or (877) 457–6233. Their Web site is www.kansasoriginals.com, where you can order something you forgot to buy.

In the town of *Dorrance* (exit 199 off Interstate 70) you'll find the *Country Inn* at 3871 198th Street. This Victorian home is close to Lake Wilson yet a world away. There is excellent biking in this neighborhood. Hosts Rich and Mary Ann Steinle offer visitors a full or continental breakfast each morning. Rooms are $55. Call (785) 666–4468.

Tom and Janet Taggart have been turning out good food at the **Bunker Hill Cafe** at Sixth and Elm Streets in **Bunker Hill** for more than nineteen years. Originally built as a drugstore in 1916, it is a unique nineteenth-century eating place. Fresh-baked raisin bread is a specialty of the house, along with catfish, Norwegian salmon, and steak.

All entrees are ordered by weight to satisfy appetites of all sizes. They serve homemade bread from the bakery they added to the back. They advertise "the best meal you'll ever have"; how's that for confidence? Hours are from 5:00 to 10:00 P.M. Wednesday through Saturday, 11:00 A.M. to 8:00 P.M. on Mother's Day, Father's Day, and Easter. Call (785) 483–6544.

Leave Interstate 70 at exit 184 and enter the Saline River Valley and the town of **Russell:** You'll see a building that looks more like a miniature stone castle than a museum, complete with turreted towers and an arched stone entry of greenhorn limestone known here as post rock. The **Fossil Station Museum** (785–483–3637) at 331 Kansas Street was built in 1907, the original block-stone stage station on the Smoky Hill Trail and formerly the county jail. It captures the spirit of the history from the late 1800s to 1930 and is open from Memorial Day to Labor Day, Tuesday through Sunday from 1:00 to 4:00 P.M., and by appointment. Admission is free, but donations are welcome.

Maybe you don't think of Kansas as oil country—think again. The **Oil Patch Museum** (785–483–6640) contains the story of the history of "black gold"; walk through an actual oil storage tank and study the geology, drilling, and production of oil. Outdoors you can see the drilling rigs and steam engines. You will find it near the intersection of Interstate 70 and South Highway 281. It's open Memorial Day to Labor Day, Monday from 9:00 A.M. to 2:00 P.M., Tuesday through Saturday from 9:00 A.M. to 6:00 P.M., and Sunday from 1:00 to 5:00 P.M. (in winter by appointment). Admission to both museums is free, but donations are welcome.

The **Gernon House** at 818 Kansas Street is one of the oldest post-rock stone houses, built in 1872 by a blacksmith and one of the original settlers. It has been fully restored, and furnished to the period.

The **Heym–Oliver House** at 503 North Kansas Street is another 1870s stone house, though this one is sawed stone, rather than faced or chipped. Ask your guide to explain the difference. It is also furnished. Hours are the same for both houses: Memorial Day to Labor Day, 1:00 to 4:00 P.M. Saturday and Sunday; by appointment Labor Day to Memorial Day. Call (785) 483–3637. Admission to all four attractions in Russell is free.

Deines Cultural Center (785–483–3742) at 820 Main was given to the city of Russell as the permanent home of the wood engravings of the nationally known artist E. Hubert Deines. The gallery also features the work of other artists, and exhibits change monthly. Admission is free; donations are welcome.

As you zip along Interstate 70, a church spire will catch your eye. St. Fidelis Church, known as the *Cathedral of the Plains,* is 9 miles east of Hays in *Victoria* at 900 Cathedral Street. This Romanesque limestone structure was finished in 1911 by German–Russian settlers. It is a remarkable feat of architectural beauty named for Capuchin Friar St. Fidelis. The church and monastery form the shape of a cross. Romanesque in design, the immense sanctuary holds enough pews to seat more than 1,000 people. Eighteen 10-foot granite columns, each weighing fifteen tons and topped with hand-carved capitals, reach to the 44-foot-high, arched and ribbed ceiling. Each family in the parish hauled six loads of stone with horse and wagon from a nearby quarry and contributed $45 to help finance construction. They hand-cut the massive sandstone blocks and dressed them in their spare time. The rose petal–shaped stained-glass panels above the doors represent harmony. They were shipped from Germany in 1916. Be sure to notice the hand-carved Austrian stations of the cross purchased in 1919 and the Italian Carrara marble altar installed in 1986. The church was dubbed "Cathedral of the Plains" in 1912 by William Jennings Bryan. It is open daily from sunrise to 8:00 P.M. Donations are appreciated. Call (785) 735–2777.

The Settlement of the Saline River Valley

*T*he earliest people to inhabit the Great Plains region lived during the Paleo-Indian period, about 12,000 years ago. These people were hunters and gatherers who roamed widely in search of mammoths and large bison. Prehistoric carvings may still be found in the weathered sandstone outcroppings in the area. European explorers and traders entered the Saline River Valley in the 1500s. A Frenchman, Etienne Bourgmont, made contact with the Padouca Indians, who hunted buffalo on horseback. During the nineteenth century the Pawnee and Cheyenne lived here. In the late 1850s white settlers began to establish homes here despite drought, invading hordes of grasshoppers, and prairie fires. In 1964 the dam built to make Wilson Lake was closed, and the waters inundated the Saline River Valley, changing it forever from open prairie to domestic farmland.

There are a dozen Roman Catholic churches in the small towns off I–70 between Russell and Hays. All but two of them are constructed of post rock, the area's unique building stone characterized by its brown streaks. These are the churches of the Volga Germans, who settled here in the late nineteenth century, each group from a different German town. Since travel by horse and wagon was so difficult, the immigrants built a church in each of the new settlements. Some older residents of this part of Kansas still speak one of the German dialects of their forefathers. All of the churches have stained-glass windows and a tower with a cross on top. All are handcrafted. Carvers shaped capitals for huge granite columns, while carpenters sculpted ornate altars of intricate design.

One of the most beautiful of the group is the **Holy Cross Shrine** at **Pfeifer** (12 miles south of Victoria), finished in 1918. Red-and-blue stained-glass windows are supported by delicate, vaulted arches and

St. Fidelis's Feather Muffins

*Y*ou can get some divine recipes from the Towers of Heavenly Recipes, *a cookbook offered by St. Fidelis Church in Victoria. It contains 278 pages of Volga-German, Russian, and other ethnic recipes along with proverbs, household hints, and German prayers from members of the parish. The proceeds are used to keep the "Cathedral of the Plains" in good repair. The book is $15, including postage. Make checks payable to St. Fidelis Church and mail to Ethel Younger, 601 Tenth Street, Victoria, KS 67671.*

These feather muffins are the church's entry in the Great Muffin Search. They truly are light as a feather!

2 cups flour	1. Preheat the oven to 350°.
3 teaspoons baking powder	2. Sift flour, baking powder, and salt.
½ teaspoon salt	3. In a large bowl, cream sugar and butter. Add egg and mix.
¼ cup sugar	
¼ cup butter	4. Add the dry ingredients alternately with milk to the creamed mixture.
1 egg	5. Bake at 350° for 20 minutes.
¾ cup milk	Yield: 12 muffins

pillars. It has been called the "two-cents church," because each family was asked to give two cents on each bushel of wheat they grew while it was being built. Many of these old churches have closed due to the area's dwindling population, but this one can be seen as part of Hays's summertime evening tours. Call the Convention and Visitors Bureau at (800) 569–4505 for more information.

The **Sternberg Museum of Natural History** is located just off Interstate 70 at 3000 Sternberg Drive in **Hays.** The museum has a huge four-story dome re-creating Earth eighty-eight million years ago. Visitors can walk from the ocean bottom to land among several animated, life-size replicas of dinosaurs and other animal life. Under the Kansas Seaway, you will see giant prehistoric marine lizards and fish that lived millions of years ago. The Discovery Room is a hands-on learning center for all ages. Touch models, use computers, and explore to your heart's content. Natural history, including recent vertebrates and invertebrates; geology; history, including objects dealing with the period of discovery, exploration, and settlement of the Great Plains; fossils—whatever your interest, you'll find it here. This is the home of the world-famous "fish within a fish" fossil. Its previous home was the Cretaceous period, some eighty-eight million years ago.

Traveling exhibits are also brought to the Sternberg Museum. One of the best known was a cast copy of "Sue," the *Tyrannosaurus rex* from Chicago's Field Museum of Natural History that toured only fifteen museums in the country.

Buffalo Herd

*F*our miles south of I–70, on the Highway 183 bypass, is a small herd of buffalo, a tiny remnant of the vast herds, numbering in the millions, that once roamed the North American plains. If you have never actually seen a buffalo, this is your chance. The herd was started in 1953 with a bull named Wild Bill and a cow named Calamity Jane (a cow is a girl buffalo, by the way). Now the herd has grown. The main bull is Max and he has many, many cows making eyes at him, and the calves keep coming. There is a life-size buffalo sculpture by local artist Pete "Fritz" Felton, Jr., entitled Monarch of the Plains, just outside historic Fort Hays. It reminds us that the Native Americans depended on the buffalo for everything—food, shelter, clothing, and tools—and felt it was worth fighting for when the railroad and white settlers began to slaughter them.

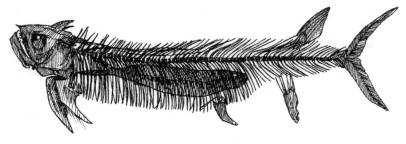

"Fish within a Fish" Fossil

Hours are Sunday and Monday, 1:00 to 9:00 P.M., Tuesday through Saturday, 9:00 A.M. to 9:00 P.M. Admission is $5.00 for adults, $3.00 for youth and seniors. It's free to members. For more information, call (785) 628–4286, or visit the Web site at www.hsu.edu/sternberg.

The Hays Convention and Visitors Bureau sponsors "Twilight Tours" each summer. Every night from June through August, a bus stops at all of the motels on Vine Street to pick up anyone who wants to take one of the seventeen free tours of the area. Guests get to see some of the ranches, a limestone quarry with a post-rock demonstration, a horse farm, historic churches, and a beautiful Kansas sunset. Call the convention and visitors bureau at (800) 569–4505 for a schedule.

Three local eateries come highly recommended by Hays residents. ***Professor's Steakhouse*** (521 East Eleventh; 785–625–9930) is open for lunch and dinner Monday through Saturday from 11:00 A.M. to 10:00 P.M., Sunday from 8:00 A.M. to 8:00 P.M.

Al's Chickenette (700 Vine Street; 785–625–7414) specializes in fried chicken and chicken-fried steak cooked to order and served with mashed potatoes, gravy, and veggies. The decor is all "Early Chicken" (you will understand when you see it). Hours are Tuesday through Saturday from 11:00 A.M. to 9:30 P.M., Sunday from 11:00 A.M. to 2:00 P.M. and 4:30 to 8:30 P.M.

Rooftops at 1200 Main Street, on the sixth floor of the Emprise Bank Building (785–628–8631), is not exactly off the beaten path, but for steaks, seafood, and a great view of the city, you can't beat it. It is an elegant place where the waiters wear tuxes and candles light the tables. Dinner hours are Monday through Saturday from 5:00 to 10:00 P.M.

Sculptor Pete "Fritz" Felten's ***Stone Gallery*** is at 107 West Sixth. The Hays native uses native limestone to create works that can be seen all over the state. He carved the figures of the four famous Kansans that stand in the state capitol in Topeka; his works can also be seen in front of the Cathedral of the Plains in Victoria and the Lindsborg Museum. The statue of Wild Bill Hickok on Hays's Main Street is his work, too. Pieces ranging in size from tabletop to life-size are on display at the gallery and in the sculpture garden outside. Most pieces are for sale. Call (785) 625–7619 for hours and other information.

Visit the unique *Boxcar Museum* on the grounds of the Hays American Legion post at Thirteenth and Canterbury. It is made from a boxcar that's crossed the ocean. Filled with food and sent to war-torn France by the United States in the 1940s, the grateful French returned it filled with gifts from every province. Open by appointment; call Ralph Walters at (785) 625–3952, or the Hays Convention and Visitors Bureau at (785) 628–8202.

The century-old *Kansas State University Ag Research Center* is at 1232 240th Avenue in Hays, just off the Highway 183 bypass. The 3,600-acre farm has demonstration plots for nonirrigated wheat and sorghum and has 800 head of beef cattle. Call (785) 625–3952 to arrange a tour and learn about the research the university is doing.

The *Tea Rose Inn Bed and Breakfast,* at 117 West Thirteenth Street, is a neatly restored 1909 Victorian with architectural features such as beveled art-glass windows and an open handcrafted staircase. But it also has all the modern amenities, including whirlpool baths and telephones in the rooms. You can stroll down the original brick-paved streets of Hays to shopping, art galleries, theaters, and church. Restaurants are nearby for lunch and dinner, but breakfast here is not just breakfast, it is a day-starting event, according to innkeeper Rose Stramel, with freshly ground coffee or fine teas. Rooms are $60 to $100. Call (785) 623–4060 or (888) 623–1125. Visit the Web site at www.tearose.net or e-mail at rs@tearose.net.

> ## Trivia
>
> *Hays was a wild town in the late 1860s, with plenty of saloons and dance halls. Wild Bill Hickok was sheriff for a few months, but left town after a brawl with some troopers. While her husband, Lt. Col. George Custer, was encamped there, Elizabeth Custer said that "there was enough desperate history in that little town in one summer to make a whole library of dime novels."*

Fort Hays State Historic Site is located on U.S. Highway 183 Alternate just south of Hays. An important U.S. Army post from 1865 to 1889, the fort was built to protect stage lines, workers on the Union Pacific Railroad, and settlers, and to serve as a supply base for other area forts. Wild Bill Hickok, Buffalo Bill Cody, and Lt. Col. George Armstrong Custer all have connections to the fort. Fort Hays was also home to the Tenth U.S. Cavalry, whose black troopers were also known as Buffalo Soldiers.

Four original buildings survive: the stone blockhouse (completed in 1868), a guardhouse, and two officers' quarter buildings. A modern visitors center displays furnishings, weapons, and other artifacts. Fort Hays is open from 1:00 to 5:00 P.M. Sunday and Monday and from 9:00 A.M. to 5:00 P.M. the rest of the week. Closed some holidays. Admission is free, but donations are welcome. For more information, call (785) 625–6812, or check the Web site at www.kshs.org.

Ellis calls itself the "Antique City of the High Plains." To back up that claim, you'll find *H & H Sentimentals Antique Mall* at 819 Washington Street (785–726–4575) and a half dozen individual shops, one near the interstate and the others downtown on Washington Street.

> **Trivia**
>
> American automaker Walter P. Chrysler worked first on train locomotives, then for Buick, General Motors, Willys-Overland, and Maxwell Motor, before founding Chrysler Corporation in 1925.

The *Bukovina Society of America's Headquarters and Museum* is also in Ellis. It is a stately two-story limestone building at Eighth and Washington Streets. The Bukovina people came here in the 1880s from the Rhine-Palatinate and Württemberg in Germany and the Bohemian forest of Austria. Although a minority in their new country, they lived in ethnic German communities and neighborhoods, preserving their language and customs. The museum has artifacts, historic photographs, and genealogy materials, and is open from 1:00 to 5:00 P.M. year-round. Guided tours can be arranged with advance notice. Call either (785) 726–4568 or (785) 726–4201.

The *Walter P. Chrysler Boyhood Home* at 102 West Tenth takes you back to the 1880s and lets you peek into the early life of the Chrysler Corporation's founder. Chrysler moved to Ellis with his family at the age of three, lived here until his teens when he went west to work, then returned to marry a local girl. The house is furnished in period style; an adjacent museum shows a short video and displays personal memorabilia.

Hours May through September are 9:30 A.M. to 4:30 P.M. Monday through Saturday, and 12:30 to 4:30 P.M. on Sunday. October through April the home and museum are open 11:00 A.M. to 3:00 P.M. Monday through Saturday, 12:30 to 4:30 P.M. Sunday. Admission is $3.00 for adults, $2.00 for seniors, and $1.00 for children ages eight to fifteen. Call (785) 726–3636 for more information.

Look for the **Landmark Craft Co-op** at Ninth and Washington Streets. It has crafts of all kinds, from weaving to woodcraft, made by local craftspeople. The hours are 9:00 A.M. to 5:00 P.M. Tuesday through Saturday. Call (785) 726–3465.

The **Ellis Railroad and Doll Museum** is at 911 Washington Street (785–726–4493). There are working model trains, including one that pulls a bright yellow Union Pacific caboose. The kids can ride on a miniature General Motors Aero Streamliner on 2.5 miles of track outside the museum. On the third floor is a collection of more than 1,600 dolls dating from 1900. They include bridal dolls, Howdy Doody, and Barbie. Hours are seasonal. April through October the museum is open from 9:00 A.M. to 5:00 P.M. Monday through Saturday, from 1:00 to 5:00 P.M. Sunday. November through March, hours are from 11:00 A.M. to 4:00 P.M. Monday through Saturday, from 1:00 to 4:00 P.M. Sunday. Admission is $2.00 for adults, $1.00 for children (under age four are free).

Trivia
If you're traveling along Highway 183, you will notice a lot of metal sculptures. These are the creation of Curly Leiker, who lives on the Sweetwater Ranch. You will see his work all over the area. He has made many life-size mailbox characters and Southwest coyotes. It is just a hobby, he says, that developed from a welding class he took at the local university back in 1970. Watch for his creations as you drive.

High Plains

About halfway between Kansas City and Denver on Interstate 70 is the town of **WaKeeney,** with a golf course, a swimming pool, antiques shops, a Christmas shop, and *two* drugstore soda fountains on Main Street (Cleland Drugs and Gibson Pharmacy). WaKeeney is known as the Christmas City of the High Plains. Every holiday season several tons of fresh greenery are made into a 40-foot tree and covered with more than 3,000 lights. Another 3,000 lights decorate the town.

The **Thistle Hill Bed and Breakfast** is 7 miles west of WaKeeney just off Interstate 70. Owners Dave and Mary Hendricks offer country comfort on a 600-acre farm. The fields near the house have been returned to native grasses, and Mary has planted a bumper crop of wildflowers.

Guests can get comfortable in front of the fireplace in the oak-floored dining room or chat with Mary in the big country kitchen while she fixes breakfast. A full breakfast, with fresh, homemade breads, muffins, or hotcakes, is part of the package; and for an extra fifteen bucks, your horse can stay, too. They've thought of everything. Call (785) 743–2644 from 6:00 to 8:00 A.M. or evenings, because it is a working farm, or e-mail wildflowermary@yahoo.com. Directions will be given when you call. The cost is $59 to $85 for a double.

A natural addition to the Thistle Hill Bed and Breakfast is the **Peaceful Prairie Shop.** It features dried wreaths, swags, and basket arrangements designed from the flowers and herbs that Mary grows in her gardens. Also available are brewed herbal soaps and pressed-wildflower and photo greeting cards, constructed right at Thistle Hill. The fragrant cottage gardens beckon you to wander along the paths to the Peaceful Prairie.

Dave and Mary also offer accommodations at their **1906 Cottage Garden Guesthouse** at 510 Warren Avenue in WaKeeney. You'll love the front porch, cottage garden, and white picket fence. The three guest rooms go for $65 each, or rent the entire house for $150. Mary will deliver a breakfast basket with homemade breads, fruit, juice, coffee, and tea. For more information on either accommodation, visit the Web site at www.thistlehillonline.com.

In **Quinter,** off Interstate 70 at exit 212, is **The Q Inn** (785–754–3820), where you can get buffalo steak or a buffalo burger. You must try this lean and tasty meat before you leave the state. Hours are 6:30 A.M. to 9:00 P.M. Monday through Saturday, 7:00 A.M. to 9:00 P.M. on Sunday.

This is the crossroads of the High Plains, where shimmering golden fields of sunflowers dazzle your eye and ring-necked pheasant thrive. Twenty-two miles southeast of Quinter is a 70-foot-high chalk spire and natural landmark known as **Castle Rock.** It's formed from calcified deposits in an ancient sea, and is extremely brittle and not safe for climbing.

Castle Rock is shown on Kansas highway maps, but getting there isn't easy. Coming from the west, it's not visible from the road. To see it, you'll have to cross a pasture that's private property and will probably need a four-wheel-drive vehicle to do so. You might do better to approach on a county road from the east and try to get a photo from the road.

Keep your eyes open. Hereabouts, in Gove, Scott, Logan, and Lane Counties, you will see great chalk monoliths rise from the earth, pale and eerie against the prairie sky. Remnants of the same inland seas that left the salt deposits near Hutchinson in southwest Kansas, these tall stone watchtowers were once the calcareous bodies of tiny sea creatures. Now they make a strange moonscape.

At the Interstate 70 and Highway 83 interchange, you can head south 20 miles and east about 7 more to see **Monument Rocks.** These chalk bluffs and pyramids reveal a wealth of intriguing fossils to paleontologists and amateur fossil hunters alike, including fish, pterosaurs, sharks, and oyster shells. A mesosaur was found here. There is no fee to visit the landmark, but it is private property, and no fossils may be removed without the owner's permission. Do not climb the pyramids, as the chalk breaks easily. For more information, call (785) 272–3840.

The history and development of **Oakley** (at Highway 83 and I–70, exits 70–76) are told here at the **Fick Fossil Museum** (785–672–4839) at 700 West Third Street, along with the prehistoric era (remember, you're in fossil country). There are railroad displays, cattlemen's brands, photographs, paintings, a general store, and a sod house that looks cozy enough to move into tomorrow. The museum contains more than 10,000 petrified shark teeth, crinoids, and an unusual collection of artwork made from fossils 100-million-plus years old and designed by Vi and Earnest Fick, including a wall of "fossil folk art" done by Vi Fick, a bas relief sculpture of a shark made of shark's teeth. Also on exhibit are a complete *Xiphactinus audax,* a large predatory fish, and some wing bones from a flying reptile known as a pteranadon (its wingspan is estimated to have been upward of 20 feet).

From May through September, the museum is open Monday through Saturday from 9:00 A.M. to 5:00 P.M. and Sunday from 2:00 to 4:00 P.M.

Chalk Monoliths

From October through April, hours are 9:00 A.M. to noon and 1:00 to 5:00 P.M. Monday through Saturday only. There is no admission charge, but donations are appreciated.

Continue west on Highway 40 from Oakley then south on Highway 25 to **Russell Springs.** Founded in 1865, it was a water stop on the Butterfield Overland Dispatch stage line, which ran through rough Indian country to connect the goldmines of Colorado with Fort Riley. The railroad replaced the stagecoach in 1911, but the town suffered an economic double whammy when it lost the railroad line in 1917 and then the county seat in 1963. But the county left the Renaissance-style stone-and-brick courthouse and it became the **Butterfield Trail Historical Museum,** which stands as a shrine to the pioneers who blazed the trail west. The museum is open the first Tuesday of May through Labor Day, Tuesday through Saturday from 9:00 A.M. to noon and from 1:00 to 5:00 P.M., and Sunday from 1:00 to 5:00 P.M. Every year over Labor Day week-end, crowds come for Old Settlers' Day and the first full weekend in June for the Butterfield Trail Ride, a two-day, 20-mile trail ride complete with a rodeo. Phone (913) 751–4242 for more information.

Elkader is a ghost town now, with only a couple of deteriorating chalk buildings indicating where it was. In the 1870s this was the starting point for fossil-hunting expeditions into the chalks. But modern-day fossil hunters should remember that nearly all of this is private property and that they should get the owner's permission before entering a pasture. This area is also home to rattlesnakes in warm weather. Enough said?

If you stay on Interstate 70 northwest to **Colby,** be sure to see the **Prairie Museum of Art and History,** at 1905 South Franklin. The "Little Smith-sonian of the West" features the famous Kuska Collection that includes dolls, glass, porcelains, textiles, furniture, and other antiques. The museum complex includes the largest barn in Kansas, a sod house, an old church, and a one-room school. The barn measures 114 by 66 by 48 feet. It was moved in one piece into the museum complex and now houses an agricultural exhibit called "From Prairie Grasses to Golden Grain." The exhibit chronicles the past century of agricultural history in northwest Kansas in more than 150 photographs, antique implements, and memorabilia.

The cavernous second level of the barn has been left empty and is used for dances and other activities and for all visitors to experience the immensity of this facility. Visit here Tuesday through Friday from 9:00 A.M. to 5:00 P.M., Saturday and Sunday from 1:00 to 5:00 P.M. April through October the museum is also open Monday, and June through August, the museum stays open until 7:00 P.M. Monday through Saturday.

Call (785) 462–4590. Admission is $4.00 for adults, $1.00 for children ages six to sixteen.

Also in Colby is *Bourquins' Old Depot Restaurant,* at 155 East Willow, next to *Bourquins' RV Park.* To find it, take exit 54 from I–70, turn north, then west onto the frontage road. Everything's made from scratch here, including bread, cinnamon rolls, and barbecue sauce from Grandma's recipe. (Barbecued pork ribs are the Friday night special.) You can also get steak, grilled chicken, and vegetarian items. Hours are 5:00 to 9:00 P.M. from April until Mother Nature closes the campground for the winter.

You can tour the *Kansas State University Northwest Research Extension Center* (785-462-7575) at Twenty-fourth Street and Experiment Farm Road, where beautifully landscaped trees, shrubs, flowers, (incuding roses), and crops are labeled for easy identification and studied for hardiness and disease resistance. Oh yes, and there is a *Factory Outlet Mall* in Colby, too. You won't have any trouble finding that.

Goodland is the site of the *High Plains Museum* at 1717 Cherry Street. Displaying the usual pioneer and Indian artifacts, the museum also has an automated replica of America's first patented helicopter, built in Goodland in 1910. You can push the buttons and watch the blades turn, and remember that people laughed at the idea of a flying machine like this when Leonardo da Vinci drew a helicopter in the 1490s. (They may have laughed at the Kansas inventor who designed this one, too, but it worked.) From October through April the museum is open Monday through Saturday from 9:00 A.M. to 5:00 P.M. and closed on Sunday. From May through September, it's also open from 1:00 to 4:00 P.M. Sunday. Call (785) 899–4595. Admission is free.

Goodland's *Carnegie Arts Center* at 120 West Twelfth displays works by area artists and sculptors and provides a home for the performing arts. Stop by Tuesday through Friday from 10:00 A.M. to 5:00 P.M. and Saturday, Sunday, and Monday from 1:00 to 4:00 P.M. No admission charge; donations are welcome. Call (785) 899–6442 for information.

Go south on Highway 27 to Sharon Springs, then west to *Weskan* and *Mt. Sunflower* and some interesting towns, or turn north on Highway 27 to continue the northern route.

Weskan gets its name from the first three letters of "west" and "Kansas." Ten miles north and 4 miles west of Weskan is, officially, the highest point in the state. Mt. Sunflower peaks at 4,039 feet above sea level. It is also the place, unofficially, to see the most beautiful sunsets in Kansas because of the soft pinks and vivid purples of the prairie here. Ed and Cindy Harold, who live near the pinnacle and own the property, enjoy sharing their mountain view with visitors. The property is part of the original homestead of the Harold family, and they have had a number of famous guests climb to the summit. Charles Kuralt called it "my kind of mountain." You won't need much in the way of gear to climb this peak—the most strenuous part of the ten-minute walk is avoiding gopher holes.

The windmills, wildflowers, and occasional coyote make this pure Kansas. Mt. Sunflower is located in a typical western pasture with cattle grazing, but you don't have to worry about any gate. Just drive over the cattle guard. To find Mt. Sunflower, take the Kanorado exit off Interstate 70 and head south. You will come to the Harolds' ranch.

Ed and Cindy Harold welcome you to climb the mountain and sign the guest book at the top. For more information, write to them at R.R. 1, Box 54, Weskan 67762, or call (785) 943–5444.

If you decide to drive to Mt. Sunflower, then you just might enjoy a stop at Sharon Springs on Highway 27. This well-shaded town in the middle of the prairie is bisected by the Smoky Hill River.

There is some very unusual scenery up here in northwest Kansas and it is very much off the beaten path. In fact, this next trek should not be taken if there is any rain in the forecast because the dirt roads turn to mud and the canyons are steep. From *St. Francis* go north on Highway 27. It will bend west then turn back north again. From the area where it turns north again, the scenery becomes sagebrush and cactus with deep dirt canyons formed by the Arikaree River, which flows across the corner of the state from Nebraska to Colorado. The *Arikaree Breakers* are canyons so deep that people come here to hang glide, believe it or not. Marie Holzwarth has on her farm one of the last inhabitable whitewashed sod houses in the state. She and her husband live in town now, but they love to show off the house, where they sometimes spend weekends. Call (785) 332–3449 and ask for Marie.

Atwood, north and east of Goodland, is nestled amid beautiful trees in the Beaver Creek Valley at Highways 36 and 25. Every morning at seven o'clock the old town whistle blows a wake-up call to late risers in this community of about 1,600 people. But nobody's sleeping in Atwood. The town is filled with people who care about the quality of life here on the High Plains.

A group of citizens bought the old 200-seat *Jayhawk Theater* when it was sold for back taxes and joined together to rejuvenate it. The woodwork was carved and cut, and a High Plains mural was painted around the ceiling. Large neon lights in blue, red, and yellow proclaim JAYHAWK on the marquee, and current movies are shown there. Call (785) 626–3372 to see what's playing.

The Ol' Depot (785–626–3114) at Highway 25 and Lake Road is a cooperative effort of thirty-nine artists and craftspeople. The depot was saved from destruction when the railroad began tearing stations down. It was moved to its present location and renovated with funds raised locally. Soon two rooms of arts and crafts were on display downstairs. Granny's Attic was opened upstairs, without much renovation, to display antiques and collectibles sold on consignment. Now both floors do an enormous business. The Depot is open Thursday from 1:00 to 5:00 P.M., Friday and Saturday from 10:00 A.M. to 6:00 P.M., and Sunday from 1:00 to 5:00 P.M.

In the 120-year-old Shirley Opera House in Atwood, Jan Stiles runs **The Mustard Seed.** Like its proverbial name, the business began small and just kept spreading. First came the health spa, which offers half-day and full-day treatments, including massage, aromatherapy, and body wraps. Stiles also sells organic beauty products, Amish-made candles, reproduction Tiffany lamps and period furniture, and a few antiques. Hungry? There's a bakery on-site, an old-fashioned soda fountain that came from a drug store in Kansas, and a whole wall of jars filled with candy. While you're trying to choose, look over the painted murals in the opera house; they're often used as background in local photos. Call (785) 626–8000 for hours and spa appointments.

The **Rawlins County Historical Museum** is at 308 State Street. Inside is a 20 by 10-foot mural by Rudolph Wendelin, caretaker of Smokey the Bear, taking you back over the history of the county. You can listen to a tape of the artist explaining the mural's history. Then you can step into **Sts. Cyril & Methodius Catholic Church,** built in 1906 and moved into Atwood as part of the museum complex. Admission is free and hours are 9:00 A.M. to noon, and 1:00 to 4:00 P.M. Monday through Friday. Also open Saturday 1:00 to 4:00 P.M. during the summer. Phone (785) 626–2885.

Spending the night? **Country Corner** (785–626–9516) on South Highway 25 is a large, two-story home where town and country meet.

Charles and Connie Peckham invite you to relax by the fireplace or watch TV in the common room. They will serve a continental-plus breakfast. The price is $50 for a room with shared bath. E-mail cpeck ham@ruraltel.net.

Wander north on Highway 25 to the town of **Ludell** for a fine bed-and-breakfast that is part of the Atwood Association. At **The Pork Palace** (785–626–9223), Francis ("Ted") and Gertie Kastens share their large, old farm home and German heritage. They offer five guest rooms and one private bath. A full breakfast is served. Their home is 13 miles northeast of Atwood (or 5 miles north of Ludell) on Highway 36. The price is $30 for a single room, $40 for a double.

The Kastens also own the **Pork Palace Guesthouse** at 103 Main Street in Atwood. There are three bedrooms and two baths available here, and guests have use of the kitchen, if they like, since the hosts don't live here. A continental breakfast is provided. Rates are $30 for a single, $40 for a double.

Trivia

Legend has it that Horace Greeley ("Go West, young man . . ."), Pat Garrett, Roy Bean, the parents of Billy the Kid, and other notable historical figures spent a stopover together at **Stage Station 15** *in Norton. The current station is a replica of that building, and you can look through glass at papier-mâché figures of the famous folks and push a button to hear the station's history. It is on Highway 36 beside the water tower.*

Highway 36 is an array of commercial sunflower fields: Acres of natural sunflowers color the side roads from **Oberlin.** As the day passes they turn their faces with the sun. It gives you the real feel of Kansas. Oberlin, at the junction of Highways 36 and 83, was the site of the 1878 massacre of forty settlers by the North Cheyenne. **The Last Indian Raid Museum** (785–475–2712), at 258 South Penn Avenue, focuses on the history of Decatur County, not only at the time of the raid, but through the 1930s and 1940s. A Native American room displays spears, arrowheads, moccasins, and beadwork. A sod house is here, and an 1885 train depot, only 100 yards from its original site, as well as a 1922 one-room schoolhouse, complete with potbellied stove and many original textbooks. A country store, doctor's and dentist's offices, a blacksmith shop, a print shop, a millinery shop—there's a whole village here. Admission is $3.00 for adults, $1.50 for children ages six through twelve. It's open April through November 10:00 A.M. to noon and 1:00 to 5:00 P.M. June, July, and August it opens at 9:00 A.M. Tuesday through Saturday.

The LandMark Inn (189 South Penn Avenue) is in the historic Bank of Oberlin building, a circa 1886 beauty downtown. Guest suites ($69 to $105) are decorated in high Victorian style. The Carriage House Loft features much simpler, but stunning Arts and Crafts–style furnishings in the living room and bedroom (complete with a Murphy bed—remember those?). In the upstairs parlor you can socialize and enjoy the fireplace. All rooms in both buildings have private baths. Call (785) 475–2340.

Teller Room restaurant, on the first floor of the LandMark Inn, has been restored to its nineteenth-century splendor with cherry woodwork and reproduction gas lights. You can almost imagine the Victorian elegance of this place in a bustling frontier town. The menu changes daily and features fantastic desserts. Lunch is served Monday through Saturday from 11:30 A.M. to 1:30 P.M. Dinner is served Thursday through Saturday evenings from 6:30 to 8:00 P.M. One Sunday a month, the restaurant opens for brunch. There's also a gift shop, the ***Oberlin Mercantile Company,*** inside the inn. Call (888) 639–0003.

Farther east on Highway 36 at Highway 283, the First State Bank of ***Norton,*** at 105 West Main Street, is the home of the ***Gallery of Also-Rans***, featuring photos and biographies of those presidential candidates (including Horace Greeley) who were unsuccessful in their bid for the nation's highest office. It is open "bankers' hours," Monday through Friday from 9:00 A.M. to 3:00 P.M. year-round, except on legal holidays. There is no charge. Call (785) 877–3341 for information.

Norton calls itself the Pheasant Capital of the World, attracting hundreds of hunters during the pheasant season every year.

You may have noticed a shortage of woodland out here, and so did the settlers. The adobe house at Prairie Dog State Park (on Prairie Dog Creek off Highway 383, near Norton at Sebelius Lake) was built in 1892 of mud and straw and still sits at its original location. Even the Kansas winds huffin' and puffin' couldn't blow it down! Today, you can picnic, fish, boat, and camp at the park. Call (785) 877–2953 for information.

Nicodemus: A National Treasure

*T*he eastern portion of Graham County on present-day Highway 24 was the first black settlement in Kansas. Nicodemus was established in 1877 by "exodusters," former slaves freed after the Civil War, who had been offered land in Kansas. The town is the last survivor of the dozen all-black Kansas settlements and was declared a National Historic Landmark in 1976. Now Nicodemus has fewer than sixty residents, and it struggles to hold on to its rich past. Since 1878, the town has pulled together for its annual Emancipation Celebration in July.

You are cordially invited to spend the night at the **Rose of Sharon Inn Bed and Breakfast,** at 603 East Main Street. Gale and Sharon Shulze will make you comfortable in their 1880 Victorian home. Call (785) 877–3010 for reservations.

Near **Calvert,** east of Norton, there are deposits of volcanic ash 20 feet thick, consisting of tiny fragments of glass or congealed lava. Ash was deposited in this area during the past few million years from volcanoes in New Mexico, Wyoming, and California; prevailing winds carried it here. Pioneers used the ash in toothpaste and cleansing powder, and mining operations are still in business here.

Barbeau House is at 210 East Washington Avenue in **Lenora,** which is south of Norton on Highway 283. This bed-and-breakfast Queen Anne Victorian was built in 1889, and many of its features are original. Hostess Lea Hall is rightly proud of this elegant home. Rooms with private baths are $65 on the main floor and $50 on the second floor (with shared baths). A full breakfast is served each morning. She also does private dinner parties for groups. Call (785) 567–4886 for reservations.

Harry and Sharyl Moos, at **Village Oak Woodcraft**, create hand-carved wooden trains, cars, and trucks—both small children's toys and more detailed executive toys—of native woods in little **Hill City,** south of Norton on Highway 283 at Highway 24. Harry uses maple, walnut, oak, and Osage orange, as well as the more exotic rosewood and ebony. Their home and shop is at 607 North Seventh Street. Call (785) 421–5622 after 5:00 P.M. or on weekends.

Hill City is also the location of the **Pheasant Inn Bed and Breakfast** at 609 North Fourth Avenue. It's in the middle of great hunting country, with plenty of game birds and deer. This charming vintage home has stained- and beveled-glass windows and hardwood floors. Host Donna Worcester offers a full breakfast to guests. The rooms are $50 to $75. Call (785) 421–2955 for reservations.

The **Pomeroy Inn** is a Hill City bed-and-breakfast where guests awaken to the smell of homemade whole-wheat and amaranth cinnamon rolls every morning—sound great? The inn has eight rooms on the ground floor, with a large lobby. On the east end of the lobby help yourself to some espresso coffee or a flavored soft drink with a pastry. Or you can drift over to the other side of the lobby and visit or watch television. Call (785) 421–2098. Rates range from $28 to $59, including continental breakfast, and all rooms have a full bath.

Krenzel Kottage is next door to the home of Troy and Robin Krenzel at

201 West Summer. It is a completely private guest house in **Morland** (population 200). The rate is $40 a night per person for one to eight guests. It is a fully furnished house with kitchen, living room, and 1½ baths, in addition to sleeping space. A continental breakfast is delivered to your door the previous evening. Call (888) 593–6369 or (785) 627–5145, fax (785) 627–5146, e-mail at dsequip@ruraltel.net, or visit the Web at www.krenzelkottage. homestead.com/kkhome.html.

Morland has some lakes with excellent fishing. It is also in the heart of a splendid upland game-hunting region with 57,000 acres of public hunting areas. Quail and pheasant are especially abundant here.

West of Hill City on Highway 24 and just north of the town of **Studly** is an English settlement dating from the time after the American Civil War, when leaflets promoting land in the western United States, especially Kansas, were distributed throughout Great Britain. The lure of 160 acres of prairie just for homesteading drew many Europeans to the vast plains. One settler, John Fenton Pratt, who arrived in 1880, built a native stone house and raised sheep. Now the state-owned **Cottonwood Ranch** is open to the public. A complex of stone outbuildings at the ranch was constructed in a pattern similar to farms in the Yorkshire, England, area, where the southern faces of the buildings were aligned and then connected with a stone wall, creating an accessible corral for livestock. The ranch is open from 10:00 A.M. to 5:00 P.M. Wednesday through Saturday, 1:00 to 5:00 P.M. Sunday for guided or self-guided tours. There is no admission charge, but donations are appreciated. Call (785) 627–5866.

A Treasure of Fossils

*O*n a knob in a Morland pasture, scientists have found prehistoric fossils of rhinoceroses and mastodons, as well as bamboo plants and bulrushes. The director of the Sternberg Museum of Natural History in Hays sees this Miocene period treasure chest as a major discovery.

How this knob was formed is still unknown. The plants and animals may have been in a riverbed, and somehow a cap of erosion-resistant rock covered the deposit. It went undiscovered until a young boy found a rhinoceros tooth and made it part of a 4-H project. The rest is history, or prehistory.

The Sternberg Museum now owns the site, called Minium Quarry, and plans to enclose it within a building. When it opens to the public, visitors will watch scientists at work in an active dig.

Sheep in Kansas

Western Kansas has been cattle country for over a century. But during the late nineteenth century there were a vast number of sheep grazing here. Both local flocks and transient ones enjoyed the Kansas grasses. Livestock grazed on open public lands at no cost to the owner. A flock could easily be herded by one man and a dog, and the sheep produced a double crop— spring lambs and summer wool. Since a ewe often gives birth to twins, raising sheep proved to be very profitable, and the sheep industry boomed here.

West of Studley on Highway 24 is the town of **Hoxie.** At 1001 Main Street, Tom and Leanna Sloan offer fine dining and a bed-and-breakfast as well at the **Main Street Inn and B&B.** This pretty blue 1890s Victorian has a wraparound porch. The main floor has private dining rooms; bedrooms are upstairs. But back to the fine-dining part: It is the finest on Thursdays and Sundays, when Leanna panfries chicken at the restaurant. Hand-breaded chicken-fried steak is always on the menu, too. Oh dear, you can almost feel the pounds gathering about your waistline. But wait! You can have a special weekend packet at the B&B that not only includes the room and breakfast, but also a masseuse to rub those extra pounds away. The pale yellow honeymoon suite has a private bath and is $65 a night, the other two rooms share a bath for $55. Another possibility for exercise (or romance) is a Leanna-prepared picnic lunch to the Sloan's lake about 12 miles east of town. You can create your own weekend packet and fill it with whatever sounds good. Breakfast can be served in your room or you can eat in the restaurant if you want to sleep late. Sunday only, breakfast at the restaurant is served from 8:00 A.M. to 2:00 P.M.; Saturday has that plus dinner from 5:00 to 8:00 P.M. Tuesday through Thursday hours are lunchtime, 11:00 A.M. to 2:00 P.M. (then siesta time) and 5:00 to 8:00 P.M., dinnertime; Fridays, 11:00 A.M. to 2:00 P.M. only. Call (785) 675–3999 for reservations at the B&B or find the inn's Web site at the Kansas Bed and Breakfast Association, www.kbba.com.

Smoky Hills

The **Dane G. Hansen Memorial Museum and Plaza,** on Main Street in **Logan,** on Highway 9, is a 1-block monument to the man who left much of his estate to the town he loved when he died in 1965. The museum features traveling exhibitions from the Smithsonian Institution and other museums, as well as permanent exhibits of Oriental art, guns, and coins. It would be considered a fine museum in a big city, and it's a surprising attraction in this small town. It is open

Not a Sign of Studly

You'll find the town of Studly, Kansas, marked on state highway maps, and indeed, the little burg is right where it's supposed to be. So why no sign on the highway marking it? So many have been stolen as souvenirs that the state highway department has stopped replacing them.

Monday through Friday from 9:00 A.M. to noon and 1:00 to 4:00 P.M., Saturday from 9:00 A.M. to noon and 1:00 to 5:00 P.M., and Sunday from 1:00 to 5:00 P.M. Admission is free. Call (785) 689–4846.

The Church of the Transfiguration at 210 Washington Street is an Episcopal Church constructed in 1890 of native limestone and surrounded by buffalo grass. This lovely church is worth a rest stop. You can get the key at the Hansen Museum and just enjoy a quiet moment there alone.

The Kirwin National Wildlife Refuge attracts birders from all over. Here 10,800 acres of grassland, shelterbelts, croplands, and open water provide roads and trails with excellent opportunities for birding. Species include pelicans, herons, owls, goatsuckers (whippoorwills), and snowy egrets. Hunting of pheasant, quail, geese, and ducks is allowed in season. The entrance is off scenic Highway 9. Call (785) 543–6673 for information.

Kirwin Lake is a reservoir off Highway 9. Here, too, you may find a variety of shore- and waterbirds, especially during migratory seasons.

On the banks of Beaver Creek is the log cabin where pioneer Kansas doctor Brewster M. Higley wrote "My Western Home" in the late 1870s. "So what?" you say. "Never heard of it," you say. Well, somewhere along the line, the name was changed to "Home on the Range," and it is now the Kansas state song. **Home on the Range Cabin** is 1 mile west and 8 miles north of Athol, on Highway 8. It has been restored and is open daily year-round from 8:00 A.M. to 5:00 P.M.

The **Old Dutch Mill** in Wagner Park is the most picturesque attraction in **Smith Center,** on Highway 36 at Highway 281. It was built in the 1870s of native logs; its burrs were made from native stones.

The **Ingleboro Mansion** (785–282–3798) at 319 North Main Street in Smith Center is a carefully restored 1879 Victorian house-turned-bed-and-breakfast. Owners Bruce and Bobbi Miles are proud of the home's stained glass, cherry, oak, and maple woodwork, as well as the impressive stairway and fireplaces. Modern conveniences are here, too: air-conditioning, VCRs, a microwave, and a refrigerator stocked with soda, juice, and microwave popcorn. There are three suites, all with private baths. Rates are $55 to $80, including continental breakfast. Call for a reservation, or visit the Web at www.ingleboromansion.com.

Trivia
Russell Stover was born at a spot halfway between Alton and Natoma. He's the man who gave us two American institutions— the Eskimo Pie and Russell Stover candies. To reach the candy-box marker commemorating him from Alton's Main Street, go 1 mile south; turn right at the river; 1 mile west, 8 miles south. At the Pleasant Plains Methodist Church turn left, then go 1 mile on a dirt road.

Osborne has a neat little bed-and-breakfast called *The Loft* at 520 North First. There are two second-story guest rooms furnished with comfortable queen-size beds and family heirlooms. A sitting room adjoins the bedrooms for your relaxation. You are welcome to hang out in the kitchen or stroll through the gardens. There's a swimming pool and walking track nearby as well as lighted tennis courts and a golf course. Hosts Russell and Irene Phalen prepare a full breakfast to fit their guests' dietary needs. Rooms are $45 for a single, $55 for a double room. Call (785) 346–5984.

In 1918 the Rock Island railroad station burned at *Courtland,* and a temporary depot was made from a boxcar. Later it was cut in half and moved, and 20 feet were added to the center. When the railroads disappeared, the abandoned station stood empty until Dan Kuhn and his wife, Carla, began to raise apples and pumpkins and looked for a market. They purchased the building and moved it again to the intersection of Highways 36 and 199, a mile north of Courtland, where it has been restored and has become the *Depot Market and Cider Mill,* 1103 30 Road (785–374–4255). You can tour the apple orchard and pumpkin patch in season, and buy apples, jellies, homemade fudge, and gift basket assortments from July through Christmas, Monday through Saturday from 9:00 A.M. to 5:30 P.M., Sunday from 1:00 to 5:30 P.M. at the store or on-line at www. kansas depot.com.

A famine in Scandinavia during the 1860s forced many Swedes, Danes, and Norwegians to move to the United States and added new flavors to the Kansas melting pot. A group of Swedes moved here in 1868 and formed the town of New Scandinavia, later renamed *Scandia.* The *Scandia Museum* on Main Street off Highway 36 tells the story. It is open Monday through Saturday from 2:00 until 4:00 P.M.

A Moose Named Kirwin

*T*here's a sign at the edge of Kirwin, east of Logan on Highway 9, that says WELCOME TO KIRWIN, THE GOOSE CAPITAL OF THE WORLD. Well, that's what it used to say. The G has been crossed out and an M added. Thousands of years ago, moose roamed over Kansas, but there haven't been any in modern times until a few years ago, when a moose named for the town showed up near herds of cattle, looking lonely and flirting with the local cows. Soon people started coming to see this unusual apparition. Now Kirwin, it seems, has moved on to greener pastures. No one is sure where the moose is these days; and the cows he mo-o-o-oned over aren't talking.

The *Pawnee Indian Village Museum*, 3 miles southwest of *Republic,* is a modern museum constructed around the floor of a Pawnee earth lodge occupied in the early 1800s. This valuable archeological site contains artifacts found there. It is a walk through history, showing evidence of the way the Pawnee lived more than 150 years ago.

The entrance, the only opening in the structure except for the hole in the roof, leads visitors back in time. You may still see the fire pit, the buffalo skull, which was the chief item of worship, the cistern-like hole where meat was stored, and iron pots that were left behind.

The Kansas State Historical Society uncovered items left by the Kitke-hahki or Republican band of the Pawnee tribe and left them just as they were found. The museum is open Wednesday through Saturday from 10:00 A.M. to 5:00 P.M., Sunday from 1:00 to 5:00 P.M. Call (785) 361–2255 for information, or visit the Web site at www.kshs.org.

In a small shop called *BEKAN* (785–527–2427), in a small town called *Belleville,* on Highway 81 slightly north of Highway 36, Bud Hanzlick creates hand-carved furniture using the most unlikely native wood— Osage orange, commonly referred to as hedgeapple. Bud creates tables,

A Sacred Heirloom

*A*round 1873 in the southwest corner of Nebraska, 1,000 Sioux warriors swarmed around a band of 400 Pawnee men, women, and children in what is now known as Massacre Canyon. The Pawnee were returning from a buffalo hunt. As the battle raged, a Pawnee father tied his five-year-old daughter to the back of a horse and lashed a sacred bundle to her back. "Take care of the bundle and it will take care of you," he told her. The girl made it safely back, and she lived on the Pawnee's reservation. Sacred bundles were always passed from mother to firstborn daughter to care for, although only the men of the family could open it or perform any of the ceremonies associated with it.

In 1987 this girl's granddaughter, Elizabeth Horsechief, donated the bundle to the Pawnee Indian Village Museum with the understanding that it would not be opened and would be displayed with respect. It is one of the few in the nation on display.

Tied on the outside of the bundle are a long pipe, arrow fragments, a meat fork tipped with a raccoon bone, and small American flags.

Careful not to open the bundle, the museum X-rayed and CAT-scanned it, revealing stuffed bird bundles, hawk bells, counting sticks, and glass beads sewn on a leather strip. It hangs today as it would have a century ago— above a buffalo skull altar.

chairs, bowls, and cutting boards that accent the natural contours and unusual beauty of this rock-hard wood.

He calls the furniture "refined rustic," and it is special indeed. He is the only person using this wood, also called *bois d'arc* or bow wood, because it fights being cut every inch of the way. It dulls saws, it's too tough to nail, and it has thorns that attack any craftsman who is foolish enough to like it. "It's as tough as the pioneers who planted it," says Bud. They used it for wheel hubs, and the Indians used it for bows because it bends without breaking.

But Bud likes the grotesque shapes it gets into, and he can guarantee it to last a lifetime outdoors on your patio. It won't rot, bugs hate it, rain and snow only make it tougher, and it is one of the hardest woods in the world. Its tight grain and color make each piece unlike any other. His pieces range from $175 to $350. BEKAN (for Belleville, Kansas) is at 901 N Street; Bud's workshop is in the backyard, and his wife, Pat, has a shop in the house, where items are displayed.

The old-fashioned soda fountain is rare these days, but there are still a few left in Kansas. The **Goose Crossing** at 1820 Main Street in Belleville is in a historic building that may have housed a drugstore as early as the 1920s. Tyra Frye, owner of The Goose, bought the building, the original marble soda fountain, cupboards, and ice-cream tables and chairs. She even bought some of the original glassware. Then she went to the library and became a soda jerk. She learned to make sodas, Green Rivers, Twisted Cokes, and Volcanos, all made from syrups, not canned drinks. Anyone who used to hang out at the local drugstore on Saturday night will want to test her fresh-squeezed lemonade and limeade on a hot summer evening

The Stained-Glass Capital of Kansas

*C*loud County was designated the "Stained-Glass Capital of Kansas" by the Kansas legislature in 1994. There is magnificent stained glass in churches in Concordia, Clyde, Glasco, Jamestown, St. Joseph, Aurora, Miltonvale, and Huscher. The rose window at the Nazareth Convent in Concordia, at Thirteenth and Washington, is in the **Motherhouse of the Sisters of St.** Joseph, built in 1903. The Motherhouse (but not the convent) (785–243–2113) is open for tours Monday through Friday from 2:00 to 4:00 P.M. You'll also find stained glass in businesses, houses, and in stained-glass studios in Glasco, Concordia, and Miltonvale. For details, contact the Cloud County Convention and Visitors Bureau at (785) 243–4290.

or the hot cocoa with a dip of ice cream in the winter. You can eat breakfast, lunch, or dinner there, too. The Goose is open from 9:00 A.M. to 5:30 P.M. Monday through Friday, Saturday until 5:00 P.M., and Thursday nights until 6:00 P.M. Call Tyra at (785) 527–5998.

Things in motion everywhere—hundreds of whirligigs, windmills, and clockworks click and whirr—can be found at the ***Boyer Gallery*** at the corner of Twelfth and M Streets. Paul Boyer is the creator of this show-motion craft display. There are bouncing dancers and ball bearings racing around a brass maze. Tiny golfers tee up inside, and a life-size mechanical lady rides a stationary bike outside the gallery's front door. Since what makes the animated creatures tick is almost as fascinating as they are, the creations have glass sides so visitors can see the intricate maze of wires and gears that keeps everything moving.

Paul began making animated carvings when he was only twelve years old. He collected timers out of old washing machines, boxes of old clockworks, and lots of ball bearings. Boyer's six brothers banded together to create a place where his work could be seen after an accident left him disabled. In fact, the gallery includes the work of all nine Boyer brothers and sisters. There are children's toys by Raymond, limestone carvings by John, wood crafts by Eldon, Duane, Leland, and Eddie, and paintings by their wives, sisters, and children. You can buy the siblings' work, but Paul's is not for sale.

The World's Largest Ball of Twine

*L*ately there have been disturbing rumors on the Internet that there is a bigger ball of twine than the one in Cawker City. They say it's someplace in Texas or Minnesota. The local people are not worried, though. They say it's no contest because the Texas ball has string and plastic stuff in it. Not pure twine from hay bales like Cawker City's. And the one from Minnesota? Well, it might have a big snowball inside. Who knows. Meanwhile, Cawker City keeps adding hay bale–twine to its ball every year. The city has its own Web site if you want to know more about this fascinating race for fame. Look it up at www.skyways. lib.ks.us/kansas/towns/Cawker/ cawker.html.

The gallery is open from 9:00 A.M. to 6:00 P.M. Monday through Saturday, 1:00 to 6:00 P.M. Sunday from Memorial Day to Labor Day. The gallery is closed January to mid-March, and open weekends only the rest of the year. Check the Web site at www.nckcn.com/boyergallery. Admission is $2.50 for adults, $1.00 for children. For more information, call (785) 527–5884.

The town of *Clyde,* west of Highway 15, is home to about 800 people. There is a museum with an old jail and a completely furnished one-room schoolhouse.

If you get hungry there is a friendly place at 325 Washington called *Last Call* (785–446–2850). It's open seven days a week from 9:00 A.M. to 10:00 P.M. Good burgers any time. Within walking distance of Clyde's attractions is *Clyde Hotel* at 420 Washington, the project of Jerry and Laura Lee Stenberg. This 1870 inn has been remodeled for comfort, yet it retains the charm of days gone by. The inn has a stained-glass window from an old Methodist church that filters the summer sunlight. In spring and summer guests enjoy a walk in the beautifully landscaped courtyard and admire the gazebo, fountain, and flowers. There are seven rooms, each with a private bath. The rooms have king- and queen-size beds. Rates are $39 to $52. Reservations are required for the continental breakfast. Call (785) 446–2231.

On *Glasco's* main street is *Hodge Podge* (113 East Main) with a good old-fashioned soda fountain with six cast-iron stools and a brass rail footrest. The dark oak back bar is more than one hundred years old. You can get a chocolate soda, milk shake, malt, or Green Dragon here. Hours are 9:00 A.M. to 5:00 P.M. Monday through Friday, 9:00 A.M. to 3:00 P.M. Saturday. Call (785) 568–2542.

Rustic Remembrances Bed and Breakfast is in Glasco 2 miles off Highway 24 and 6 miles from the junction of Highways 81 and 24. All the rooms are furnished with antiques, and the large deck and patio give you a quiet spot to relax. This is a working farm. Owners Madonna and Larry Sorell raise Belgian draft horses, mini donkeys, Jacob sheep, turkeys, seven breeds of chickens, and llamas. The home is a century old and Madonna is a spinner and weaver; she offers classes for these forgotten arts. Larry collects antique machinery. There are four rooms with shared bath. Rates are $45 to $75. Call (785) 568–2777.

If you want to miss the interstate altogether, go west on Highway 24, the scenic route west. If you have the time, it's more interesting to travel on than the interstate.

Kansas's Prisoner of War Camps

*D*uring World War II, there were several POW camps located in Kansas. One was near Concordia. Two German prisoners escaped from the camp and were heading for Mexico, according to the video *Stalag Sunflower (made at Emporia State University). The authorities knew of the escape but did not pursue the prisoners for a couple of days. Then* they picked them up, took them back to the prison, and pulled down a wall map. They pointed out where they were and how far they had walked (they hadn't even crossed the county line, yet). Then they pointed out how far it was to the Rio Grande. The Germans realized that America is a bit larger than Europe, and no further escape attempts were made from that camp.

St. John's Catholic Church at 701 East Court Street in **Beloit** was completed in 1904 and is believed to be the first church in the United States featuring flying buttresses, the same architectural feature that makes the cathedral of Notre Dame so impressive.

The completely restored **Little Red Schoolhouse** on Highway 24 in Beloit is original, built in 1871. It is affiliated with the National Library of Congress and contains the Living Library Museum, with Old State Printer books, Lorraine Wooster editions, and other historic educational material. It is open May through September, Sunday through Friday from 1:00 to 4:00 P.M.

Glen Elder has a unique castle-like structure on the National Register of Historic Places called (believe this?) the **Castle Filling Station**, which was built in 1912 on the northeast corner of the New England–style town square.

Want to try some buffalo meat? Slip into **Butterfield's Buffalo Meat** 1 mile west and .50 mile south of the junction of Highways 24 and 14. Larry Butterfield, Sr., will wrap up a couple of steaks for your next dinner. Call (785) 738–2336.

The lovely oasis of **Glen Elder Reservoir/Waconda Lake** is 10 miles west of Beloit on Highway 24. It has fishing, hunting, a prairie dog area, and camping facilities.

In **Cawker City** on Highway 24, on the north side of the lake, the wide main street has been declared a State Historical District. Here you will see the old wooden storefronts of a frontier community, as well as evidence of a Jewish past.

Cawker City is also famous for having the world's largest ball of twine. (Yes, you read that right.) Twine parties on Labor Day weekend bring folks out to add inches to the over-40-foot ball of twine. The sphere has been part of the town since 1960, when it was brought in by Frank Stoeber, who began it in 1953. The city fathers gave it a spot on Main Street, where it catches the eye of people passing through town.

The Carr Creek Valley on **Ringneck Ranch** is the setting for Keith and Debra Houghton's pheasant-hunting lodge near **Tipton** on Highway 181, south of the lake. Excellent hunting, complete with local guides, dogs, and comfortable accommodations, makes for an enjoyable experience.

The ranch has accommodations for fifty-four people. Arrive in time for a family-style dinner with homemade bread, fresh pies, and grilled steaks, and meet your hosts. Morning brings biscuits and gravy, and then it's off to the fields with your guide to hunt along creeks and through sorghum fields. The ranch has been featured on ESPN and PBS.

Keith and Debra book hunters during the October through March season. Their managed game-bird habitat is a "controlled shooting area," licensed by the Kansas Wildlife and Parks to harvest game birds in excess of the state limits of four birds because of the extensive habitat and breeding here. There are 10,000 acres of the best quail, pheasant, and prairie chicken habitat imaginable. Four-wheel-drive field vehicles and good bird dogs are provided as part of the package. All you have to bring is your shotgun and some clothes.

The ranch has four new suites, each with private bath, ranging from $45 to $49. Please call for room prices in the main ranch house. Hunting licenses can be obtained at the ranch. Fee is from $275 to $375 a day for hunters. For $150, nonhunters may use the ranch facilities and, if they like, the new "Crazy Quail" shooting game that throws clay targets in many diverse directions to keep the edge on your shooting, or just for fun. Guests are welcome to enjoy a stay at the working ranch in the off-season, too. Call (785) 373–4835 for more information and reservations. Check out the Web site at www.ringneckranch.net, or e-mail them at ringneck@wtciweb.com, or fax (785) 373–4059.

Blue Hill Gamebirds is also located in Tipton. They raise about 20,000 pheasants per year. They sell about that many chicks, too. So you can see that the hunting around here is very good. Summer is hatching season; call Don and Virginia Montgomery at (785) 373–4965 if you want a tour.

Tipton has many interesting things for a town of about 300. The **Tipton Grocery,** at 406 Main Street, is famous in this part of the state for its old-fashioned German sausage, made fresh in the store by hand. The recipe is a closely guarded secret, handed down for several generations now. Fred and Vali Smith (Vali came here from Germany when she was eighteen) are the owners. Hours are 8:00 A.M. to 5:30 P.M. Monday through Friday, 8:00 A.M. to 4:00 P.M. Saturday. Call (785) 373–4125.

Kenny Hake restores World War II antique jeeps. He is actually known all over the world for his fine work. King Michael and Queen Anne of Romania once came to visit to collect, reminisce, and buy Kenny's restorations.

He also restores some very rare WWII aircraft. Aviation buffs are intrigued by his trips to Siberia, the Far East, and other places to collect remnants of aircraft that would be lost forever without his extensive and faithful restorations. He can be reached at his business, Kent Manufacturing, in Tipton (785–373–5181).

Hungry? Tipton has a fairly new restaurant at 501 Main Street called the *Headquarters* (785–373–4645). It offers lunch and supper and is open for continental breakfast in the mornings. (Sundays it opens at 5:00 P.M.)

The *Garden of Eden* (785–525–6395) in *Lucas* on Highway 18 is a most unusual place. Once the home of S. P. Dinsmoor, at Second and Kansas Streets, the house is made of post rock and resembles a log cabin. It is surrounded by scores of primitive concrete figures, all made by Dinsmoor after he reached the age of sixty-four.

Garden of Eden

Dinsmoor, a disabled Civil War veteran, spent twenty-two years constructing this amazing display (unique doesn't begin to cover it), using more than 113 tons of cement, native limestone, and various woods. At the front of the house stand Adam and Eve with outstretched arms, forming an arched entrance to the yard. A concrete serpent coils in a tree above them, a concrete devil watches from a nearby rooftop, and above all this is a red, white, and blue (concrete) American flag that actually turns with the prevailing winds. At age eighty-one, Dinsmoor married twenty-year-old Emily and had two children. He died when he was eighty-nine.

Dinsmoor's body lies in a concrete coffin (which he also made) with a glass top in a niche in the mausoleum wall. The body of his first wife lies below him in a steel vault entirely encased in concrete. The mausoleum is guarded by a concrete angel.

The monumental art forms are worth the drive. They have been featured on *Ripley's Believe It or Not* and in *People* magazine, as well as on every network morning show. You can take Highway 232 north from Interstate 70, a pretty drive by Wilson Lake and fields of golden milo, surrounded by post-rock fences. Turn west on Highway K–18; there are plenty of signs to guide you. The Garden of Eden is open May through October from 10:00 A.M. to 5:00 P.M. and in winter from 1:00 to 4:00 P.M. Admission is $4.00.

The *Grassroots Art Center* displays the works of grassroots artists, who are self-taught and often use materials that they find around them. Some call it "recycled art." Many grassroots artists are retired and fill their yards with their works, much as the strange Mr. Dinsmoor did. Most are perceived as odd by their neighbors and most of their works are destroyed at their death.

The center is in three adjacent post-rock buildings on Main Street and will soon expand into a third. It is a community endeavor in this small town (population 475) to encourage self-taught artists.

The center has just completed a post-rock courtyard, which is filled with examples of how the native limestone was used for building homes and fences. Some of the stones that decorate the homes are very ornate.

The center was built to show the works of Inez Marshall, of Portis, who carves and paints native limestone. She feels an inner voice when she touches a piece of stone. Her works are often whimsical and humorous (her Model T Ford has working headlights).

A striking display of Ed Root's glass-encrusted concrete creations fills the lobby of the center. His crushed-glass yard ornaments—a mailbox and a weather vane, for example—are made from available materials such as crushed Milk of Magnesia bottles or the family's dishes.

A farmer from Luray, Leroy Wilson, is another artist whose works are displayed there. He spent twelve years painting the walls and fixtures in his basement in colorful mosaic patterns. On display are the vanity and walls retrieved from the basement before his house was sold after his death.

The center is open May through September from 10:00 A.M. to 5:00 P.M., Monday through Saturday and from 1:00 to 5:00 P.M. Sunday. From October through April, the hours are 10:00 A.M. to 4:00 P.M. Thursday through Saturday and 1:00 to 4:00 P.M. Sunday, or by appointment. Admission is $4.00. Call (785) 525–6118.

The *Lucas Inn* at 229 South Main Street has twelve rooms for rent near Lake Wilson. Call Carol Schneider at (785) 525–6358.

There is also a bed-and-breakfast in Lucas. The *Stone Cottage Farm Bed and Breakfast and Antiques Shop* is at 5010 Highway 232. Becky Thaemert and Roland Spencer can be reached at (785) 525–6494.

The almost lost art of making sausage and bologna is still alive and well in Lucas. Doug and Linda Brant, of *Brant's Meat Market* at 125 South Main Street, will give you samples of their specialty meats fresh from the smokehouse. These are family recipes passed down for three generations. This is a perfect spot to stop for picnic supplies. For more information call (785) 525–6464.

Yesterday House Museum on Main Street in *Sylvan Grove* features the largest barbed-wire collection in the region as well as the history of post-rock country. It is open May through October on Saturday and Sunday from 2:00 to 5:00 P.M. Admission is free. Call Vera Meyer for information at (785) 526–7270.

The Nielsen family has lived and farmed this land in *Denmark,* near Sylvan Grove, since 1870; their children are the fifth generation to live at the historic farm home built of native limestone. It is now the *Spillman Creek Farm and Lodge,* and Merrill and Kathy Nielsen welcome hunters to the farm, which is walking distance from a 120-year-old Lutheran church that still maintains an active congregation. Call (785) 277–3424 after 6:00 P.M. for information on upland game and pheasant hunts.

Leo "Duane" Vonada and his son, Damon, own the *Vonada Stone Quarry,* at 532 East Quail Lane (785–526–7369) near town. As part of the Post Rock Tour mentioned at the beginning of this chapter, they will demonstrate the way early settlers found, quarried, and cut post rock using old-time tools in the original quarry on their farm north of Sylvan Grove. Signs, corner-post art, and engraving are also available there. A post rock with your name on it is about $100. They also make sundials, beginning at $210, and limestone benches for $225 and up. There is an interesting display of milling equipment on the farm, with a vertical mill and drill press used in making tools in the early 1900s.

Like the posts that line the fields, thick-walled post-rock homes and buildings predominate in this part of the mostly treeless prairie. In frontier days, trappers and buffalo hunters improvised dugouts built into the hillsides; railroaders utilized similar shelters. Later, the homesteaders found them still inhabitable when they came through in covered wagons.

A stone post weighs nearly 400 pounds; it takes two men to load one into a wagon. Even with modern equipment, post-rock buildings like the Lincoln County Courthouse in Lincoln would be a wonder. A self-guided tour available at the courthouse leads you through interesting places nearby.

Get off of I–70 at the Lincoln exit 221. Go 14 miles to where Highways 14 and 18 cross. The restoration of the stately 1906 **Woody House Bed and Breakfast** in **Lincoln** at Highway 18 and North Street, preserved the authenticity of this historic 1906 Queen Anne home and retained its original charm in a peaceful farm setting. The elegant interior has curved glass windows, a decorative staircase, and a bathroom with its original fixtures. The rooms are furnished with antiques.

The place comes with an old-fashioned porch, where one can enjoy a lazy swing in a hammock. Three guest rooms, one with a summer terrace, invite guests. Ceiling fans and gentle breezes cool the rooms, and central air-conditioning helps on hot days. A generous continental breakfast is included in the $40 to $50 price. Each room has a wash basin and the full bath is shared. Ivona and Michael Pickering are the innkeepers; call them at (785) 524–4744. Visit the Web site at www.bbchannel.com/bbc/p225488.asp.

Betty's Place (785–792–6323) on 314 Main Street in **Barnard** is well known and worth the 20-mile drive from Lincoln, especially on Thursday, when fried chicken is the specialty. It has been featured on the front page of the *Los Angeles Times* travel section. The cafe seats about sixty people, and on Thursday between 90 and 125 meals are served to the noon-hour crowd. Owner Betty Harlow gets up at 2:00 A.M. to bake homemade cinnamon-pecan rolls, bread, and pies. She has been doing this for more than twenty years, so she's pretty good at it now. Betty's is open six days a week from 6:00 A.M. to 2:00 P.M.; closed on Sunday.

Just 2.5 miles southwest of *Minneapolis* is a National Natural Landmark made up of more than 200 Dakota sandstone concretions known as *Rock City*. Nowhere in the world are there similar rock formations as large or as numerous. Some are almost perfect spheres; others have elliptical forms, with names like Kissing Rocks and the Widow's Tunnel. There are balanced rocks, pyramids, and palaces with diameters of more than 27 feet. Once called "dinosaur marbles" and "Jayhawk eggs," the rocks have appeared in geology textbooks from as far back as the 1870s. Rock City is open May through August from 8:00 A.M. to 6:00 P.M. daily. Be sure to take your camera because now there is a walking trail. There is a $2.25 charge per car. Call the chamber of commerce for information at (785) 392–3098.

Minneapolis, by the way, has been designated the Official Boyhood Home of George Washington Carver. You can find the details of the town's contribution to Carver's career at the "Making of the Man" display at the *Ottawa County Historical Museum* (785–392–3621) at 1105 South Concord. A local dinosaur is also in residence, along with other fossils, meteorites, and Native American and pioneer artifacts. There's even a 1917 Ford tractor. Hours are 10:00 A.M. to noon and 1:00 to 5:00 P.M. Tuesday through Saturday.

The town was built in the late 1800s and each of the homes and buildings that line Main Street has a story to be told: bad stories of bankers running off with money and good stories of lining the street with hay to quiet the town so the buggy traffic wouldn't bother a sick woman's rest. The *Blue Store Emporium* at 307 West Second Street had its beginning when a Chicago merchant established it to unload clothing and other items after they had gone out of fashion in Chicago. Today it houses an old-fashioned soda fountain with a full lunch menu. There is a hand-carved full-size wooden eagle done by a local artist. Antiques, organic herbs, and, best of all, a fudge factory can also be found in this historic building. Hours are Monday through Friday from 8:00 A.M. to 3:30 P.M. Phone (785) 392–3491.

You will want to take the self-guided *Red Post Tour*. With a red post at every turn, you will be drawn through the picturesque scenery, unique landmarks, and rural heritage of the area. Stop by the Minneapolis Chamber of Commerce at 213 West Second Street to pick up the map, or call (785) 392–3068 for more details.

A local rancher constructed a huge buffalo statue from fifty tons of concrete and rebar. It stands on the rolling hills of eastern Ottawa County. Watch for it in your travels.

There's a bed-and-breakfast 2 miles north of **Wells** (11 miles east of Minneapolis) on a blacktop road. ***Trader's Lodge Bed and Breakfast and Fine Dining*** is at 1392 210th Road. Hosts Neal and Kay Kindall welcome you to their lodge of fir and native stone decorated with furs and Native American art, some of it handcrafted by Neal and offered for sale. The lodge is set in the rolling hills, only 4 miles from Ottawa State Fishing Lake on a wheat and cattle farm.

Guests are welcome to enjoy the massive native stone fireplace in the large family room. You can bike or hike the hills on the blacktop road and enjoy the brilliant sunset from the large wooden porch. Rooms are $65 and $85. Call (785) 488–3930 or (866) 360–1813 for directions and reservations. Visit at the Web site at www.come.to/traderslodge.com.

Bennington is east of Highway 81 on Highway 18. You can enjoy a great meal or spend the night at ***Our Old House Restaurant and Bed and Breakfast*** at 104 East Bennington Street. The Popelkas invite you to enjoy this old Victorian home and small-town hospitality. Call (785) 488–3999 for reservations.

PLACES TO STAY IN NORTHWEST KANSAS

ATWOOD
Crest Motel,
601 Grant Street,
(785) 626–3213

BELOIT
Waconda Budget Motel,
Junction Highway 24 and Highway 17,
(785) 738–2231 or
(800) 538–5998

COLBY
Comfort Inn,
2225 South Range,
(913) 462–3833

Country Club Drive Motel,
460 Country Club Drive,
(785) 462–7568

Holiday Inn Express,
645 West Willow,
(785) 462–8787

Ramada Inn,
1950 South Range,
(785) 462–3933 or
(800) 750–7160

GOODLAND
Best Western Buffalo Inn,
830 West Highway 24,
(785) 899–3621 or
(800) 433–3621

Howard Johnson Hotel,
2218 Commerce Road,
(785) 899–3644 or
(888) 495–9452

HAYS
Best Western Vagabond,
2524 Vine Street,
(785) 625–2511 or
(800) 432–2776

Econo Lodge,
3503 North Vine,
(785) 625–4839

Hampton Inn,
3801 Vine Street,
(785) 625–8103

Holiday Inn,
3603 Vine Street,
(785) 625–7371

Super 8 Motel,
3730 Vine Street,
(785) 625–8048 or
(800) 800–8000

OAKLEY
Best Western Golden
Plains Motel,
3506 Highway 40,
(785) 672–3254 or
(800) 528–1234

OBERLIN
Frontier Motel,
207 East Frontier Parkway,
(785) 475–2203

RUSSELL
Dumler RV Park,
883 Front Street,
(785) 483–2603

Russell's Inn,
Interstate 70 and
Highway 281,
911 South Fossil,
(785) 483–2107

SALINA
Baymont Inn & Suites,
745 West Schilling,
(785) 493–9800

Country Inn & Suites,
2760 South Ninth Street,
(785) 827–1271

Days Inn,
407 West Diamond Drive,
(785) 823–9791

WAKEENEY
Super 8 Motel,
709 South Thirteenth
Street,
(785) 743–6442

**PLACES TO EAT IN
NORTHWEST KANSAS**

COLBY
Village Inn,
2215 South Range,
(785) 462–6683

CONCORDIA
Jammer's Sports Bar &
Grill,
1431 East Sixth,
(785) 243–3100

HAYS
JD's Country Style Chicken,
740 East Eighth,
(785) 623–2830

Montana Mike's,
3216 Vine Street,
(785) 628–8786

OAKLEY
Colonial Steak House,
I–70 & Highway 83,
(785) 672–4720

Mitten Café,
Highway 40,
(785) 672–4111

OBERLIN
Janey's Frontier Restaurant,
209 East Frontier Parkway,
(785) 475–3429

RUSSELL
Red Carpet Inn Restaurant,
Junction I–79 &
Highway 281,
(785) 483–2107

Selected Chambers of Commerce and Visitors Bureaus

Atwood Chamber of Commerce,
(785) 626–9630 or (800) 422–9630

Hays Convention and Visitors Bureaus,
1301 Pine, Suite B, Hays 67601-3554;
(785) 628–8202 or (800) 569–4505

Colby Convention and Visitors Bureau,
350 South Range, Suite 10; (785) 462–7643

Concordia/Cloud County Visitors Bureau,
606 Washington; (785) 243–4290

Oakley Area Chamber of Commerce,
700 West Third Street; (785) 672–4839

Oberlin Chamber of Commerce,
132 South Penn Avenue; (785) 475–3441

Salina Area Chamber of Commerce,
120 West Ash, Box 586; (785) 827–9301

SALINA
Bistro Café,
1200 East Crawford Street,
(785) 827–2728

The Cozy Inn,
108 North Seventh,
(785) 825–9407

Grandma Max's,
1944 North Ninth Street,
(785) 825–5023

SCANDIA
The Kaffe Haus,
Highway 36,
(785) 335–2543

TIPTON
The Head Quarters,
506 Main Street,
(785) 373–4645

WAKEENEY
Real Country Cafe,
I–70 & Highway 283,
exit 127,
(785) 743–5473

Index

Entries for Eatin' Places and Sleepin' Places appear in the Special Indexes beginning on page 268.

INDEX

INDEX

INDEX

INDEX

INDEX

Eatin' Places

INDEX

Sleepin' Places

INDEX

About the Author

Heartland native Patti DeLano has been traveling the globe since she was twenty. A flight attendant for Trans World Airlines for ten years, she gave up flying to raise a family. She and her late husband, Bob, a pilot for TWA, traveled extensively and, after his retirement, took to the roads to see the small towns of America.

Now she is spending time on the Gulf of Mexico—off the coast of Venice, Florida—on sailing vessel *Serafina de Mare* (Angel of the Sea), a 38-foot Islander Freeport, as she and her new husband, Tom, get ready to sail in search of off-the-beaten-path places in the islands of the Caribbean.